BRITAIN
IS
BETTER
THAN
THIS

ALSO BY GAVIN ESLER

NOVELS

Power Play

A Scandalous Man

The Blood Brother

Deep Blue

Loyalties

NON FICTION

How Britain Ends

Brexit without the Bullshit

Lessons from the Top

The United States of Anger

BRITAIN
IS
BETTER
THAN
THIS

Why A Great Country
Is Failing Us All

GAVIN ESLER

An Apollo Book

9 7 5 3 1 2 4 6 8

A catalogue record for this book is available from the British Library.

ISBN (FTPBO): 9781804547724
ISBN (E): 9781804547700

Printed and bound in Great Britain by
CPI Group (UK) Ltd, Croydon CR0 4YY

Head of Zeus Ltd
First Floor East
5–8 Hardwick Street
London EC1R 4RG

WWW.HEADOFZEUS.COM

For Anna, and for all those who prefer to solve problems rather than create them.

'We persist in regarding ourselves as a great power, capable of everything and only temporarily handicapped by economic difficulties. We are not a great power and never will be again. We are a great nation, but if we continue to behave like a great power we shall soon cease to be a great nation.'

Sir Henry Tizard, British government scientific adviser, on the post-war future of the United Kingdom (1947)

'Without regret for the past, without anxiety for the future, we walked gaily across a carpet of flowers which concealed the abyss beneath.'

Louis-Philippe, comte de Ségur on the French Revolution

Contents

PART ONE

Inspirations and Irritations

I

'Why are things so... so shit?'

Britain is better than this. We all know it. We also know that
something has gone seriously wrong in the country almost 70
million of us call home. If we do not act soon the United Kingdom
of Great Britain and Northern Ireland, to give it the full name on
British passports, may be beyond repair. How can it be that a great
and diverse country like ours, with so many good and competent
people and such a strong sense of identity suffers from our current
malaise? How can a 'United' Kingdom at times feel so disunited?
And how after the passing of Queen Elizabeth II can we change our
head of state seamlessly – without gunfire, riots or revolution – and
yet our political system remains sclerotic and unfit for the twenty-
first century?

There is an uncomfortable British paradox. We're clever, creative
and successful. One British university – Cambridge – has more Nobel
Prize winners than any country in the world outside the United
States and Britain itself. Yet many of us feel that our demonstrably
clever and competent country has lost its way; that when change
comes it may be change for the worse; that many of the people in
top positions in the great institutions of our democracy are men and
women we would not trust to look after our children or our bank
accounts, and when we find out they have lied to us they continue
in power or even end up being promoted. We reward failure and we
have become used to scratching our heads and asking ourselves how
in the 2020s a great country ends up with a series of failed prime
ministers, failing governments, corruption scandals and repeated
examples of political and economic self-harm.

Survey after survey of public opinion shows that the great
institutions of British democracy, from parliament to the media
and big business, are no longer trusted as they once were. The unity,
even the existence, of the United Kingdom is now in doubt. Growing
numbers of people in Scotland, Wales and Northern Ireland no
longer wish to be part of our union. Significant numbers in England
don't seem to care if the others leave. Where once we had delusions

of grandeur, we now often have delusions of competence. We even seem to have weaponised nostalgia, with some in public life insisting that only by grasping at past faded glories can we magically secure a better future. This book will argue the opposite. We need not be pessimistic. Decline is not inevitable. Disunion may be averted. A better Britain really is possible – but only if we face up to the reality that our British malaise is not merely the fault of the people we put into power. It's not them. It's us. We tolerate uselessness, deceit and failure in a system of governance that allows unsuitable people to flourish. It's not enough to change prime ministers if we retain the system that rewards incompetence and lying. The bad news is that if we do nothing, things will get worse, perhaps under a determined and ideologically driven leader who knows how to abuse what we think of as British democracy. The good news is that if we now honestly confront the failings within this still great nation, we can reinvent our old democracy and put things right.

The Awkward Question

Inspiration for this inquiry into the British malaise began with an awkward question. It came from an elderly upper-class English woman who approached me while I was sitting in sunshine in the grounds of Dartington Hall, near Totnes in the west of England. I was flicking through notes for a talk I was about to give at a literary festival, thinking how wonderful it was to live in a country with so much beauty and so much talent. Dartington is glorious, a country estate dating back to medieval times. The grounds extend to 1,200 acres. I spent the day marvelling at the countryside, walking in the forest through deer-filled meadows leading down to the trout, otters and kingfishers of the River Dart. The subject of my talk was a book I had written on the divisions within our dis-united kingdom, *How Britain Ends*. The title was an observation, that Scotland and Northern Ireland may soon go their separate ways, rather than a recommendation.

'Sorry to interrupt your reading,' the elderly woman said politely. She had the cut-glass accent reminiscent of Queen Elizabeth II. In my head I called her 'Elizabeth' too. 'I hope you don't mind, but may I ask you a question?'

'Of course.'

'So...' Elizabeth spoke hesitantly, as if an unfamiliar word was about to stumble across her tongue. 'Can you please tell me... why are things so... so *shit*?'

I blinked in astonishment, then laughed and asked her what she meant. Elizabeth explained in detail in what was almost a stream of consciousness about her pride in being British, then she hit on the modern British paradox. Britain 'has been' a great country, she said – 'just look at Dartington Hall!' – but now everything was a mess. Nothing worked the way it was supposed to – the National Health Service (NHS), the police, the economy, the government. The prime minister (then Boris Johnson) told lies. Past politicians lied occasionally, Elizabeth said, but nowadays they lied much more often, shamelessly and without penalty, 'taking us for fools'. The 'bad eggs' used to resign when they were caught out. Now even those who were exposed as corrupt or incompetent somehow clung on to power. Politicians preferred to create problems rather than solve them. Elizabeth remembered a time when British governments were filled with clever people – 'not all of them, but quite a lot'. They seemed competent, even if she didn't always agree with their policies. Nowadays leaders could not be trusted.

I shuffled my notes and mumbled sympathetically but was unable to provide a coherent answer to her question, yet Elizabeth's observations rang in my head for months. Every problem that she mentioned seemed to become more obvious as the days went by. The negative impact of Brexit deepened. A friend in London, a wine importer, talked of the painful post-Brexit bureaucracies he encountered. The pound fell. Prices on imports went up. An exporter with a small company in Scotland spoke of taking on an extra member of staff 'just to fill in the effing forms'. Exports went down. Former loyalist paramilitaries in the Shankill area of

Belfast told me of 'young lads' bent on trouble because the Northern Ireland Protocol agreed as part of the Brexit agreement made them feel 'different' from the rest of the UK. They feared it was a step towards being swallowed up by the Irish Republic. Near where I live in Kent, refugees were coming ashore in record numbers with no one in government able to fix the broken asylum system. I found an empty dinghy used by asylum seekers on the beach near my house. I also found myself repeatedly stuck behind long lines of lorries at Ashford or Dover, transport tied up by the new Brexit bureaucracy. News headlines were repetitive misery. The UK's GDP was forecast to suffer a 4 per cent decline. We had the lowest growth in the G7. We witnessed the shambolic withdrawal of British troops from Afghanistan, the consequences of the war in Ukraine, the first strike by the Royal College of Nursing in its history, unrest across the NHS, industrial action on the railways and elsewhere, billions of pounds wasted on coronavirus contracts, devious dealings – oh, and lies about it all. Such a lot of lies.

Partygate and the unravelling of Boris Johnson's administration was only a surprise because it took so long for his decades of ethical failings and deceit to bring him down. What followed Johnson was the unedifying contest between Liz Truss and Rishi Sunak with Truss – as the world knows – becoming prime minister and lasting for just over forty days. The first major event of her new government was its political suicide. Her Chancellor and friend Kwasi Kwarteng offered a 'mini-budget' that unravelled even as he was speaking in the House of Commons. It tanked the pound, spooked the bond market and made the United Kingdom appear an unreliable place to invest money and do business. All in a day's work for a country that traditionally boasted about political stability and yet had eighty ministerial resignations, four Chancellors of the Exchequer and three prime ministers in four months. British exceptionalism came to mean exceptional turmoil, exceptional incompetence and exceptional discontent. Every news bulletin, every serious newspaper, even casual conversations with friends, neighbours or local dogwalkers compounded the sense of malaise. Elizabeth's question still lacked an answer. Why were things so... so shit? Why had so many British people lost trust in the institutions at the very heart of our supposedly 'world leading' democracy? The United Kingdom was in democratic recession.

Institutional Failure

The NHS, the BBC, the civil service, judges, the police, water and energy companies, airlines, banks, financial institutions, nurses, doctors, train operators, control of British borders all made headlines for the wrong reasons. Senior civil servants told me how difficult it had become to 'speak truth to power' and that the unwritten British constitution was permitting unprecedented abuses of the norms expected from government ministers. MPs complained they were unable properly to hold government ministers to account. Senior judges privately told me of their worries about underinvestment in the criminal justice system, political interference and the consequences of judges being labelled 'Enemies of the People'. This outrageous slur was offered by a newspaper – the *Daily Mail* – notorious for supporting Hitler and British fascism in the 1930s – in 1934 it ran the headline 'Hurrah For The Blackshirts'. Why was the *Mail* – owned by someone not even resident in Britain for tax purposes – repeating a Nazi meme? Had it really come to this?

In 2022 criminal barristers went on strike for the first time in British history after receiving pay cuts. Courts were so disrupted that some cases went untried for years. Minor cases often never came to court at all. Sewage was spewing into our rivers and seas, prompting a backlash from environmentalists, swimmers and anglers. Surfers Against Sewage mapped the worst spills so we could all see one answer to the question 'Why are things so... so shit?' and avoid the effluent on our beautiful coasts and rivers, including the Wye, the Calder and the Wharfe. Creaking infrastructure, some dating from Victorian times, was literally cracking, allowing billions of litres of tap water to be lost from ageing pipes. By August 2022 the water industry and its financial regulator, Ofwat, calculated that water companies lost an average of 2.938 billion litres of water *a day* in 2021–22, amounting to 1.06 trillion litres over the year, an ocean of waste.

My neighbours complained about difficulties in seeing a doctor. One friend with breathing difficulties was told that she could not get a doctor's appointment for *four weeks*. Another friend told me of an eighty-year-old neighbour lying in the street for more than an hour with a broken hip, waiting for an ambulance. Finding an NHS dentist was almost impossible. Teachers spoke of schoolchildren too hungry to learn. The number of food banks to feed the less well-off expanded so much that in the 2020s the UK had more food banks than branches of McDonald's.

Beyond coronavirus and industrial action, our lives were also disrupted by increased bureaucracy for those travelling abroad, chaos at ports and airports, fruit and vegetables rotting unpicked in farmers' fields, the cost of living crisis and the steepest rise in inflation for forty years. It came with the biggest fall in the pound against the dollar for thirty-seven years. It is certainly true that international economic dislocation caused by the war in Ukraine contributed to rising energy costs and other economic disruption.

It's also true – as we will explore – that there has been a democratic recession worldwide in the twenty-first century, part of a measurable loss of trust in governments and democratic institutions everywhere. In what follows we will see numerous parallels with America's democratic crisis. But as my interlocutor, Elizabeth, had suggested, in the United Kingdom this catalogue of misfortune was often worse than in other places. And it was not a visitation from a virus or foreign enemy. It was often a consequence of self-harm, something we were doing to ourselves. That jarred brutally with our self-image as a great nation. The philosopher and constitutional theorist A. C. Grayling estimated that the British democratic system has influenced political systems in at least fifty countries around the world, but by the 2020s foreign press coverage suggested we had become an international joke.

To take just one, relatively minor, example: those supposedly worthy people elevated for life to the upper house of the British parliament, the ever-expanding House of Lords, included donors who gave large sums of money to the Conservative Party, a retired cricketer, the son of a former KGB agent, and a former member of a revolutionary communist group that supported the IRA bombing campaign in England, who later became a fervent advocate of the UK leaving the European Union. The chairman of the Conservative Party admitted he had paid around £5 million in back taxes, including a penalty. A successful businessman at Goldman Sachs, Richard Sharp, who donated £400,000 to the Conservative Party, admitted he also acted as an 'introduction agency' to help facilitate a loan of £800,000 for prime minister Boris Johnson. A few weeks afterwards Mr Sharp was appointed chairman of the BBC. He had previously been Rishi Sunak's mentor at Goldman Sachs. In the ensuing row prime minister Sunak asked William Shawcross, the Commissioner for Public Appointments, to inquire into the affair. It then turned out that Shawcross's daughter Eleanor is head of the policy unit for... Rishi Sunak. Mr Shawcross (rightly and honourably) recused himself from the inquiry. And around the same time two of the most obviously disgraced prime ministers of the past century, Boris Johnson and Liz Truss, appeared to be plotting, separately, a comeback.

Now take one step back. Assume that – as all the people named here insist – none of them has done anything wrong. All this is just normal for the United Kingdom in the 2020s. Isn't that the problem? The more I thought about Elizabeth's question, the more it seemed that the scandal in the United Kingdom in the twenty-first century is not that which we forbid. It is that which we allow. We even pretend that all this is normal. If the United Kingdom were a person you would diagnose a nervous breakdown. As a nation we find ourselves nostalgically pining for a glorious yet imaginary British past while avoiding hard decisions and reforms in the present, precisely those reforms necessary to ensure a better future.

Part of the problem is what might be called the 'Politics of Distraction'. It is a pattern of disinformation used as a deliberate political strategy. Boris Johnson is a master of this. The Politics of Distraction involves three related ideas. The first is 'Dead Catting'. A public figure makes a comment so distracting that it is like throwing a dead cat on the table. This is designed to change the national conversation. And it works. Second, 'Strategic Lying'. This is when a leader tells lies or misleads the public not in error or with an occasional falsehood but as a clear political strategy. This steals news headlines and deflects attention from real problems. Third, 'Truth Decay'. This is the inevitable consequence of British public life being so deluged by a blizzard of information, misinformation and disinformation that as ordinary citizens we do not have the time, inclination, energy or skills to separate truth from falsehood. In the end we simply shrug, perhaps don't care, and ultimately lose trust in the very institutions we need to make democracy work. For a brief flavour, here's an odd, yet telling, example of how the Politics of Distraction works in practice. More serious examples will follow.

The Politics of Distraction

In 2022, faced with the war in Ukraine, the lasting economic damage and disruption of Brexit, and the residual costs of the coronavirus pandemic, British government ministers began a public consultation process. They wanted anyone interested to fill out an online questionnaire on whether the UK should return to the imperial system of measurements, including pounds, ounces and gallons. Two minutes on Google would confirm that no country in the world – with the possible exception of Myanmar, a military dictatorship on the other side of the world – retains anything comparable to the antiquated British imperial system of measurements. The Empire is long gone, and in science and international business so are outdated British measurements based at times on human body parts, including the 'foot'. The United States (and to a lesser extent Liberia) does retain measurements in 'gallons' but common terms such as this disguise the fact that US standards are utterly different from British measurements with the same name. A US gallon is 3.785 litres. A British imperial gallon is 4.546 litres. American AR-15 assault rifles (Armalites) fire ammunition calibrated not in inches, but millimetres (5.56×45mm), although Americans spell it 'millimeters'.

The problem the British government metric 'consultation' was designed to solve does not exist. De-metricating the United Kingdom would not simplify trade with any nation. The consultation was phoney, as well as pointless. It was organised by the 'Brexit Opportunities Minister' (sic) Jacob Rees-Mogg as part of what has become a pattern of British ancestor worship. Respondents to the survey complained that there was no option to advocate total conversion to metrication rather than the hybrid system Britain retains. We fill up our cars in litres, but fuel economy figures are often expressed in miles per (British) gallon. We buy a pint of beer in a pub, yet we manage to drink whisky, gin, rum and vodka in measures of 25, 35 or 50 millilitres, and a large glass of wine at 250 ml. Somehow we survive. The survey was a typical Dead Cat event. These turn up from time to time as a deliberate distraction aimed at capturing a few headlines. It has also become the habit of recent British governments to invent 'problems' that they may be able to 'solve' in order to distract from real problems that are much more complex and intractable.

To take one other egregious example, around the same time as the vacuous imperial measurements survey, the then Transport Secretary, Grant Shapps suggested cutting the frequency of tannoy announcements on trains. The chronic problem on British railways was, and remains, underinvestment and poor services, notably on the West Coast Main Line. There were also disruptive strikes, organised because rail workers' pay lagged behind inflation. The tannoy problem was barely a problem at all; a distraction that eventually dissolved in ridicule. Shapps then deftly changed the conversation. He wondered whether British bicycles should have compulsory number plates, like cars. The only country that has such plates is North Korea.

The prime minister at the time, Boris Johnson, was himself a master of the Politics of Distraction. In his long political career Johnson consciously, constantly and deftly changed the British national political conversation by throwing putrid Dead Cats around, stories which often did as they were designed to do, capture newspaper headlines and then quietly die. Examples include (but are not limited to) suggesting a Garden Bridge across the Thames in London (and spending more than £50 million on considering it), another bridge (or tunnel) from Scotland to Northern Ireland, a new London airport on the sea, and endless eye-catching but ultimately non-existent building projects. To combat crime, Mr Johnson promised that more than 20,000 'extra' police would be recruited. The number 20,000 often appears in political promises. It is big enough to make a headline yet small enough to be almost credible. The Conservative government in 2010 had previously promised to *shrink* police forces in England and Wales by precisely 20,000 police officers as an austerity measure. Coincidentally 20,000 was the figure chosen in August 2021 as the number of Afghan refugees who could theoretically be resettled in the UK under the Afghan citizens resettlement scheme (ACRS). This came after the debacle of the precipitate withdrawal of British forces from Afghanistan, putting at risk those who had helped Britain in the war effort against the Taliban. The House of Commons Library reports: 'Four people have been resettled under pathway 2, as at the end of September 2022.'[1] That is 19,996 short of the target figure of 20,000.

To fix the acute problems in the NHS, forty 'new hospitals' were promised, leading to much discussion about whether any of these new hospitals would eventually exist in reality. They didn't. The few new buildings were generally extensions to existing hospital facilities. Inconveniently, health service professionals repeatedly pointed out that even if the fantasy building programme were to begin, the 'new hospitals' would have to be staffed by fantasy doctors and non-existent nurses. There is an acute shortage of both. The government then put a cap on the number of doctors to be trained at universities. A British Medical Association (BMA) report said: 'It's frightening that we've reached a point where we're short of 49,162 full-time equivalent doctors, but even more terrifying to think this number could hit 83,779 by 2043, as our research suggests.'[2]

What follows, then, is not a recitation of government failings. Nor is it an examination of the familiar problem of useless individuals in government promising much and then failing to deliver. The key point is to consider the consequences for British democracy of a blizzard of deliberate distractions, Strategic Lying and the loss of trust in the institutions of democracy, resulting in decayed standards of truth and a loss of trust in British public life. Truth Decay is now so obvious and omnipresent that lies and deceit often barely register because no one believes what they are told in the first place.

Getting a Grip: Strategic Thinking v. Strategic Lying

In his book on modern British failure, *Hard Choices: What Britain Does Next*, the UK's former National Security Adviser and Ambassador to France, Lord (Peter) Ricketts points out that the United Kingdom in the past fifty years has been dogged by a lack of strategic thinking. He argues that government ministers – and he has worked with many of them – are unable or unwilling to plan coherently for the next generation. Their political horizons extend only as far as the next General Election. Their policy announcements are often focused merely on the next day's news headlines. In an extreme example of short-termism *The Economist* suggested that the prime ministerial career of Liz Truss might be shorter than the lifespan of a supermarket lettuce. The tabloid newspaper *The Daily Star* considered this a challenge. They posted pictures of a lettuce in competition with the prime minister. The lettuce lasted longer. When the reality of public life is beyond satire, we need to remind ourselves once more that Britain was not always like this. British governments of course failed in the past – appeasement in the 1930s, the Suez Crisis in the 1950s and economic stagnation in the 1970s are obvious examples. Britain's problems are also far from unique, but they are especially acute and are made much worse by a kind of national complacency about our 'world beating' or 'world leading' system of governance replete with glorious 'traditions' in the 'Mother of Parliaments' which is the 'envy of the world'. That supposed envy is in very short supply in the 2020s.

Yet the best of our traditions do offer clues for a better Britain in the future. Early Victorian leaders stumbled through a series of government failures as a result of corruption, nepotism and incompetence in the British civil service. The Palace of Westminster, as we will see, was so decayed that much of it burned to the ground. The Victorians acted ruthlessly. They rebuilt parliament and brought about sweeping systemic changes to British institutions beginning with the reforms instituted by the Northcote–Trevelyan Report of 1854. These set the course of British public life for generations, professionalising the machinery of government so that the UK was indeed considered truly world leading, generally free from corruption, and remarkably stable. The challenges of the 2020s are different in detail from those of the 1850s, but the problems are just as significant. Possibly they are even more acute. In the 1850s the British Empire was expanding. In the 2020s in the United Kingdom the evidence of decline is all around us, blighting our everyday lives.

What follows, then, is an attempt to get a grip on the systemic problems at the heart of British democracy by recognising that the core of our current difficulties is not merely that unsuitable people are reaching positions of power and influence. It is the failing sclerotic system that permits this to happen, again and again. And the rest of us are at fault for not fixing it. We will conclude with suggestions about what kind of democratic revival may still be possible. There is also some good news. We may have lost trust in the British system, but we have not lost trust in each other. The Office for National Statistics concluded in 2022 that trust between British people remains positive and healthy while trust in British governments has declined precipitately: 'Three-quarters (75 per cent) of the UK population reported that they are trusting of most other people, higher than the average among the OECD countries who participated in the survey (67 per cent). One-third (35 per cent) of the UK population reported that they trust their national government, lower than the average across the OECD countries (41 per cent). Half (49 per cent) of the UK population said they did not trust the national government.'[3]

We can build on this. The end of our twenty-first-century Elizabethan Age has exposed many problems. Fortunately there is a way ahead.

The Way Ahead

Assessing the United Kingdom's unwritten (or more accurately uncodified) constitution, the constitutional lawyer Sam Fowles concludes gloomily that Britain is a 'vanishing democracy'. We are experiencing, Fowles says, a slow moving 'democratic crisis' with an 'unbalanced constitution' in which 'the norms and institutions that underpin our democracy are undermined through a lengthy war of attrition'. Fowles notes that this cannot merely be a high-principled constitutional debate among politicians and lawyers in court. Failure to live up to democratic standards and norms of behaviour has practical consequences for all of us: 'In 2020 Moody's downgraded the UK's credit rating on the basis of a weakening in the UK institutions and governance. It is the first time in history that this has occurred. Something is clearly wrong.'[4]

Something is indeed clearly wrong but one optimistic note should cheer us up. We have faced the knowledge that something is clearly wrong with our institutions not just in the Victorian period but many times since then. In the 1940s Britain seized the opportunities of the turning point forced upon us by the Second World War. Clement Attlee's government resolved to create a new Britain, a 'New Jerusalem', with new institutions to solve old problems. We invented the NHS, reformed education, created the welfare state and built new homes, new universities and new towns. Attlee's domestic reinvention coincided with that other great shock to the British national psyche, the retreat from Empire. We created the Commonwealth, helped create NATO and – after a major piece of strategic planning from the government of Harold Macmillan – for a time entered into a joint venture with our European partners through what became the European Union. Now at our own turning point in the 2020s, we can once again realistically define a new role for the United Kingdom. But we can succeed only if we remember an insightful comment at the time of the Attlee administration by Sir Henry Tizard, rector of Imperial College and a government scientific adviser. In 1947 Tizard warned of the danger of leaders failing to shift the British people from their imperial mindset.

'We persist,' Tizard said,

in regarding ourselves as a great power, capable of everything and only temporarily handicapped by economic difficulties. We are not a great power and never will be again. We are a great nation, but if we continue to behave like a great power we shall soon cease to be a great nation.

In the twenty-first century the United Kingdom and its political leaders have fallen into Tizard's trap. The United Kingdom in the 2020s is not a great power and has not been a great power since before Tizard's day. We can nevertheless hope to be a great nation, but only if we honestly confront our domestic divisions and repair our constitutional weaknesses. No one can fix the roof if they refuse to accept clear evidence that it is leaking. What follows is an honest assessment of the damage. The repairs or reformation will take a lot longer, but an appetite for change is in the air.

2

A State of Disunion

On the day of Queen Elizabeth II's Platinum Jubilee celebrations my neighbours held an informal street party, much like those enjoyed by millions of British people all across the country. The roads were closed. The bunting was out. Coronation chicken was on the menu along with British beer, varieties of fizz and good-humoured jokes about the event nicknamed 'Platy Jubes'. A couple of locals made speeches.

Another neighbour produced mementoes of her grandfather. He had been an official at Queen Elizabeth's coronation in 1953. I was asked to repeat a story from when I was the BBC Chief North America correspondent during the Queen's state visit to Washington DC. Her Majesty walked up to me at a drinks event and, to my astonishment, thanked me for my 'very clear diction' on television broadcasts. I was stunned. I blurted out, 'Thank you, Ma'am... the Queen's English.' The Queen laughed, possibly in sympathy. But behind the festivities, and the untrammelled goodwill towards Elizabeth II, we all knew our Elizabethan era was coming to an end. Within a few short weeks she would pass into history, our longest reigning monarch, spanning the end of Empire, the creation of the Commonwealth, the entire course of the long Cold War, the UK's entry into Europe and its eventual withdrawal. The Queen's passing meant that a country resistant to change found itself at what Germans call a *Zeitenwende*, a time shift, or turning point. Our *Zeitenwende* was to reveal Britain's strengths and also our chronic economic, political and ultimately constitutional weaknesses. Above all, at a historic turning point it is necessary to decide which way to turn.

Zeitenwende: *The End of Our Elizabethan Era*

On 8 September 2022 Queen Elizabeth II died at the royal estate at Balmoral in Scotland. She was ninety-six and had served our country for seventy years, the only monarch most British people had ever known. She was succeeded by King Charles III and these historic events occurred just two days after the United Kingdom found it had also acquired a new head of government. Liz Truss emerged as prime minister after weeks of an uninspiring and divisive contest with her rival Rishi Sunak. Sunak repeatedly (and prophetically) questioned Truss's economic competence and fitness for office. The Conservatives had been in power for twelve years. They boasted that their secret weapon was loyalty, although the real secret of Conservative success has always been pragmatism seasoned with ruthlessness. The strength of a two-party system means that it is pragmatic to stick together even if you despise your own colleagues, as many do. Traditionally winning candidates who become prime minister reach out to supporters of the loser, then the loser's supporters profess fealty to the winner. Truss formed her new government by shunning Sunak and his supporters, refusing to offer them key cabinet positions. But the weakness of the two-party system is – as George Washington predicted in his farewell address to the American people way back in 1796 – that political parties fracture into factions. The Conservative 'party within a party', the European Research Group (ERG) on the right, was balanced by rival cliques coalescing around the Conservative centre. For Conservatives, while the official Opposition is the Labour Party, the real *enemies* are colleagues on their own benches.

Beyond the tedious internecine strife, of more immediate public concern was the fact that the British constitutional and electoral system had failed to deliver what we were brought up from childhood to believe as the United Kingdom's greatest strengths – stability and competence in public life. September 2022 truly was Britain's *Zeitenwende,* a remarkable month in which Truss became the sixth British prime minister in sixteen years and the fourth Conservative prime minister in the six years since the 2016 Brexit vote. It was also the month in which Truss took decisions that immediately consigned her to the dustbin of history. In October 2022 the inept 'mini-budget' of Truss's friend and Chancellor of the Exchequer Kwasi Kwarteng, plunged even Conservative MPs and supportive newspaper columnists into despair. Truss was forced out of Downing Street after just seven weeks, becoming by far the shortest serving prime minister in British history. She even beat the record of George Canning. He at least had the excuse that he died after four months in office in 1827.

What was exposed in 2022 was not merely the political death of an unfit prime minister. It was the constitutional and other failings of the system of governance of the United Kingdom that produced her. Truss reached the highest political office in one of the world's richest democracies after securing a mere 81,326 votes, from a group of people whose sole qualification for deciding the identity of the next prime minister was the fact that they each voluntarily paid £2.09 a month to become members of the Conservative Party. Many of them are elderly; they are almost all white. This is how the British system 'works'. In late 2022 the sense of gloom was inescapable. During the forty-four days of the Truss reign of error, the failures of the system and our uncodified constitution were obvious, embarrassing and ridiculed all around the world. These failings jarred with our traditional British self-image. They were a sharp corrective to all those dreary civics lessons in schools in which our teachers asserted the glorious facts about the United Kingdom's unwritten constitution bringing unique advantages of flexibility and stability in a polity generally free from corruption.

The Data of Decline

Liz Truss promised an administration which would deliver 'growth, growth, growth'. By the time she left office, the OECD calculated that the UK would record the lowest growth in the G20, with the sole exception of Vladimir Putin's Russia. Given Russia is led by a corrupt dictator in a Kremlin kleptocracy fighting both economic sanctions and losing the war in Ukraine, the fact that the UK's economic growth stood marginally above this failing state was hardly a reason for British national pride.[5] The Office for Budget Responsibility (OBR) confirmed that leaving the European Union was so damaging in the long term that it was cutting UK GDP by 4 per cent. We would all be poorer. The *Financial Times* calculated Brexit would cost £100 billion in lost output annually, a loss of £40 billion in revenue to the Treasury per year. Less tax revenue meant less to spend on the NHS. The NHS was already failing to meet targets, failing to treat patients quickly, failing to ensure enough hospital beds to cope with the annual winter beds crisis and even failing to ensure that ambulances reached emergency patients within a reasonable time. The UK also lagged behind all other G7 nations in economic recovery from the coronavirus pandemic.

And yet the official delusions continued. Government ministers kept insisting that in some unfathomable way the United Kingdom was 'levelling up' to make poorer regions richer. The data of decline demonstrated the opposite. Since 2010 health care outcomes and life expectancy in poorer areas of England had gone significantly backwards. In 2010 the Marmot Review, by Sir Michael Marmot, Professor of Epidemiology at University College London and past president of the World Health Organisation, outlined significant health improvements in England from 1997 to 2010. Ten years later, in February 2020, the Health Foundation thinktank found that situation had gone into reverse. English people in the 2020s could increasingly expect to spend more of their lives in poor health. Health outcomes under Conservative governments after 2010 declined most significantly among the poorest 10 per cent of English women. Far from 'levelling up', the health gap between rich and poor was growing. Even *between* poorer areas there was a gap which meant that 'living in a deprived area of the North East (of England) is worse for your health than living in a similarly deprived area of London, to the extent that life expectancy is nearly five years less'.[6]

In the 2020s the sense of British decline was compounded by increases in the cost of living, higher interest rates (and therefore higher mortgage payments), and by strikes affecting everything from train staff and Border Force workers to ambulance drivers and nurses. Shortages of doctors and nurses were acute, leading to at least 105,000 total NHS vacancies by July 2022.[7] The British malaise in the twenty-first century, in other words, was both clear and omnipresent.

Politics had become personal. It affected everyone and every part of people's lives, from supermarket shopping and transport failures to travel and trade, to caring for the sick and elderly. The reality of the slogan 'Levelling Up' was that very little was going up except prices. Incomes in real terms were going down.

There was similar vacuity about the other favourite slogan of the post-Brexit governing class, the notion that the country could now be described as 'Global Britain', unshackled from the chains of Europe.

In August 2021 British forces were rapidly evacuated from Afghanistan following a decision taken not in London but in Washington to end the defence of that country against the Taliban. The British government was informed rather than consulted. The Taliban swept back into Kabul. At the same time the UK's military forces were shrinking to levels not seen since the early eighteenth century, at the end of the War of the Spanish Succession (1714). The Defence Secretary Ben Wallace was pressed to defend army numbers being cut to 72,500. He admitted that UK defences were 'extremely vulnerable' and noted that 'if we just want to stay at home and do a bit of tootling around, we've got an armed forces big enough'. Talk of Global Britain meaning the British army 'tootling around' at home sounded uncannily like the old BBC TV programme *Dad's Army*. It summed up the degree of cognitive dissonance in a country that talked constantly of greatness and yet in the public sphere exhibited astonishing weakness and seemed actively to promote failure and self-harm.

Brexit was one result of this. It had become a feast of vacuous self-congratulation. Johnson's chief negotiator, David Frost, boasted in 2020: 'I'm very pleased and proud to have led a great team to secure today's excellent deal with the EU.' He called it the 'biggest and broadest trade deal in the world'. By 2022 Frost was repudiating his own deal. In the tradition of promoting failure, he was now 'Lord Frost', so at least Brexit was of benefit to someone. Frost passed the blame for the failures of the deal to the influence of the Labour Opposition, conveniently forgetting that the Conservative Party had a landslide majority of roughly eighty seats when Brexit was negotiated. When challenged on social media on why he had originally described his own disastrous deal as 'excellent', Lord Frost did not respond to me or anyone else. Prime Minister Boris Johnson had also declared that the deal was 'excellent' and that he had managed to 'Get Brexit Done'. Yet he too tried to reopen the process, threatening to break an international treaty as a result of his own decision in 2019 to announce that the Irish border would, in customs and trade terms, now be moved to the Irish Sea. At a stroke Johnson overturned a century of British history and Ulster unionism by dividing Northern Ireland from the rest of the United Kingdom, then he blamed Ireland and the European Union for what he himself had agreed.

Inevitably relations with the UK's most important trading partner began to unravel, but so did the promise of 'world beating' post-Brexit trade agreements with other countries. A Japan trade deal was announced, but it simply copied the existing Japan–EU deal. A new Australian deal was also announced as a great achievement, yet British farmers were immediately outraged that it would – as everyone predicted – undercut animal welfare and food standards in the UK. George Eustice, the Environment Secretary who played a part in securing the deal, admitted in November 2022 (after he had left the government) that 'the truth of the matter is that the UK gave away far too much for far too little in return'. You may wonder why 'the truth of the matter' could not have been revealed when Mr Eustice was in the government. The broken promises and the attempt to fool the public on the consequences of the biggest decision taken by British voters in decades was only one part of a much bigger picture – of deceit, and as we will see, of the collapse of truth. The inevitable loss of trust is one of the reasons for our current malaise.

Rocket Man

In his first speech to parliament as prime minister in July 2019 Boris Johnson put rocket boosters on everything: 'Our mission is to deliver Brexit on the 31st of October for the purpose of uniting and re-energising our great United Kingdom and making this country the greatest place on earth.' The Johnson government however did not deliver Brexit by that date. The yawning chasm between rhetoric about 'the greatest place on earth' and the reality of Britain in the 2020s was obvious. Frustrated by his failure to keep to his self-imposed timetable, Johnson then 'prorogued' or suspended parliament, an action deemed illegal by the Supreme Court. In Scotland, as we will see in detail later, a senior judge made clear that Johnson had lied to HM the Queen on the prorogation. Yet the judgement of the Supreme Court, one of the key checks and balances against unfettered executive power in the United Kingdom, did not instil a degree of humility in the Queen's ministers. Quite the opposite. Conservative politicians insisted that the power of judges needed to be curbed. The *Daily Mail*'s notorious front-page splash that judges were now 'Enemies of the People' was one of many attacks on the judiciary.

The impact on public trust in British democracy was profound. By 2019, according to the Eurobarometer:

> levels of confidence among the UK public had dropped to just 19 per cent – fewer than one in five Britons tend to trust their national parliament. Among all European legislatures, the UK parliament is now one of the least trusted... more than three times as many Danes, Finns, Netherlanders and Luxembourgers expressed a high or fair degree of trust in their legislatures as Britons did in their own parliament. The average level of trust across all European countries, 34 per cent, was nearly twice as high as in the UK.[8]

Arrival at 'greatest place on earth' was now postponed indefinitely, due not to unforeseen circumstances but problems anyone paying attention had predicted long in advance. By 2020, however, the Brexit agreement that David Frost called 'excellent' was eventually delivered. It allowed Johnson and his party to celebrate that at last they had, in one sense, 'Got Brexit Done' even if trust in British democracy was undone.

Within a few weeks, the inadequacies of this version of Brexit became obvious. There was trouble on the streets of Northern Ireland for a reason that anyone familiar with the last century of British and Irish history could have predicted: unionists in Northern Ireland were deeply aggrieved at being treated differently from the rest of the United Kingdom, something they and their forefathers had fought against since the late nineteenth century. Johnson tried unilaterally to alter the sections known as the Northern Ireland Protocol, enshrined in the 'excellent' agreement with the European Union. The Northern Ireland Secretary Brandon Lewis was forced to agree in parliament that the proposed new British legislation 'does break international law in a very specific and limited way'. That's because the Johnson government under its Northern Ireland Protocol Bill planned unilaterally to change UK domestic law so that British courts did not have to take into account European law in ways clearly specified by the Brexit withdrawal agreement. That would override the special legal status given to the agreement on Northern Ireland.[9]

This deceit, chicanery and bad faith had profound implications for how the UK was seen abroad, even if at home the delusional Boosterism continued. On 1 January 2020 the New Year's Day edition of *The Daily Express* assured readers that the decade ahead could be the 'Roaring Twenties'. Evidence of the 2020s 'roaring' proved difficult to detect. (Incidentally, the 1920s in Britain roared briefly but it was punctuated by a bitter General Strike, and marked elsewhere by the fascist coup in Italy, the rise of Nazism in Germany and around the world by the beginnings of the Great Depression.)

By mid-2022 Boris Johnson was gone, unseated by backstairs intrigue in his own party as a result of his many ethical and other failings. These were exposed in banal and sordid form by his indulgence of drunken parties at 10 Downing Street while the rest of the country was enduring the miseries of isolation and lockdown during the covid pandemic. Key members of Johnson's staff were filmed laughing and joking about how they might spin the news to explain why the Downing Street parties were not really parties. All this meant that the United Kingdom experienced the kind of political turmoil and economic failure less like the Roaring Twenties and more an echo of the 'stagflation' 1970s, a time when stagnation and inflation meant Britain was known as 'The Sick Man of Europe'. Yet the incompetence and venality at Westminster in the 2020s was much more damaging than fifty years previously since it disrupted as never before the presumed unity of the United Kingdom as a voluntary union of four nations. As the Westminster parliament's own definition of the UK put it, the United Kingdom's coherence was always vague: 'There is no single definition of what constitutes the Union between the four nations of the United Kingdom. Unlike in most other countries, the essential components or elements of this Union have never been set down or codified.'[10] Dr Andrew Blick, Lecturer in Politics and Contemporary History, King's College London wrote:

> There has never been a specific moment at which the UK has sought decisively to write down the key values and rules of its system. While all constitutions develop over time, the UK constitution stands out for the extent to which it appears to be an accumulation more than a specific planned construction.[11]

The vagueness of this 'accumulation' with 'no single definition' even of the union at the heart of the United Kingdom is a vagueness we will see running through all major constitutional questions in Britain. This 'accumulation' rather than 'construction' known as the UK constitution began to unravel in the 2020s. One reason was that leaving the European Union was opposed by most voters in Scotland and Northern Ireland, leading to loud demands for a second independence referendum in Scotland, greater support for independence in Wales, and the emergence of the Irish republican party Sinn Féin as the largest political grouping in Northern Ireland. In this lopsided union, the Conservative Party held firm in Westminster even though it ran no major local government authorities in Scotland, Wales or Northern Ireland. Conservatives have very few MPs in those nations or regions and the Westminster government has been in constant contention with the devolved parliaments in Belfast, Edinburgh and Cardiff. The forces of disunion were strengthening.

Ever since the devolution agreements of the 1990s the Westminster parliament has often seemed increasingly irrelevant to the daily lives of the roughly 10 million UK citizens who live in Scotland, Northern Ireland, and Wales. Support for Welsh independence increased from 14 per cent in 2014 to 25 per cent in 2022.[12] The Labour First Minister of Wales, Mark Drakeford, an anti-independence unionist, publicly asserted the dangers when he said that the union of the United Kingdom as it is currently constituted 'is over'. When the First Minister of Scotland, Nicola Sturgeon, demanded a second independence referendum, Liz Truss suggested that as prime minister her strategy would be to 'ignore' Ms Sturgeon because the First Minister was 'an attention seeker'. The United Kingdom Supreme Court ruled emphatically in November 2022 that the Scottish government had no legal authority to call a second referendum, because that power resided only with Westminster. This unsurprising legal verdict was interpreted very differently politically north and south of the border. English politicians, commentators and newspapers saw it as a major setback for Sturgeon and the Scottish National Party (SNP). SNP politicians and commentators saw it as a boost for independence. That's because Ms Sturgeon was able to capitalise on resentment that a law passed by Westminster prevented Scotland from voting on whether to remain part of the UK's 'voluntary' union.

Independence supporters pointed out to me that the European Union was also a voluntary union of nations. The EU did not try to prevent an inconvenient vote on anyone leaving because (as Scottish nationalists told me) the European Union is democratic and has its own written constitution, unlike the UK. The idea that a Conservative government that represented only a tiny minority of Scottish people (six out of fifty-nine Scottish seats at Westminster) could block a vote on leaving the 'voluntary' union known as the United Kingdom merely proved how undemocratic the United Kingdom had become, they said. Whether this argument is convincing, appealing or even useful, the resentment caused was clearly significant. For the first time ever, four consecutive opinion polls by the end of 2022 showed a majority of Scots were now in favour of independence. Scottish unionists, including the former Labour leader Gordon Brown, suggested that the choice for the UK was to become 'a reformed state or a failed state' especially since a majority of Scots had not voted Conservative since 1955. Two well-known Scottish Conservatives told me that the 'only thing' that could keep Scotland in the union in future would be 'a Labour government'. Another prominent Scottish Conservative politician, a strong unionist whom I have known for years, said of their Conservative government colleagues as (quote) 'what a f- – – ing shower'.

In England, Conservative grandees including former Hong Kong Governor Lord (Chris) Patten and former Chancellor George Osborne bemoaned the state of the union. They claimed that the Conservative Party was no longer a truly British party but an 'English nationalist' party, dividing the country with competing nationalisms. In Northern Ireland for the first time in its 100-year history more citizens identified as Catholic than Protestant. The biggest Northern Ireland political party was, by 2022, Sinn Féin, founded as the political wing of the IRA. The six counties of Northern Ireland were created separate from the Irish Free State in 1921 to avoid precisely this outcome, by keeping Catholics in the minority and ensuring that Irish Republicans would never be in government. By the 2020s Irish nationalists began to feel that after a century of partition in Ireland the tide of history was flowing towards them and Irish unity. The United Kingdom as currently constituted appeared to be entering a death spiral, driven by alienation from the incompetence of the governing class at Westminster.

The Changing of the Guard

There was some good news – mostly in what did *not* happen. In the course of a few days in 2022 the United Kingdom changed its head of state with the accession of King Charles III; changed its head of government with the arrival of Liz Truss to replace Boris Johnson in Downing Street; changed key government ministers in Truss's new cabinet, then changed the captain and crew once more as Rishi Sunak became prime minister and the merry-go-round slowed for a while. The British paradox was also apparent. We were clearly still a great nation, but we were just as clearly labouring under a failed democratic political system. In all these changes, as we have noted, there was no revolution, no riots or violence, and very little fuss beyond traditional British flummery, uniforms, parades and respectful queues; no gunfire, except cannon celebrating the accession of King Charles III. Beyond a few minor protests the biggest public upset came when the new king was filmed losing his temper over a leaky fountain pen. It was a somewhat comic moment of humanity amid the solemnity.

On the day of Queen Elizabeth II's funeral I interviewed the constitutional scholar Sir Anthony Seldon and discussed the success of the transition between our heads of state. Seldon told me that King Charles had achieved the first and most important task of any British monarch by ensuring the royal succession, probably to the end of the twenty-first century. But there was also some less than good news, both for the new monarch and the new prime minister. Beyond the irritations of tabloid stories about 'Harry and Meghan' – Prince Harry and his wife Meghan Markle, and their apparently fraught relationship with other members of 'the Firm' – there were real scandals and controversies. Some touched on the new king.

Prince Charles, as heir to the throne, had unwisely accepted what was reported to be €3 million as a 'charitable donation' delivered in a suitcase stuffed full of cash from a Qatari billionaire. Charles's charitable endeavours meant he also took funds reported to be £1 million from the family of Osama bin Laden. This came despite objections from his advisers at Clarence House and the Prince of Wales Charity Fund (PWCF). In Prince Charles's favour, bin Laden's wider family had for a long time – at least since the 2001 attacks on the United States – disowned Osama. Sir Ian Cheshire, chairman of the PWCF said that the 2013 donation of cash in a suitcase was 'carefully considered' by the fund's trustees. It is difficult to see how taking millions in suitcases stuffed with cash was truly 'carefully considered'. It might be traditional behaviour in the House of Pablo Escobar, but did not suit the House of Windsor. And it got worse. As the world knows, Prince Charles's brother, Prince Andrew, had been stripped of his royal duties as a result of his association with an American paedophile and sex trafficker Jeffrey Epstein. Andrew denied any wrongdoing but nonetheless paid Virginia Giuffre, one of Epstein's victims, a reported £12 million.

King Charles III moved quickly to try to pull together the union of the United Kingdom. He visited Edinburgh, Belfast and Cardiff amid fears that perhaps our Elizabethan Age was drawing to a close with a kind of fearful symmetry. The first Elizabethan Age ended in 1603. The Stuart king in Scotland, James VI, became King James I of England. A new nation was born, a nation that would conquer half the globe in the greatest empire the world had ever seen. After he became King of England, James I wisely engaged in his own rebranding when in 1604 he proclaimed: 'We have thought good to discontinue the divided names of England and Scotland... and resolve to take... the name and style of *King of Great Britain*.'

The first Elizabethan Age brought the United Kingdom together, but the end of the second Elizabethan Age showed signs of a change in the opposite direction. And the world noticed. On social media a popular meme showed Conservative government ministers dancing and singing to the tunes of *The Muppet Show*. Former US Treasury Secretary Larry Summers, a good friend of Britain, concluded that, like the Brexit vote of 2016, the self-inflicted wounds and failures of British democracy were causing irreparable damage to the country's image:

It makes me very sorry to say, but I think the UK is behaving a bit like an emerging market turning itself into a submerging market... Between Brexit, how far the Bank of England got behind the curve and now these fiscal policies, I think Britain will be remembered for having pursued the worst macroeconomic policies of any major country in a long time.[13]

When Rishi Sunak replaced Liz Truss as prime minister in October 2022 the political chaos continued. Among the many scandals that came to public attention, a newly promoted minister, Gavin Williamson, was forced to resign after just a few days back in office. He achieved the astonishing record of being removed from high political office by three successive prime ministers in four years. This also appeared to be regarded as normal in 2020s Britain. How do you become Gavin Williamson, you may ask? Mr Williamson was often described in British newspapers as 'formerly a fireplace salesman' and was repeatedly 'feeling the heat', in his serial resignations. For some reason he followed the pattern of being rewarded for failure. He became a Knight of the Realm, *Sir* Gavin Williamson. (No – I don't know why either.)

'Which Muppet Will be Prime Minister by Christmas?'

Just before Christmas in 2022, a stranger came up to me on a train journey and asked: 'Which Muppet do you think will be prime minister by Christmas?' The answer was unfortunately embedded in the question. If Britain is governed by Muppets – and I was beginning to have sympathy with this point of view – then the specific identity of the Muppet-in-Chief doesn't much matter. It is the rotational system for delivering interchangeable Muppetry to high political office in Westminster that is itself the problem. The System (with a Capital S – we will define more coherently later) has failed us repeatedly. Our prolonged economic, financial and political crises in the twenty-first century are – as we will see – not occasional errors of judgement from a few politicians of dubious ability. They are rooted in our crisis of ethics, competence and standards. This crisis allows – in fact encourages – unsuitable, untalented, unqualified and at times unethical people to reach the top.

The consequent loss of trust in the institutions of democracy means that our ethical crisis is, in reality, a constitutional crisis. Democracies which survive find ways to stop bad, useless or rotten people from abusing power. They do this by having a robust constitution with checks and balances to enforce norms of behaviour and respect for rules. In Britain, we don't have a constitution intelligible to most citizens. Some, as we will see, argue that we do not have a constitution at all. What we do have is a system that permits the prime minister to act as judge and jury of his or her own conduct, provided they retain the support of a majority in parliament. This is often dressed up in the somewhat closed world of traditional British commentary on the subject as an exceptional British achievement admired round the world. If this was ever true, it certainly is not true now.

What is true is that instead of an instruction manual for conduct in government we have a series of sonorous yet vague constitutional platitudes designed not to inform but to conceal. These include 'the Crown in Parliament', the 'separation of powers', the 'royal prerogative', 'executive privilege', 'sovereignty' and many more. Often these phrases are used in ways to suggest that British citizens should accept that all this is glorious and remarkably successful in practice even if unintelligible in theory. The excuse for constitutional opacity in the 2020s is that in some miraculous way centuries ago, it led to the creation of the greatest empire the world had ever seen. In Walter Bagehot's famous phrase about royalty, 'We must not let in daylight upon magic.' To which, in an age in which the constitutional magic has decidedly faded, one can only respond: you cannot be serious.

This book, therefore, is an exercise in letting daylight fall not upon magic but upon sleight of hand, the shocking abuses that are possible in a failed British system of governance based on a series of illusions and delusions dressed up in language most of us find impenetrable. The blurred lines of our failing constitution don't just allow abuse, they encourage it. The United Kingdom's supposed constitutional 'rules' either do not exist in any meaningful fashion, or if they exist they are not always agreed, or if they are agreed they are often so vague that they can be challenged or ignored by the most powerful person of all, the prime minister. And even if the supposed constitutional rules do exist, are clear, and are not challenged or ignored, well... then they can be changed. All it takes is a prime minister in command of enough votes in parliament. We boast about this and call it 'flexibility'. You could use a more common synonym and suggest the British system is so flexible it can easily be bent.

We will explore these alternative descriptions later. But the series of unfortunate events of 2022 revealed in dramatic form something which has been obvious for years. The great Whig historian Lord Macaulay once wrote of the 'pure gold' of the English unwritten constitution. Modern commentators and outside observers have been less kind. Former Irish Attorney General, Senator Michael McDowell, was one among many who offered a scathing analysis about the hollowness of Britain's supposedly 'world leading' and 'world beating' system of governance:

> The revelation that UK chancellor Kwasi Kwarteng committed Britain to a programme of unfunded tax cuts and unfunded borrowing without even discussing the abolition of the 45 per cent tax rate for the highest earners with the cabinet had many Irish people scratching their heads. Ireland has a written Constitution which radically differs from the non-constitutional agglomeration of conventions that some in the UK describe as 'the British constitution'... The British cabinet system of government has been permitted to mutate and decay to the extent that the late Tory politician Lord Hailsham famously described the office of prime minister as an 'elective dictatorship'... The sad fact is that the UK has utterly degraded its internal systems of governmental checks and balances. All this has been developing for the last half century. Boris

Johnson's ill-fated spell in office marked the high point of prime ministerial autocracy.[14]

British politicians and newspaper columnists debated why the Cameron, May, Johnson and Truss governments were such a rapid succession of failures. One former British cabinet minister, a lawyer of considerable reputation, described Boris Johnson from the start as always reminding him of some of the people he used to see 'in the dock in court'. But as Senator McDowell observed, the far more significant yet unaddressed question was very different. It is the existence of what 'some in the UK describe' as the British constitution. What on earth is that supposed constitution if it permits the shenanigans and 'prime ministerial autocracy' that we have endured for years, and which foreign observers like McDowell seem to think doesn't even exist?

Before looking in more detail at our beloved idiosyncrasies, it is worth examining one underreported piece of data of Britain's decline. It indicates why an Irish Senator could so clearly see Britain's relative failure in the twenty-first century.

Back in 1973, Ireland together with the UK joined the forerunner of the European Union, the European Economic Community. In terms of GDP per capita the Irish Republic was then considerably poorer – roughly two-thirds as wealthy – than the UK. It was still a backward, primarily agricultural country. But by early 2022, when Senator McDowell wrote his critique of Britain's constitution and economic policy, Ireland's GDP per capita was predicted to be roughly US$83,800, whereas UK GDP was put at US$41,900.[15] Another calculation (using different criteria) later that year by World Economics reassessed Ireland's GDP per capita as the highest in Europe at US$125,000, with the UK figure at $52,000.[16] By November 2022 the British OBR forecast the UK's growth for 2023 as lower than any of the twenty-seven countries of the European Union. Top of the growth figures, at slightly more than plus 3 per cent was the country once dismissively known in England as 'Poor Little Eire'.[17]

3
Idiosyncrasies

Westminster is, as most of us recognise, quite simply weird. Voters in only two European countries elect their national legislatures by the Westminster First Past the Post system (FPTP). One is the United Kingdom. The other is Belarus, the dictatorship of Vladimir Putin's ally, Alexander Lukashenko. The modern parliaments in Scotland, Wales and Northern Ireland, like other Western European democracies, use forms of proportional representation, and are also shaped differently. Westminster pretends that it has a 'two-party' system, with government and opposition facing each other traditionally 'two sword lengths apart' – 3.96 metres. But the two-party system is itself an ancient fiction, kept alive (just) by FPTP. According to the UK parliament website the following parties had members in the House of Commons since 2019: the Alliance Party, Conservative Party, Co-operative Party, Labour, Liberal Democrats, Plaid Cymru, Scottish National Party, the Green Party, the Democratic Unionist Party, Sinn Féin and the Social Democratic and Labour Party. Modern European parliaments, with significant numbers of minority party members, tend to favour a horseshoe shape. When the Scottish parliament was set up in 1997 the first First Minister Donald Dewar praised the horseshoe idea as one likely to allow robust debate while being conducive to consensus. 'We have always said the Scottish parliament will be marked by a new kind of politics where constructive debate as well as proper party rivalry will be important,' was how Dewar put it.

In the 'old kind of politics' at Westminster, MPs praise the parliamentary committee system because it allows them to cooperate positively across party lines, unlike the Them and Us posturing in the House of Commons chamber which TV viewers and spectators mostly see:

> In a (committee) meeting the members sit around a horseshoe shaped table with the chairman in the middle. This is a less adversarial layout than the Floor of the House and encourages committees to act in a more collaborative fashion. In general select committees like to proceed on the basis of consensus.[1]

Implicit in this praise of the consensual committee system is that the 'Floor of the House' behaves in ways that are exactly the opposite of collaborative. It rewards adversarial politics, the tedious braying of Prime Minister's Questions, and MPs who act confrontationally because with government and opposition facing each other there are only winners and losers. Consensus is not important. But the idiosyncrasies of the Westminster system go far beyond encouraging politicians to create problems for the other side rather than solving them together. Voters in England make up 84 per cent of the British population, yet they lose out the most. That's because all three devolved parliaments in the UK ensure much fairer elections. Proportional representation (PR) tends to allow small parties formally or informally to become a key part of governing coalitions and more easily represent their voters' interests. The Westminster system means those who vote for small parties often can't elect any representative who speaks for them.

This is at the heart of England's democratic deficit. Westminster MPs are often elected not *because* it is the wish of a majority of voters in their constituencies, but *despite* the majority opinion. In Kent where I live, for example, there are seventeen constituencies. In the 2019 General Election, sixteen of these constituencies elected Conservative MPs. Only one, Canterbury, returned a Labour MP. The Conservative Party took 532,000 votes across the county. That means on average it takes 33,000 votes to elect one Conservative MP in Kent. But it takes seven times as many, almost a quarter of a million votes, 221,000, to elect the county's one Labour MP, Rosie Duffield, the first Labour MP in Canterbury's history. The Liberal Democrats took 92,000 votes across Kent in 2019. They were rewarded with nothing – no representation whatsoever. Whatever the merits of Liberal Democrat candidates, voting for them is a 'wasted' vote in Kent and elsewhere. If Lib Dems and Labour were elected with the same number of votes as Conservatives in Kent, they could expect two Lib Dem MPs and six or seven for Labour. What is true of Kent is true everywhere in the UK for Westminster elections.

The Electoral Reform Society calculated that in the 2019 election across the entire UK it took:

- 864,743 votes to elect the lone Green MP
- 642,303 votes to elect zero Brexit Party MPs
- 334,122 votes to elect each Liberal Democrat
- 50,817 votes to elect each Labour MP
- 38,300 votes to elect each Conservative MP
- 38,316 votes to elect each Plaid Cymru MP
- 25,882 votes to elect each Scottish National Party MP

Willie Sullivan of the Electoral Reform Society said that:

When it takes nearly 900,000 votes to elect one party's MP, and just 26,000 for another, you know the system is not just struggling, it's bankrupt. Millions of voters have gone totally unrepresented, with worryingly warped results in many areas.[2]

What is also 'worryingly warped' is that – with the exception of Belarus – nobody else in Europe thinks the British 'bankrupt' system is democratic. And Belarus isn't a real democracy.

More widely, in the 2015 General Election the pro-Brexit UKIP party created by Nigel Farage managed to secure 3.8 million votes across the UK (mostly in England, and many in Kent). UKIP ended up with just one MP in the House of Commons, Douglas Carswell, who then left the party. That meant almost 4 million British citizens who took the time and trouble to vote UKIP in 2015 were not represented in the House of Commons. Again, this is normal. It's how the British system works.

Obviously, it does not actually work in reality. It's a turn off. A neighbour of mine, a man in his forties who runs a small business on the Kent coast, told me he had stopped voting 'years ago' because 'it was just a waste of time' and 'anyway, they [meaning politicians] never listen'. My neighbour voted for Brexit in 2016 because, as he told me then, 'Maybe they will listen now.' Later he had reasons to regret that choice, since he planned to buy a property in Greece, and realised that doing business outside a common market and customs area is extremely difficult. He gave up. Of course my neighbour's story is merely an anecdote. It's not scientific or psephological research. But his apathy speaks for millions who could vote (the voting age population) yet who choose not to do so. Campaigners for reform of the system, including Tom Brake of Unlock Democracy, Neal Lawson of Compass and many others, argue that the result of FPTP is that most voters, most of the time, just like those in Kent, do not get the MP they vote for. Most British people, most of the time, do not get the government that they vote for either. That is also just how British democracy 'works'. As Tom Brake told me, 'What's the point if you feel your vote is perpetually wasted?' Yet 'the point' is that our antiquated system is useful for some people. Not voters, obviously. Politicians.

The febrile December 2019 General Election focused on one emotive issue, Boris Johnson's 'promise' to Get Brexit Done. The result was great public interest in the election. According to the Office for National Statistics: 'The total number of UK Parliamentary electoral registrations in December 2019 was 47,074,800, an increase of 1,299,100 (2.8 per cent) from the previous year.'[3] If this really was a crunch election on a matter of great importance setting the post-Brexit course for the UK for a generation, turnout was still just 67.3 per cent or two-thirds of the voting age population. The excitement was so high that a third of registered British voters, around 16 million of us, didn't vote. Post-war UK election turnout peaked back in 1950 at 84 per cent and has slipped ever since. Losing a third of your audience is considered a catastrophe for television programme ratings, yet is regarded as just fine and normal in British elections. In this at least the UK is not unique. As we will see in Chapters 4 and 5 the loss of trust in elections and democracy itself extends far beyond the UK, and is particularly notable in the United States.

Whatever the many and varied reasons for all those millions of missing voters in Britain in 2019, the implications were clear. The Johnson government's parliamentary 'landslide', a majority of eighty seats, was based on support from just 43.6 per cent of the vote. That translates to 29 per cent of the voting age population, just over a quarter. The MPs elected in this supposed geological upheaval would decide the shape of Brexit, a profoundly important issue for years to come. Yet nearly three-quarters of possible UK voters did not vote for the Johnson 'landslide', although that is not how most newspapers portrayed the vote. As for Boris Johnson, he accepted the voters' verdict with characteristic modesty and another misplaced geological metaphor:

'We must understand now what an earthquake we have created. The way in which we have changed the political map in this country. We have to grapple with the consequences of that.' Johnson added that 'no one can now refute' that we have a 'stonking mandate' to deliver Brexit and 'no one can possibly dispute that it is the will of the British people to get Brexit done'.

Measuring the 'will of the British people' by the decisions of fewer than a third of registered voters is yet another idiosyncrasy considered normal in Britain. And that's the problem. We have become so inured to accepting constitutional nonsense that we don't even examine the basic arithmetic.

Yet if you think the way in which the British decide the political complexion of the House of Commons and government is eccentric or shameless, it is a model of reason compared to the composition of the upper chamber of the supposed Mother of Parliaments, known to MPs as 'the other place', the House of Lords. The House of Lords is where democracy goes to die. To understand why we need to take one step back.

The only democracies anywhere in the world to have unwritten or, more accurately, uncodified, constitutions are the UK (an uneasy union of different nations and at least five – some say six – different electoral systems with a total population of 68 million); Israel (population 9 million) and New Zealand (population 5 million). But no country anywhere in the world has a legislative chamber quite as bizarre as the House of Lords. It is part hereditary, part Church of England bishops, as well as big-money party donors, cronies, and superannuated or failed politicians. The only two sovereign states in the world to award clerics of the established religion votes in their legislatures are the UK, with twenty-six seats reserved for bishops, and the Islamic Republic of Iran. Iran is a totalitarian theocracy. There are also in the Lords many very distinguished and admirable business people, academics, scientists and former senior civil servants too. But the House of Lords is the only upper house of a bicameral parliament anywhere in the world with *more* members than the lower house. If a camel is jokingly described as a horse designed by a committee, the House of Lords is part camel, part humpback whale, and 100 per cent fossil. Failed attempts at Lords reform give some indication not just of the difficulty of making any real change to Britain's constipated constitution, they also show how abuse of the quasi-democratic British system is not merely tolerated but perversely encouraged.

By 1999 the House of Lords was utterly discredited. It had expanded so much with new Life Peers that it contained 1,273 members. Fortunately most of them did not turn up for debates, because there would have been nowhere to sit. The House of Lords Act that year expelled more than 600 of their Lordships, but the numbers crept up again immediately. There is – I am not making this up – no upper limit. In theory the Lords could expand exponentially forever. Perhaps we could democratise the chamber by making every one of the 47 million people who vote in a UK General Election new members of the House of Lords? If you think that is crazy, here's the current system which we accept as part of the way we are governed. In 2011 a parliamentary committee recommended capping the number of Lords at 300. A decade later the proposed cap was 600. There are now a shade over 800 Lords and Ladies. Some 200 of them are hard-working, conscientious and talented. After a career in journalism, I know some members of the Lords and admire those I do know. I can think of several dozen that I find hugely impressive, irrespective of party affiliation. Others, not so much. About half do not even bother to attend regularly. They are rarely missed.

Back in 2007 the House of Commons voted to make the House of Lords an entirely elected second chamber. The Lords – predictably – disagreed. By September 2021, three-quarters of the British public backed scrapping or overhauling the Lords. In 2022 the Labour leader Sir Keir Starmer committed his party to give the public their wish, but don't hold your breath. For more than a century it has always been easier to promise Lords' reform than to achieve it. In the British tradition, the difficulty of fiddling with the composition of an unelected upper chamber that is useful for 'promoting' failed political rivals as well as cronies leads most prime ministers to think they have better things to do with their time than Lords' reform. The result is an archaic constitutional dog's breakfast at the heart of British democracy. The structure of the chamber as it exists is therefore worth considering in detail.

The average age of peers currently is seventy-one. That's several years beyond the age of eligibility for a state retirement pension. The Electoral Reform Society tried to explain the 'modernisation' of the House of Lords at the end of last century, and yet their explanation merely reveals the ludicrous construction of a Gilbert and Sullivan fancy dress operatic comedy. We must pretend the next paragraph makes sense.

The House of Lords Act of 1999 removed all but 92 hereditaries, then numbering 750, breaking a 700-year-old right for all peers to sit on and vote from the red benches. The remaining 92 were elected by all the previous hereditary peers in the House grouped by party affiliation – 42 Conservatives, 28 Crossbenchers, three Lib Dems, two Labour and 17 others. These numbers are set. When one Conservative resigns, a new Conservative is elected. The decision to retain 92 hereditary peers was a forced compromise from then-Prime Minister Tony Blair, who, in his planned House of Lords reforms, had sought to remove all of them but was forced to back down following opposition from the Lords themselves, instead agreeing to let a small number remain as a temporary measure ahead of further reform. Yet over two decades later the number of hereditary peers remains the same.[4] *

A democratically elected British government bowing to opposition from *within* the House of Lords to reform *of* the House of Lords is not by any means the greatest peculiarity of the British parliamentary system, although it is emblematic of the United Kingdom's inability to bring about constitutional change. A more significant brake on constructive change is the systemic problem that Senator Michael McDowell noted when he quoted the former British Lord Chancellor Lord Hailsham's observation that Britain is, or risks becoming, an 'elective dictatorship'. There are important caveats to this bold statement. Unlike a real dictatorship or authoritarian state, there remain significant checks and balances within the British system, at least in theory. But, as we will explore in more detail (in Chapter 5, Truth Decay: Strategic Lying, Dead Cats and Our Democratic Recession) there are also many ways in which a rule-breaking prime minister who refuses to obey traditional norms of behaviour can avoid scrutiny or dismiss its consequences. Boris Johnson demonstrated that peculiar talent for three years.

One other block to Lords' reform or constitutional innovation is a simple matter of political psychology. I asked a very senior civil servant why, after Tony Blair's enormous election victory in 1997 Blair did not commit to electoral reform and proportional representation. The senior civil servant answered enigmatically.

'179.'

'I don't understand,' I responded. 'What do you mean, 179?'

'Tony Blair's majority in 1997 was 179 seats,' the senior civil servant explained. 'He won by a landslide and then began to see some of the

---

* The Lords themselves agreed on a plan a few years ago to cut the size rapidly to below the Commons. The only reason it failed was because the then Prime Minister, like all before and since, refused to give up their power of patronage to appoint peers at will.

good points of the system which up till then he had assumed needed to be changed.'

A Leader of the Opposition like Blair may commit publicly to widespread constitutional reform, but once in government the prospect of running an 'elective dictatorship' becomes sufficiently appealing that few prime ministers retain the appetite to kick away the ladder up which they have so recently climbed. There are also other enormous – yet bizarre – privileges of power. An outgoing prime minister, even one dismissed in disgrace like Boris Johnson, may leave a mark on British politics and parliament for decades to come through the tradition known as the resignation honours list. In his list, Johnson was able to recommend as fit for a peerage two of his loyal advisers who, given their ages, could be politically active in the Lords for a good half century – the Conservative Party's former political director Ross Kempsell (then aged thirty), and Charlotte Owen (then twenty-nine) a former prime ministerial assistant. They were intended to become the youngest life peers in history, appointed by a prime minister so unpopular at the time of his leaving power that he was trusted by only 11 per cent of the population and distrusted by 75 per cent.[5] We will hear a little more about Ross Kempsell's talents later. But how is all this apparently acceptable and unchallenged? In part it is the invocation of tradition, the dressing up of political expediency quite literally with men in tights and archaic uniforms, and equally opaque language about Lord Macaulay's 'pure gold' of an 'unwritten' constitution. You may prefer a different metaphor in the twenty-first century, that of putting lipstick on a pig. I prefer hocus pocus. Either way, the effect is magical and transformative.

The dictionary definition of 'hocus pocus' is 'meaningless talk or language designed to confuse or mislead, trick or confuse people about the reality of a situation'. It comes from post-Reformation Protestant scepticism about the Catholic Latin Mass in which the bread and the wine of the eucharist are celebrated and the communion wafer held up with the words *hoc est corpus meum* ('this is my body') – the literal transmutation of bread into the body of Christ. By the 1700s the theological discussion of transubstantiation was corrupted into 'hocus pocus' as a cod-Latin phrase used by magicians, conjurers and tricksters. The aim was to deceive the gullible, at least in Protestant eyes. Today's equivalent is the incomprehensible constitutional language through which the United Kingdom is governed.

If anyone is unclear what these phrases actually mean, here's an explanation from the House of Commons website in which you may hear echoes of the Holy Trinity:

> Along with the House of Commons and the House of Lords, the Crown is an integral part of the institution of Parliament. The King plays a constitutional role in opening and dissolving Parliament and approving Bills before they become law.[6]

The king opens parliament in a rather lovely ceremony. The monarch reads out a speech written by the government outlining its programme. He then 'approves' bills before they become law, but – you may wonder – does the option of the sovereign truly 'disapproving' bills and putting them in the wastebin actually exist in reality, or only in theory? Is this something realistically on offer, or is the monarch's 'constitutional role' more like that of a nodding donkey? And – without attempting to be rude about any of those involved in those solemn occasions in which the emperor, or rather monarch, certainly does have plenty of clothes – when all these functions are stripped of arcane ceremonial traditions, how far is the constitutional role of the monarch as described here simply that which could be performed by a literate janitor 'opening' parliament and reading some words written by the government of the day? What, even, do we mean by 'the Crown' in such matters, beyond the name of a historically inaccurate but watchable TV series? Here again is an attempt at an explanation of the Crown's constitutional role from the House of Commons Library while Queen Elizabeth II was on the throne: 'The Crown is one of the oldest institutions in the United Kingdom and remains *a significant part of its constitution. It has, however, no single accepted definition.*' [my italics]

Oh, that 'no single accepted definition' caveat again. We will see that repeatedly. If there was 'no single definition' of gravity or death or a red traffic light or theft we might be in trouble, but when it comes to constitutional matters this is just normal. So we know 'the Crown' is 'significant' but we do not really have a clue what it is. Then:

The term has been used to describe a physical object or as an alternative way of referring to the monarch in their personal or official capacity. At its most expansive, the Crown *has been taken* as a proxy for 'the government' or what in other countries would be known as 'the State'.

In this explanation 'the Crown' is *not* the government but it is a 'proxy' for the government, or indeed for 'the State' which is, of course, not exactly the same as 'the government'; while the Crown is also a physical object and a way of referring to the monarch in either (or both) their 'personal or official capacity'. This isn't getting much clearer, I suspect, for most readers.

There is more (or less):

There are, as a result, many distinct Crowns – of Canada, Australia and other countries where the Queen Elizabeth II is head of state – all connected via the *'personal union'* of the current monarch, who marks her Platinum Jubilee during 2022. The terms 'the sovereign' or 'monarch' and 'the Crown' are related but have separate meanings. The Crown encompasses both the monarch and the government. It is *vested in the Queen, but in general its functions are exercised by Ministers of the Crown* accountable to the UK Parliament or the three devolved legislatures. [my italics][7]

Remember: this verbal porridge is from the House of Commons Library. It asserts that the Crown has functions which are 'exercised' by government ministers yet somehow 'vested' in the queen (or, now, the king). The dictionary definition of 'vested' is to 'confer or bestow (power, authority, property, etc.) on someone'. Yet if power is exercised by ministers, it can hardly be conferred, bestowed or 'vested' in the queen or king, except in some miraculously symbolic form, perhaps as communion wine really is (or is a metaphor for) the blood of Christ. That must be what 'personal union' means. The British monarch is turning into St Patrick's shamrock, three leaves in one body. So let us fix on the comforting certainty that there is 'no single accepted definition' of anything at the heart of the system of British governance, but there certainly are a lot of words to let you know that no one knows anything for sure.

A generous conclusion might be that the works of constitutional scholars and the House of Commons Library are designed to impress rather than to inform. It is certainly doubtful that any of this glorious verbiage would stand up to the scrutiny of the close reading technique of a twentieth-century literary scholar like F. R. Leavis. A less generous conclusion would be that no one really has a clue what any of this means, but if there is sufficient hocus pocus surrounding it then the expectation is that you and I will not ask too many questions. We will instead marvel at the verbiage just as we are impressed by glorious uniforms and men in tights, the marching bands, clip-clop of the Household Cavalry and the horse drawn carriages. It is a 'tradition' or at least a traditionally accepted convenient disguise for a constitution that at its heart involves a con trick for which we need to accept one caveat. There is a long-running British tradition that our ineffable British constitution miraculously works in practice even if it is shaky in theory.

Unfortunately evidence of the British system working in practice in the 2020s is hard to detect. To labour the point, it is surely easier to understand the concept of the Holy Trinity – Three in One and One in Three, the Father, Son and Holy Spirit – than these tortured quasi-explanations of the Crown in Parliament, or the differences between the sovereign or monarch or the Crown, especially when some of this encompasses both the sovereign (or monarch) and the government (or executive) and maybe parliament (the legislature). And in some esoteric way the House of Lords fits into all this, although perhaps not for long.

After years as a journalist and writer asking politicians and others about some of the central conceits at the heart of the British system of governance I have come to one fixed conclusion. Rather like the making of sausages, the more you inquire what goes into the process, the less likely you are to want to accept the product, especially now when – as we will see in more detail later – whatever we pretend is the British constitution seems incapable of working successfully in theory or in practice. The serious point is that there is, inevitably, enormous confusion about how power is arranged in Britain – public confusion, my own confusions, confusion within the House of Commons Library, admitted confusion in the work of some excellent constitutional scholars and the confusion of all those who tell us there is 'no single accepted definition' of anything in the entire system. What makes it worse, in practical terms, is that this confusion is celebrated as if it were a peculiar British genius, evidence of excellence rather than mere eccentricity, or more malevolently of a desire to exert control. Walter Bagehot the author of *The English Constitution* (not the *British* Constitution, by the way), always provides later writers with a good quote to fit any and all circumstances. His observation on the Crown/monarch/ sovereign is now worth expanding: 'Above all things our royalty is to be reverenced, and if you begin to poke about it you cannot reverence it... Its mystery is its life. We must not let in daylight upon magic.'

Bagehot is writing specifically about royalty here, of course – the Crown, at least in one definition. But why not 'let in daylight' when what really is being 'reverenced' is power, and – by the way – it is definitely *not* the power of the titular head of state, the monarch? It is the power you find at the heart of that old lawyer's question, '*cui bono*?' – 'who benefits' from this constitutional word salad, the jumble that we must not examine too closely? The answer to that at least is clear. The beneficiaries are the executive, the government and most especially the chief executive, the prime minister. The hocus pocus enables a prime minister to claim that his or her real powers exist somewhere in the clouds of smoke. The confusion, the 'magic', is deliberate. It is part of the pretence that the mysteries of the British constitution are too wonderful to explain clearly to the likes of you and me.

But – and this is where we are now – what if the magic ceases to entrance us? Bagehot and other constitutional scholars often seem to channel the great Christian saint, St Anselm of Canterbury who squared the circle of disbelief in the Holy Trinity with the words: '*Neque enim quaero intelligere ut credam, sed credo ut intelligam*.' Roughly translated this means: 'I do not seek to understand in order that I may believe, but I believe in order that I may understand.' In constitutional terms we are to shut up and just believe, and all will be well. Except of course, it isn't.

Our concern, however, is not letting daylight into the magic of royalty. Our concern is to protect against the viral outbreaks of corruption and incompetence which eat away at our democracy and which are treated with constitutional faith healing. Power is what we are concerned with here. It might be 'vested' with the monarch, Crown, sovereign or any other approximate synonym or metonym. But in reality power resides with those who pretend – and may even convince themselves – that they have been elected with a 'stonking mandate' and who further pretend they are accountable to parliament until things go wrong. When their unethical and even illegal conduct is exposed, those in power may choose to assert that they also have the power to decide that their own conduct has been just fine all along, because there is constitutionally no 'one accepted definition' of lying, stealing, graft, corruption, nepotism, ethics or failure. We are not trying to let daylight in upon magic, because there is no magic. What daylight exposes is wrongdoing. What follows next, then, is – choose your metaphor – a bit of daylight, or disinfectant, splashing on where power really lies, namely on the occupant of 10 Downing Street. This is not to rehearse the uselessness of any one individual. It is to demonstrate why the British system of governance does not deserve the confidence of the people of the United Kingdom.

It's the System, Stupid

In one of the first acts of the short-lived Liz Truss government, King Charles III was prevented from addressing the COP27 Climate Summit in Egypt. The King, despite years of interest in environmental issues, felt obliged to obey – no matter what powers are supposedly 'vested' in his office as monarch, sovereign, head of state or Crown. The King did as the government ordered – although, interestingly in this case, someone, somewhere leaked the fact that he was not allowed to go. One can only ask, again, *cui bono?* Who benefited from the leak? Whatever the source, this was just one example of a very different observation of Walter Bagehot. He wrote that the monarch has the right to be consulted, to encourage and to warn. Implicit in that list is also the right to be ignored. And here we come upon another convenient fiction, the 'royal prerogative'. Even in Victorian times this was regarded as constitutional moonshine. Here's Bagehot elegantly noting that Queen Victoria 'has a hundred such (prerogative) powers which *waver between reality and desuetude*, and which would cause a protracted and very interesting legal argument if she tried to exercise them'. [my italics]

By the twenty-first century the modern constitutional scholar, the Canadian-born Anthony King – whom I admire and will quote frequently for the brutal clarity of his observations – observed that the British royal prerogative 'refers principally to the age old fact that unlike the governments of many other countries, British governments, *imagining that they are actually sovereign... can legally ratify treaties and declare war without bothering to consult anybody else*, including the two houses of parliament'.[8]

The key phrase is 'without bothering to consult anybody else'. This is the dressing up of executive fiat in fancy clothes. The royal prerogative, if it has any meaning in reality, has little to do with the monarch. It has everything to do with sonorous words acting as a disguise for the hard reality of prime ministerial executive power. This has the benefit (for a prime minister) that it comes with the avoidance of legislative or other scrutiny. Lord Hailsham's emotive phrase 'elective dictatorship' is merely a colourful way of describing this power. Translated into modern English, the royal prerogative is 'exercised' when a prime minister decides that something he or she is doing is far too important to let anyone else – most especially those interfering representatives of the people in parliament – have a constitutionally relevant view of the wisdom of the activity. These traditional convenient fictions of the British constitution are convenient for the executive, the government and prime minister. The convenience for the rest of the population is dependent on the fiction remaining unchallenged and the smokescreen of constitutional verbiage remaining as impenetrable as the Latin Mass to the medieval peasantry. All this obviously presents dangers for British democracy. Again, Boris Johnson is useful, if only as a warning.

Even if the British constitution of the twenty-first century is incomprehensible to most British citizens, it is generally respected. We are repeatedly told (with almost liturgical fervour by some of those in power) of the glories and 'traditional' genius of the 'precedents' which form part of how we are governed. It is worth unpacking this vocabulary. A precedent is something that happened in the past. There is no particular magic to this. If that something-in-the-past is repeated a second, third and fourth time it becomes a regular event that we may eventually call a tradition or a precedent. My parents set a precedent by having a cooked family breakfast on a Sunday. When my father became keen on golf, that 'tradition' fell into abeyance. When the coronavirus lockdown eased, my wife set a precedent by suggesting we meet our friends on a socially distanced Wednesday evening in a local pub garden. This precedent became a much-loved tradition, involving various rituals or norms of behaviour, including that the first person to arrive bought the first round of drinks. (The nice bit was that people wanted to arrive early in order to buy their round. British people are on the whole very decent.) Traditions, as we will see in detail in Chapter 7, are always invented. They can therefore be dis-invented or ignored. A tradition can also become a block on positive change when it becomes embedded but no longer useful. It is traditional for British voters to go to the polls on a Thursday, but since polling takes place on the premises of state schools, a Thursday election involves huge disruption with the shutting of state schools for the day. The reasons for this tradition are spelled out by the Electoral Reform Society:

> Until 1918, polling at General Elections took place over several days and at one time different constituencies could complete polling on different days, thereby – it was alleged – creating a bandwagon effect for a successful political party. The 1918 Representation of the People Act restricted polling to one day (except for Orkney and Shetland until 1929). Since 1918 a General Election has always been on a Thursday, except for 1918, 1922, 1924 and 1931. The reason for choosing Thursday, it is said, was as follows. On Fridays the voters were paid their wages and if they went for a drink in a public house they would be subject to pressure from the Conservative brewing interests, while on Sundays they would be subject to influence by Free Church ministers who were generally Liberal in persuasion. Therefore choose the day furthest from influence by either publicans or Free Church clergymen, namely Thursday.[9]

This century-old tradition is now pointless. In a world of credit cards, monthly salary payments and limited influence from brewers, pub owners or Christian ministers why do we disrupt our children's education to vote on a Thursday? A sensible reinvention of this tradition would be to encourage postal and online voting and switch to in-person voting (for those who like a long walk to put a cross on a piece of paper) to Sundays, when schools are empty. This more sensible approach will almost certainly not happen in my lifetime, or ever, unless there is a scandal or a crisis. That's because our tradition of ancestor worship means even obsolete British traditions are unaccountably revered. The conservative thinker Edmund Burke neatly summarised the idea that democracies must evolve or die: 'A state without the means of some change is without the means of its conservation. Without such a means it might even risk the loss of that part of the constitution which it wished most religiously to preserve.'[10]

The failure even to discuss the out-of-date idea of Thursday voting is just a tiny example of what has become the dangerous constitutional sclerosis of the United Kingdom in the 2020s. Some British constitutional traditions, of course, are glorious and lovely. The state opening of parliament is – arguably – one example. At least it is harmless. TV viewers enjoy the spectacle. The same is true of the coronation, even though Prince Charles became King Charles III the moment his mother died in September 2022. The coronation that took place in May 2023 was in strict constitutional terms not necessary. We already had a monarch as head of state whether there is the highly choreographed spectacular of a coronation or not. Edward VIII proved as much. He became King in January 1936. There was no coronation. He abdicated the following December, a king who was never crowned, yet no one disputes that Edward VIII 'reigned' as king, monarch, sovereign and head of state of the United Kingdom. Other traditions, however – those involving unchecked executive power camouflaged by sonorous constitutional language – are a real and present danger. Boris Johnson illustrated the danger quite beautifully even if he personally was too indolent, too self-obsessed and too lacking in an ideology to cause irreparable damage. What follows is an explanation of some of the flaws in the system that allow someone like Johnson to flourish, and which in the hands of someone more ruthless and less incompetent could comprehensively undermine our rickety democratic system.

How Johnson Did It

The most interesting fact about Johnson's career as a journalist and politician is that his failings and deceit were worn openly. As anyone who cared to follow his career trajectory will know, it was replete with examples of unethical behaviour, law breaking, lies, greed and narcissism. None of this prevented his political advancement. On the contrary, Johnson's many scrapes and japes aided his career by ensuring that everyone in Britain knew who he was. Notoriety and fame are close bedfellows. To recap very briefly: Boris Johnson was fired twice for lying, once as a journalist for making up quotes in *The Times*, and once for lying about the affair he conducted with a colleague, Petronella Wyatt. He called the accusation an 'inverted pyramid of piffle', before the affair was confirmed publicly by Ms Wyatt's mother. Johnson has never been able to say how many children he has fathered and by whom. He was recorded in a telephone call with a friend from Eton, Darius Guppy, apparently conspiring to have a journalist beaten up. In his newspaper columns for the *Daily Telegraph* he wrote entertainingly but inaccurately about the European Union standardising condom sizes and banning British sausages. He described gay men as 'bum boys', referred to Africans as 'piccaninnies', while Muslim women in burkas appeared to him as 'letterboxes'. Former colleagues of Johnson told me first-person stories about Johnson lying to them face-to-face without any signs of shame, regret or guilt, even when confronted about his lies. And so on. Yet Johnson was considered a fit and proper person by his Conservative colleagues to become Mayor of London, a Member of Parliament, Foreign Secretary and finally prime minister of the United Kingdom. As political journalists put it, in Johnson's case the lying and outrageous behaviour which would have doomed other politicians was 'priced in'. His saving grace was that for *Telegraph* readers and many voters Johnson was always entertaining, but also ruthless in using the idiosyncrasies of the British political system to ensure his self-preservation. In this he was shameless but also instructive. He revealed extraordinary constitutional weaknesses.

In November 2020 after a Cabinet Office inquiry, Boris Johnson's first Ethics Adviser, the Independent Adviser on Ministers' Interests, Sir Alex Allan, challenged the prime minister about the unethical behaviour of the Home Secretary Priti Patel. Ms Patel's behaviour included shouting and swearing. Sir Alex was clear:

> My advice is that the Home Secretary has not consistently met the high standards required by the Ministerial Code of treating her civil servants with consideration and respect. Her approach on occasions has amounted to behaviour that can be described as bullying in terms of the impact felt by individuals. To that extent her behaviour has been in breach of the Ministerial Code, even if unintentionally.[11]

Johnson seized on one word, 'unintentionally'. He insisted that, despite the conclusion of his Ethics Adviser, in Johnson's *own* judgement the code had *not* been breached and therefore did not warrant Patel's resignation from the cabinet. The prime minister asserted his full confidence in the Home Secretary. He even sent a WhatsApp message to Tory colleagues to 'form a square around the Prittster'.[12]

Sir Alex Allan resigned. In this, Johnson embodied a phrase used by US President George W. Bush. Faced with demands to sack his loyal Defense Secretary Donald Rumsfeld, President Bush refused to do so. He responded to critics by saying: 'I'm The Decider and I decide what's best.' In Johnson's case, The Decider had decided, and there was no way in which a mere 'Ethics Adviser' – note the word 'adviser' – could overturn such a decision. But to paraphrase Oscar Wilde's Lady Bracknell, to lose one Ethics Adviser may be a misfortune, to lose two sounds like carelessness.

By the summer of 2022 Johnson did lose his second Ethics Adviser. Lord (Christopher) Geidt's letter of resignation was full of exasperation that Johnson was judge and jury of 'your *own* conduct under the Ministerial Code'. Geidt noted that 'This would be especially important in the event that the Metropolitan Police found against you, which they did, and/or that Sue Gray's report included criticism of behaviour within the scope of the Ministerial Code, which it did.' Sue Gray's report was yet another inquiry into Johnson's conduct as prime minister. Gray, being a serving senior civil servant, reported to Boris Johnson himself. He was her boss. How could she possibly sanction him? Noting that any prime minister who deliberately breached the code to suit his own political ends would be 'an affront' Geidt eventually found his own position untenable: 'This would make a mockery not only of respect for the Code but licence the suspension of its provisions in governing the conduct of Her Majesty's Ministers. I can have no part in this.'[13]

Geidt quit, having exhausted all other alternatives. Allan quit for the same reason. Sue Gray was side-lined. Johnson stayed. His Ethics Advisers advised but advice is not binding on a prime minister who does not want to hear it. Under the British system the only real sanction on a shameless prime minister comes when their own MPs have had enough. In this case the degree of tolerance of bad behaviour by Conservative MPs (who felt they owed Boris Johnson their political careers) was legendary. They benefited from sticking together within the same creakingly rotten system, although by the summer of 2022 Boris Johnson, after more scandals, did eventually lose the confidence of the Conservative parliamentary party and was forced to quit. Senior officials privately praised Geidt and Allan for attempting to do the impossible, namely to keep a rule-breaking, norm-defying, lying prime minister within the guidelines of decent behaviour in our flawed democracy. They failed, but they did try. Fortunately there are plenty of good people within our failing system of governance.

The important lesson in all this is not about Johnson himself. He is in a sense irrelevant. It is those failures of the system that for so long permitted unethical and even illegal conduct, including parties in Downing Street during the coronavirus lockdown. That system remains broadly unchanged. (We will explore this further in Chapter 9.)

The real scandal, as always, is not what is forbidden, but what is allowed. Our sclerotic constitutional system proved itself open to abuse on relatively minor issues of behaviour, with Ethics Advisers allowed to advise but then be ignored. Perhaps that is not surprising in a system in which the head of state may be consulted and also politely marginalised.

It could be worse. Consider how, in the Hailsham 'elective dictatorship' scenario, a future British prime minister not as lazy and more certain of their own ideology than Boris Johnson, could abuse our failed system, ignore or constructively dismiss Ethics Advisers (and many other officials) while clinging to power with Trump-like determination. Dr Hannah White, Director of the Institute for Government, spotted the problem: 'The most important lesson that Johnson's three years as prime minister have taught us is how uniquely vulnerable this type of constitution may be to concerted manipulation by a determined populist leader with a large Commons majority and a calculated agenda.'[14]

We are not there yet. But the British malaise is, as White notes, systemic and constitutional. Boris Johnson's abuse of the system in that sense was a warning. The Old Etonian bluffer turned out to be a canary in the coalmine. We may not always be so lucky.

In the nineteenth century, Alfred, Lord Tennyson famously praised the United Kingdom – (he, too, meant England) – and its uncodified constitution as:

A land of settled government
A land of just and old renown
Where freedom slowly broadens down
From precedent to precedent.

Around the same time the constitutional theorist A. V. Dicey described the idiosyncratic precedents, or norms of behaviour, which traditionally acted to guide conduct in British (again, he meant English) public life as, 'The fruit not of abstract theory but of that instinct which... has enabled Englishmen, and especially uncivilised Englishmen, to build up sound and lasting institutions much as bees construct a honeycomb.'[15] As a result of these, and other, celebrations of the idiosyncrasies in our democratic system, many British people seem unaware that in the twenty-first century British exceptionalism is regarded internationally as dangerous eccentricity. The Johnson–Truss years may have diminished the power of that delusion at home, although belief that our antiquated traditions guarantee 'settled government of just and old renown' persists against all recent evidence. Yet even before the infamous Year of Three Prime Ministers 2022, the UK's record of political stability was shaky.

From the birth of the Federal Republic of Germany in 1949 until 2020, there have only been eight Federal Chancellors. In that same period the United Kingdom had sixteen prime ministers. By 2022 it was up to eighteen. In the sixteen years from 2005 until 2021 Germany had one Chancellor, Angela Merkel. In that time the United Kingdom had five prime ministers, a coalition government and was under the shaky administration of Theresa May, a leader who failed to secure a stable parliamentary majority. What our idiosyncratic traditions certainly do guarantee is that good advisers – Geidt, Allan, and others including Sir Kim Darroch (as we will see) as the UK ambassador in Washington – are sacrificed, while repeated political scandals and examples of executive incompetence go unpunished.

We used to believe, for example, that the United Kingdom was largely free from corruption. Boris Johnson continued to insist that was still the case even as he and his party were drowning in sleaze and scandals from 2021 onwards. 'I genuinely believe', Johnson said, 'that the UK is not a remotely corrupt country, nor do I believe that our institutions are corrupt.' The coronavirus procurement scandals, the symbiotic relationship between rich donors to the Conservative Party and various kinds of preferment have since dented such complacency.

Transparency International is a global movement to end international corruption. It notes that British society as a whole is relatively free from corrupt practices. Most British people would be shocked if any public servant – a police officer, a judge, a local government employee, a teacher or doctor – demanded a bribe. But we are no longer shocked by corruption in British politics among MPs and between people in government and various cronies:

> Although corruption is not endemic in the UK, it is correct to say that in some areas of UK society and institutions, corruption is a much greater problem than recognised and that there is an inadequate response to its growing threat. The report found that *the growing threat of corruption is often met with complacency,* and that key institutions are refusing to confront the problem. [my italics]

Transparency International added that of particular concern were political parties and parliament where 'the response to the increasing corruption risk is often incoherent and uncoordinated'. [16]

British political greed and corruption stories in the twenty-first century have been on the front pages of newspapers and leading TV news bulletins for many years. They involve dodgy Russian money; donations to the Conservative and other parties by people of great wealth who subsequently find themselves elevated to the House of Lords; cronyism; tales of influence and access being bought and sold by MPs; the parliamentary expenses scandal; lucrative government contracts, including some awarded during the coronavirus crisis to party donors; bullying, groping and various sex scandals (too numerous and sometimes too weird to mention in detail); payments of £840 for a single roll of gold-encrusted designer wallpaper for the prime minister's apartment in Downing Street; and endless other examples of what is euphemistically called 'sleaze'.

Trust in MPs, in parliament, and in the British system of governance has been undermined. So has the UK's reputation abroad and our self-image as a country built essentially on the honesty and probity of those in positions of power, with merely a few bad apples.

We're also cheap. In an award-winning podcast series called *The Big Steal*, I worked with the celebrated anti-corruption campaigner

Bill Browder. He has campaigned bravely against Russian corruption, the influence of Vladimir Putin and money from Russian oligarchs entering British politics. Browder is the architect of the US's Magnitsky Act. It is named in memory of his Russian friend and colleague Sergei Magnitsky who was in effect murdered in prison by the Russian state for investigating the corruption of Vladimir Putin and his Kremlin cronies. The Magnitsky Act allows US authorities to crack down on Russian oligarchs and other corrupt individuals. It has been replicated in many countries, including in Britain. In April 2022, at a meeting in London, Browder told me that 'people here [in the UK] are very inexpensive to corrupt'. They can be bought, he said, for as little as £50–75,000. Browder explained that such sums of money, for a Russian oligarch are like 'a tip to a concierge' yet they are enough to buy political influence by greasing palms within the British establishment.

By November 2021, after numerous scandals became public, more than three out of four British people admitted they were concerned about corruption in public life.[17] Some 76 per cent of British voters said they were worried about government corruption, defined as 'dishonest or fraudulent conduct by those in power'. Among Conservative voters the figure was 72 per cent. Among Labour voters it was 90 per cent. By May 2022 in the main editorial page cartoon in *The Times*, prime minister Johnson was shown rowing a boat along the river Thames surrounded by sewage and pornography. The Houses of Parliament were caricatured as sinking under effluent. The caption read: 'The Great Stink 2022'. The *Guardian*, around the same time, referred to Boris Johnson as a Pinocchio politician with an extendable nose. One columnist, sketch writer John Crace, started referring to Johnson 'the Suspect'. After fines were issued, including to the prime minister, for parties in Downing Street, Crace took to referring to Johnson as 'the Convict'. Johnson was the first British prime minister to have been found guilty of breaking the law while in office. The political campaign group Led By Donkeys, in one of its videos which I narrated, exposed the extent of donations by those with Russian connections to leading members of the British

Conservative Party. In March 2023 Led By Donkeys helped set up a fake Korean company that contacted MPs and recorded some MPs asking for £10,000 a day for unspecified services and advice to the non-existent company.[18] By July 2022, the month of Johnson's announcement that he would resign, the satirical magazine *Private Eye* published the 'Boris Johnson Memorial Issue' featuring on the cover a blocked toilet covered in excrement. The headline read: 'The Prime Minister's Legacy in Full'.

Beyond satire, serious authors, broadcasters and podcasters, including some who regard themselves as traditional Conservatives, catalogued Johnson's lies and misleading statements along with other examples of sleaze and alleged corruption in book and documentary form. Newspapers offered what they said were the 'Timelines of Tory Scandals' in long and depressing reads.[19]

At this point we need to remember that political life in the United Kingdom wasn't always like this, but complacency about the supposedly high standards of those in public life in Britain has been widespread for years. Delusions about the glories of the British system of governance is equally widespread. In a speech in Brussels on 17 February 2020, the man who negotiated the British deal to leave the European Union, David (now Lord) Frost compared the superior British system of governance to that of the mere mortals condemned to inhabit France, Germany, Italy, Sweden and other less fortunate European nations. Frost claimed that the most important feature of the British constitution is that our system 'just evolved'. Our greatness came about as a result of effortless grace, unlike other European countries where the system of government was the result of radical change, wars, revolutions and deliberate constitutional constructions. Part of this is undeniably true; part is traditional British mythmaking. The bit which is true is that revolutions or defeat in war often require the creation of new constitutional settlements. It happened with the War of Independence in the United States after 1776, and in Germany, Turkey, France, Japan, post-Franco Spain and post-communist Russia, among many other nations in the twentieth century. But the complacent British narrative usually concludes that the gentle evolution of precedents and accepted norms of behaviour in the UK has successfully, if vaguely, defined relations between the monarchy, the executive, the legislature and the judiciary to create a uniquely stable, corruption-free and exceptional British kind of democracy. One obvious flaw in this argument is that political stability has not been a notable feature of British life in recent years.

Traditional English constitutional theorists – Walter Bagehot, A. V. Dicey and others – imply that this exceptional British system may not work in theory yet it works triumphantly in practice. The flexibility of the British system did, after all, help create the most powerful empire in world history. But David Frost's presumption that the British constitution 'just evolved' is nonsense. From the Cromwell Protectorate to the Restoration and the Glorious Revolution of 1688, the 1707 Union of Parliaments, the 1832 Reform Act, votes for women, reforms to the House of Lords and devolution in the 1990s, the most significant constitutional changes in Britain came not from some idiosyncratic 'evolution' but – rather as in other countries – from political and social discontent, riots, protests, suffragism, wars, economic shocks and street violence. The Union of Scottish and English parliaments in 1707 led to vigorous resistance in Scotland. The birth of what became the Irish Republic and the creation of Northern Ireland was baptised in blood during the Anglo-Irish War and Ireland's Civil War. Much of this remains unfinished constitutional business even now, a century later, and the shadow of the gunman in Northern Ireland has not been banished. As the Constitution Unit at University College London (UCL) put it:

> Codified constitutions are typically produced following a major historic turning point, such as the grant of independence, revolution, defeat in war, or complete collapse of the previous system of government. None of these things have happened to the UK, which is why it has never had cause to codify its constitution.

They add one caveat: 'Our one revolution, in the seventeenth century, did briefly produce a written constitution: Cromwell's Instrument of Government.'[20]

The idea that 'the grant of independence, revolution, defeat in war' have not occurred in the United Kingdom is incorrect, as the history of Ireland (part of the UK 'granted' independence in the 1920s after the 1916 Easter Rebellion) makes clear. The British failure to remember historic military defeats is itself a kind of amnesia. It affected me personally as a postgraduate student of Irish literature. In one seminar I expressed views similar to those of the UCL Constitution Unit, about the United Kingdom never having to face 'a major historic turning point' caused by 'defeat in war'. An Irish-American friend immediately reminded me not only that the shattering loss (for Britain) of the American colonies from 1776 onwards was certainly defeat in war, but so was Afghanistan in 1842, and that the Anglo-Irish war of the 1920s was fought on what then was the soil of the United Kingdom. It led to the break-up of the UK. British people also tend to believe that the United Kingdom has not been invaded or occupied since 1066. On 5 November 1688, William of Orange landed at Brixham, near Torbay in Devon, with 14,000 Dutch, French, Swedish, Finnish and Brandenburger soldiers. He deposed King James II in what was clearly an invasion, and certainly a revolution, even if it was welcomed by most Protestants. It was called the Glorious Revolution, which is obviously a clue. The idea that none of these events, right up to the loss of Empire, constituted a 'major historic turning point' after military failure is another comforting yet unfortunate British delusion. What is undeniable is that the vagueness or opacity of the British constitution means that, unlike the United States, constitutional matters tend to be boring as well as incomprehensible for most British people.

Anthony King rightly argued that the United Kingdom's uncodified constitution, built on a haphazard accretion of laws, precedents and norms of behaviour, has resulted in a general lack of interest about constitutional matters. (That, as we will examine later, is because no one actually knows what the constitution *is*, or even, for some, if a British constitution exists.) Politicians and most citizens, King argues, 'Do not even notice that constitutional change... is taking place' and that the word 'unconstitutional' has therefore 'no precise meaning in the UK, if indeed it has any meaning at all... those who protest, as people occasionally do, that the British constitution has been violated are not saying anything precise. They are merely expressing disgruntlement with some new state of affairs'.

King himself is precise. He notes that the British constitution did not 'just evolve', but neither is it a fixed document which can be 'changed'. It is a flexible system that can be 'amended'. Changing something would be an admission there must have been something wrong. Amending something suggests only that the United Kingdom's system of government was once almost-perfect but now it is pluperfect. But King does add his own list of profound constitutional changes or, rather, amendments:

> The most important of these included the Act of Settlement 1701 (which among other things legally established the independence of the judiciary), the Act of Union 1707... the Parliament Act 1911... the Government of Ireland Act 1920... the Parliament Act 1949... the European Communities Act 1972... etc.[21]

The salient question now therefore is not whether the British constitution merely 'evolved' without all these shocks. David Frost's analysis is obviously untrue. Nor does it really matter whether it is written or unwritten, codified or uncodified, understood or misunderstood. It is whether the British constitution with all its many idiosyncrasies is fit for the challenges of the twenty-first century. It clearly is not, as we will see.

A subsidiary, but also important question, is whether in a democracy the uncodified British constitution should be made more intelligible to most British people, stripped of hocus pocus, so that we can have an operators' manual for our democracy. Perhaps no one cares. Perhaps the British in the 2020s are content with the way in which the United Kingdom is governed. Perhaps as a nation we are happy that – rather like The Holy Trinity – our salvation is guaranteed. Personally, I doubt it. We really are better than this, which is why next we will examine some of the innovations introduced into our public life by those who have taken advantage of our constitutional porridge to benefit themselves. For now we need to note that the British constitution manages to be vague, complex and for many of us boring all at the same time. This is not an accident. The obfuscations and complexities suit those in power once we begin to understand that it means they can make up that which is 'constitutional' as they go along to suit their own best interests. The lack of clarity about the 'magic' at that point begins to make sense. And the British constitution starts to become very interesting indeed.

4

Innovations

'It would help us to get a little way on the road if we had a clearer idea of where we wanted to go.'

Harold Macmillan

The Brexit referendum of 2016 was an innovation. To put it charitably, it was an attempt to fix some of the problems that had been building within Britain, most notably in England, for years. The idea behind the referendum was, obviously, to offer a choice between what was known – retaining membership of the European Union – and what was unknown, undefined and contentious even among the people advocating it: leaving the EU.

The use of referendums as a direct consultation with voters in the United Kingdom's representative democracy was a constitutional innovation in itself, a blunt instrument to solve difficult political problems. In the case of Brexit, it was pitched as an 'advisory' referendum. Members of Parliament subsequently considered the result to be binding upon themselves. This was a direct contradiction not only to the way in which the referendum had been announced but also to historic Conservatism and the parliamentary tradition enunciated so clearly by Edmund Burke. He famously explained to the electors of Bristol in 1774 that the job of a Member of Parliament was as a representative not a delegate: 'Your representative owes you, not his industry only, but his judgment; and he betrays, instead of serving you, if he sacrifices it to your opinion.'[1]

A referendum, in the British context, shows how the vagaries and vagueness of our constitution can have practical and serious implications on the lives, happiness and prosperity of all of us. The central thesis of this book is that the United Kingdom really does need to reinvent the way our system of governance works, but innovation requires that we first think very carefully and strategically about what we wish to achieve and how that may be achievable.

The Brexit experience was exactly the opposite. British democracy is based on the sovereignty of parliament, but a referendum implies that parliament cannot be sovereign if MPs are forced to subject themselves to the 'people's will', as Burke foresaw. A referendum therefore is a device which sits very oddly within whatever the British constitution is supposed to be. In the case of Brexit, we botched it. When the Brexit mess became obvious, leaving the European Union became increasingly unpopular and 'the people's will' changed. Many of those who voted for it and even some of those who campaigned so energetically for it seemed bewildered by the result. Rather like one of those old Trotskyites unable to accept that communism was a disaster, Nigel Farage and other Brexit campaigners kept insisting that Brexit would have succeeded if only it had been done 'right'. But the trouble is that Brexit is simply a six-letter word expressing a negative desire – to leave the EU. It was never a policy. In terms of constitutional failure, the larger point is that unless referendums are carefully constructed in a parliamentary democracy they can offer ill-defined binary choices on emotive issues to a fickle electorate, and as in the Brexit case create many more problems than they can possibly 'solve'.

The first referendum in British history was held in 1975. It was to solve the difficult political issue of membership of the European Economic Community, the forerunner of the European Union. The referendum was called by Labour prime minister Harold Wilson merely to manage internal conflicts in his own party. Many Labour MPs wanted to leave the European Economic Community, seeing it as a capitalist cabal – a position that Jeremy Corbyn has adhered to for his entire political career. The UK joined the EEC under Conservative leadership in 1973. In the 1975 referendum it was absolutely clear to voters what they were voting for or against. They chose the status quo, to remain in the EEC.

The referendum device was used again in 1998 to try to ensure peace in Northern Ireland. There were referendums on both sides of the Irish border on the implications of the Good Friday Agreement. In the north a referendum was a constitutional innovation, but at least the terms were made plain for all. A thirty-five-page document was posted to every home in Northern Ireland. It explained to voters what they were voting for or against. In the Irish Republic referendums are more common and their status defined in law within the Republic's written constitution. Voters there were asked if they agreed to repeal Articles 2 and 3 of that constitution, the parts claiming sovereignty over Northern Ireland. The referendums north and south were therefore simple to understand and both electorates voted to end the conflict. But the relative stability that followed was undermined by the Brexit referendum of 2016 because Northern Ireland, like Scotland, voted to remain in the EU, while England and Wales voted to leave. The Irish border which had been argued about and at times fought over since the partition of Ireland in the 1920s became contentious once more. Moreover, the referendum of the people of Northern Ireland in 1998 in favour of peace and power-sharing was rendered irrelevant by mostly English votes in the Brexit referendum of 2016. This was and remains a constitutional calamity. It threatened to put lives at risk by reinvigorating violence in Northern Ireland. Something similarly divisive, although without the undercurrent of violence, occurred in Scotland. There the 2014 independence referendum was based on years of discussions. A document about how independence would work was produced and debated by the SNP and others. Scotland's First Minister Alex Salmond argued that Scotland should retain the monarchy, the pound and the Bank of England. Scottish voters rejected independence as potentially the riskier option and stuck with the status quo. One of the most telling arguments that I heard repeatedly from doubtful independence voters was the threat that if Scotland left the UK it would be seceding from an EU country and therefore place itself outside the European Union, perhaps for years. Scotland continues to be overwhelmingly in favour of being part of the EU. In the Brexit referendum of 2016, every one of Scotland's thirty-two electoral districts voted to remain. Nevertheless Scotland was taken out of Europe against its clearly expressed will, again by English votes. The referendum was therefore a constitutional calamity for the union of the United Kingdom twice over.

One other referendum – often forgotten – took place in 2011 to change the FPTP voting system for Westminster elections. Again, the principles were clear. Should we keep FPTP or switch to a fairer system, details of which were clearly outlined during the campaign? The Liberal Democrats insisted on this referendum as a condition of their participation in David Cameron's coalition government, but faced with implacable hostility from Conservatives, and with the

Labour Party refusing to take a position either way because many Labour MPs were opposed, the best chance of electoral reform for a generation was lost. (We will return to why this referendum failed to engage British voters later, in Chapter 9.)

The 2016 Brexit referendum was therefore a hugely divisive innovation, not merely between Leave and Remain voters but because its result undermined the result of two previous, and much clearer, referendums in Scotland and Northern Ireland. It was uniquely vague and uniquely unsettling.

In my conversation with the constitutional scholar Anthony Seldon on the day of the funeral of Queen Elizabeth II, Seldon was blunt about this. Brexit, he said, 'ushered in the biggest domestic upheaval that this country has seen – at the same time as the territorial integrity of the United Kingdom is at threat with Ireland possibly uniting and indeed Scotland breaking away'. Seldon added that a further negative consequence was the way in which expert opinion within the civil service was ignored and at times derided by politicians. He spoke of 'the attack on the civil service that Brexit has unleashed. We've seen a Permanent Secretary fired from the Treasury and the civil service under attack as never before since the Northcote–Trevelyan reforms in the nineteenth century'.

The nineteenth century attacks on the civil service were motivated by bureaucratic incompetence. The Northcote–Trevelyan reforms put that right. By the twenty-first century the Brexit attacks were for the opposite reason. Honest officials questioned the wisdom and at times even the legality of government ministers' decisions on Brexit. Some civil servants, as Seldon well knew, were punished for honestly expressing legitimate concerns. Their unease was well-founded. What 'Leave' meant to voters was deliberately unclear: there could be as many versions of Leave as there were Leave voters. That meant most of them would be unhappy when the result failed to live up to their expectations. It did. And they were.

It was as if every Leave supporter agreed that we should all go and climb a mountain, but once we set off, everyone wanted to scale a different peak. Some said it would be absurd to leave the Single

Market and Customs Union. Others wanted a 'clean break' from the EU, although what that meant was never made clear. No country in modern times has made a 'clean break' with its nearest neighbours, except perhaps North Korea. (And truly not even them. They are dependent on China.)

The contradictions and dangers of Brexit were most obvious on the island of Ireland. Peace was based on the fact that for Ulster unionists the Irish border existed on a map, but for Irish nationalists, as long as both Ireland and the UK were together in the EU, the border was just a wiggly line on a piece of paper. It had no impact on anyone taking the road from Buncrana to Derry or Dundalk and Drogheda to Armagh or Newry. It was Schrödinger's border, dead and alive at the same time. Brexit, therefore, by undermining both peace in Ireland and the settled will of the Scottish people to remain in the European Union after an advisory referendum, while simultaneously making the entire United Kingdom poorer, is one of the most peculiar acts of self-harm carried out by any government since the beginnings of the British state in 1603. It means that the United Kingdom in the 2020s is more divided against itself than at any time since the secession of the twenty-six counties of the Irish Republic in the 1920s. It is hardly surprising that Brexit blighted the careers of four British prime ministers in a row, Cameron, May, Johnson and Truss. But all this was, apparently, the 'will of the people'. Or was it?

In 2016, at the time David Cameron called the Brexit referendum, Europe rarely featured in voters' priorities. Cameron wanted the referendum not because voters needed it, but because he did. He was faced with a Conservative Party management problem. In the 2015 General Election the Tories had been outflanked on the right by Nigel Farage's upstart party and their remarkable tally of 3.8 million UKIP votes. This should have been a moment for a statesman to reflect on the future of Britain and how out of date British constitutional democracy had become when all those millions of votes secured just one UKIP Member of Parliament. Cameron, however, was not thinking about Britain's future. He was thinking about his own, and the threat to his premiership from a resurgent English nationalism stealing Conservative votes. To outflank UKIP he came up with the cunning plan of a referendum, complacently – a word that must appear often in this account – assuming that he would win. He lost and resigned.

Once the referendum was won, UKIP disappeared, but not because Cameron's plan to absorb the English nationalist rebellion succeeded. On the contrary the Nigel Farage brand of euro-loathing found a new home by absorbing large sections of the Conservative Party. Their vehicle was a party within the party, the European Research Group (ERG). 'Research', as we will see later, is a word that adds credibility to any venture. 'Research' is what scientists do. British people don't trust politicians but do tend to trust scientists, although the ERG 'research' – if it existed – did not involve any rigorous tests of the basic hypothesis that Britain would be better off with Brexit. As one irritated English voter memorably told the BBC, we 'went to bed in Great Britain and woke up in Little England'. Cameron's replacement, Theresa May, tried to face down the UKIP-influenced ERG rebels within her own party, but compounded the political self-harm by deciding to call a General Election. That meant dealing with yet another constitutional innovation, the 2011 Fixed Term Parliament Act (FTPA).

The FTPA specified that British General Elections were to take place once every five years. This was a significant twenty-first-century constitutional change, full of good intentions. The idea was to end the manifestly unfair 'elective dictatorship' tradition by which a prime minister can call an election at any time they think they have the best chance of winning. The FTPA ended that abuse. It brought Britain into line with modern democratic countries where the most powerful government leader has, in one way or another, a fixed term in office, and cannot set an election date according to his or her own best interests. For US presidents and German Chancellors it is four years; for American Senators six; for French presidents, five. Being able to call an election was therefore an exceptionally attractive big stick for a prime minister, but that was removed by the FTPA. An election was not scheduled until 2020 but Theresa May decided she needed to find a way to secure her own personal mandate from voters to keep her own fractious party in line for the tough Brexit fights ahead. There was a get-out clause in the FTPA. If two-thirds of the House of Commons voted for an election that would get round the FTPA's five-year timetable. The change required support from the Labour Party and its leader Jeremy Corbyn. He agreed. With Labour's complicity, Theresa May secured her election date three years early. The two major parties in the two-party system were in agreement about their own best interests. They maintained the 'tradition' whereby an election may be called at the whim of a sitting prime minister not because this is fair or democratic, but because Corbyn's Labour leadership in opposition assumed that the same system heavily biased in favour of the government and a sitting prime minister would benefit Corbyn himself if he ever managed to get into power. It all turned out disastrously for Theresa May. The Curse of Brexit claimed another political life. She destroyed her comfortable Conservative majority in the Commons and was forced to rely on uncertain support from Northern Ireland's Democratic Unionist Party. Her weakness empowered the anti-EU rebels within her own party. Mrs May was comprehensively undermined by the ERG and others. She was forced to quit and in July 2019 was replaced as prime minister by one of the key plotters against her, Boris Johnson, who began the next part of the downward spiral that led to our now familiar crises, scandals, lies and rotating prime ministers.

It's worth repeating that these changes were brought about by factions, forces and pressure from within the Conservative Party itself. A succession of British prime ministers were chosen not by British voters but by Conservative MPs and Conservative Party members according to rules that they drew up and altered for their own convenience, not ours. As the constitutional lawyer Sir Jonathan Jones KC – the former Treasury Solicitor and Permanent Secretary of the Government Legal Department – put it in a speech on public law and the constitution, allowing a tiny and unrepresentative group from a faction in one political party to decide who should lead the British people is just the way the British do things:

> There's nothing 'unconstitutional' in that. Under our constitution we elect MPs, not governments or Prime Ministers, and there are no relevant legal or constitutional rules on how political parties choose their leaders. But it certainly doesn't make for stability or good governance.[2]

Jones added that those Conservative Party members who chose a succession of leaders for almost 70 million British citizens, and did so without 'relevant legal or constitutional rules', made up just 0.3 per cent of the British population, a minority of a minority of a minority. This self-selected group were governed only by their own rules which inevitably reflected their own interests. Sometimes Conservatives decided that only MPs could choose their leader. At other times they threw the vote open to the party membership as a whole. (The Labour Party also has its own idiosyncratic ways of electing a leader. Jeremy Corbyn became a candidate in 2015 with the lowest support from MPs but some wanted to ensure a contest embracing the left of the party. Corbyn then triumphed becoming Leader of the Opposition, although not of course, the prime minister of 68 million.)

All this might matter less if as many British people were members of political parties nowadays as there are – say – members of the National Trust (5.95 million in 2019–2020) or go fishing (over one million fishing licences were sold in 2010–2021 according to the Environment Agency Annual Fisheries Report for that year).[3] But political party membership in Britain is a minority sport. The numbers have collapsed since the mass membership days of the 1950s. Nowadays the Labour Party reports around 432,000 members (December 2021) and the Conservative Party around 172,000 (September 2022). In 1953 the Conservative Party had a reported membership of 2.8 million; in the same year, Labour claimed over a million members plus millions more affiliated through trade unions. Those days are long gone.

In terms of choosing a succession of failed leaders, it will come as no surprise to learn that Conservative Party members are not the average person in the British street. They are mostly prosperous (social classes A and B are over-represented in the party membership), older folk (over fifty), mostly white (97 per cent), mostly male (two-thirds), mostly resident in the southeast of England. The votes of just 92,000 Conservative members secured Boris Johnson the job of Britain's prime minister in 2019 – about the same number of people that can fit into Wembley stadium. Even fewer, around 81,000, put Liz Truss into Downing Street in 2022. The word 'oligarchy' is often misused to mean rule by the rich, and as a term of abuse directed at Russian billionaires. Rule by the rich is technically 'plutocracy'. An oligarchy is more correctly the rule by *a few*. Britain in that sense is indeed an oligarchy. For years, endorsed or otherwise by a General Election, British leaders emerge as a result of the whims, prejudices and vagaries of very few people in the unelected Conservative Party oligarchy or of their counterparts in the Labour Party. Of course political parties should choose their own leaders. But there is no reason why the people of the United Kingdom should accept that such a leader automatically becomes prime minister of the rest of us, without a commitment to a General Election. This is surely idiotic. Either way, the opportunities for complacency and abuse don't end there.

The Invention of Tradition

It may seem advisable, as Sir Jonathan Jones suggests, for a British party leader suddenly thrown into Downing Street to hold a General Election. It may even be laudable, but it is not inevitable. Labour's Gordon Brown succeeded Tony Blair seamlessly as prime minister in June 2007. It was inconceivable that any challenger from within Labour could have gathered more than a handful of anti-Brown protest votes. Brown became prime minister one might say by acclamation. He did consider calling a General Election a few months later, but as newspapers and TV channels reported, 'Brown bottled it'. He thought he would lose, and – in the British tradition – the prime minister is 'The Decider'. Brown decided to hang on until the last possible moment, May 2010. And then voters decided he should go.

By 2019, for Boris Johnson the calculation was different. He thought he might win an election, but only if he held it quickly before the effects of the Brexit debacle became clear to voters. That's why, just like Theresa May, Johnson was so keen to get round the FTPA, passed just eight years before. For Theresa May using the clause that allowed her to sidestep the act with support from Jeremy Corbyn, was not a solution available for Boris Johnson. His parliamentary majority was very slim, and Labour showed no signs of being as compliant with him as they were with May. Johnson therefore decided he could scrap the act entirely. This was possible with a bare majority in parliament. Johnson's new law stated: 'An early parliamentary General Election is to take place on 12 December 2019 in consequence of the passing of this Act' and 'That day is to be treated as a polling day appointed under section 2 (7) of the Fixed-term Parliaments Act 2011.' Two sentences changed the constitution of the United Kingdom. In Britain change is just that easy. It is a triumph – you may conclude – for British flexibility and pragmatism. An important change to electoral law dating from 2011 was found to be unworkable, twice, so eight years later it was excised. An alternative view is that this 'flexibility' is chicanery. It allows the British system to be abused by any prime minister with even a slender majority who seeks personal advantage by bending the electoral process to his or her own timetable. As Anthony King argued, the British do not 'amend' the constitution, since that suggests it must have been flawed. We just change it. And since no parliament can 'bind' its successor, the 2011 FTPA was sidestepped in 2017 and scrapped without fuss in 2019. Everyone is fine with this, even if it allowed Boris Johnson personally to decide when citizens should get a chance to vote in a General Election, by gaming the system and dressing up his own self-interest as a restoration of a British 'tradition'.

The Conservative 2019 'landslide' of an eighty-seat majority resting on 43.6 per cent of those who voted and 29 per cent of the entire British voting age population was hailed as a personal triumph for Boris Johnson. Friendly newspapers described him as an astoundingly popular vote-winner. There is no evidence for this. The former YouGov pollster Peter Kellner pointed out that at the time of Johnson's 'thumping majority' (of House of Commons seats) his personal popularity stood at *minus* 20 per cent. His opponent, the Labour leader Jeremy Corbyn, was even more unpopular, at an astonishing minus 44 per cent 'approval'. Comedians revived an old joke. The British people chose 'the evil of two lessers'.

More seriously, no single British political party in living memory has gone into government based on the votes of a majority of the British people. Cameron's 2010 government did have majority support from voters but only because it was in coalition with the Liberal Democrats. Tony Blair's enormous majority of 179 seats in 1997 was – like that of Johnson – based on a plurality, the endorsement of around 43 per cent of voters. And the peculiarities of Britain's failing democracy go much deeper. There is, for example, no single British 'electoral system'. Our innovations – devolution, referendums and the truly strange method of voting for hereditary peers to work in the House of Lords – result in, as Peter Kellner concludes, the United Kingdom now having half a dozen electoral systems:

> We have... acquired a constitution that gives rise to a new set of controversies, for in recent years it has become one of the most complex in the world. We employ at least six different electoral systems to choose people for public office. England, Wales, Scotland and Northern Ireland are all run according to different rules. Referendums, once unheard of in the United Kingdom, now play a spasmodic role in deciding major issues without the government having made any real attempt to

establish coherent principles for drawing the line between direct and representative democracy. And today's bizarrely constituted, theoretically indefensible but somehow workable House of Lords demonstrates that in society as well as in biology, evolution has the power to trump intelligent design.[4]

These six different electoral systems occur side by side in a state within which there are several different nations, an uncodified constitution and referendums held according to rules made up for the convenience of the prime minister in charge. We have made a political virtue out of situational ethics. The result is a deepening sense of disunion. Different systems inevitably produce different electoral verdicts in different geographical areas, especially when those geographical areas have strongly different senses of identity. This haphazard accretion is what we call British democracy. It was always likely to pull the various bits of the United Kingdom in different directions. And that is what has happened. Voters in Scotland and Northern Ireland legitimately complain they have been taken out of the EU against their will. Voters in Wales complain that they are barely regarded at all by the government in Westminster. Voters in England complain that all the other parts of the United Kingdom are 'subsidised' by English taxpayers, and have devolved administrations which suck on the taxpayers' golden teat and then just, well, complain.

Since Brexit became a reality in Northern Ireland the underlying tensions have become more obvious. There have been problems with cross-border trade (between Northern Ireland and the rest of the United Kingdom), flashes of violence, political instability, the suspension of power sharing, and significant damage to the UK's reputation for both competence and fair dealing. In a meeting with the Irish prime minister Leo Varadkar on the Wirral in 2019 Boris Johnson allowed the Irish border to be moved into the Irish Sea. He did this to permit frictionless trade on the island of Ireland to continue without a glimmer of understanding that the friction would continue but be moved to within the UK itself. This (reasonably) was seen within the unionist community as a threat that their core British identity was being undermined. I was in Belfast a few days after Johnson's meeting with Varadkar. Unionists were saddened, enraged and astonished. When I returned to Belfast again the following year, former loyalist paramilitaries in the Ulster Volunteer Force, men in their late middle age, told me feelings were running so high in loyalist areas it was hardly surprising that 'young lads' were causing trouble, burning buses and threatening violence. A British prime minister who had demonstrated no previous interest in the problems of Northern Ireland had undermined the biggest unionist grouping, the Democratic Unionist Party (DUP). The DUP had campaigned in favour of Brexit yet were in such disarray that they voted against every type of Brexit to come before the House of Commons, including a No-Deal Brexit. The republican party, Sinn Féin, once the political wing of the Provisional IRA, replaced the DUP to become the biggest party. The irony of a British prime minister and his allies in the biggest unionist party destroying the very basis on which Northern Ireland had been constructed was not lost on the people in both parts of Ireland, nor among Irish-Americans, including the president of the United States, Joe Biden. It's worth considering for a moment why this matters.

The six counties of Northern Ireland became a political entity separate from the twenty-six counties of the Irish Republic in 1921. Those six counties were plucked out of the ancient Irish province of Ulster while three Ulster counties – Donegal, Monaghan and Cavan – remained in the Republic. This was shamelessly sectarian. If all nine counties of Ulster had remained part of the United Kingdom, Catholics would have been in the majority in Northern Ireland, a position unacceptable to Protestant unionists in the 1920s, although it appears to be happening anyway in the 2020s. The dominance of those who define themselves as Protestants has been eroding for years.

The creation of Northern Ireland and therefore the partial dismemberment of the United Kingdom in the 1920s rarely features in history lessons taught to British school children. This inglorious part of British history doesn't seem to exist in the political consciousness of most twenty-first-century British politicians either, although presumably even someone as ill-informed as Lord Frost cannot pretend that the forced territorial loss of 22 per cent of the land mass of the United Kingdom in the 1920s after the Anglo-Irish war is an example of a state which 'just evolved'. As a percentage of land mass the secession of Ireland was greater than the 13 per cent of territory lost by Germany in the 1919 treaty of Versailles. Anthony King remains a rare exception to the general British silence about this loss of land considered part of the United Kingdom since 1801: 'Constitutional historians have paid oddly little attention to this momentous event,' King writes, 'even though in terms of land mass, though not of population, it was equivalent to Germany losing Bavaria or France losing the whole of both Brittany and Normandy.'[5]

For the British the result of one of the biggest domestic political failures in history was not a major rethink of what had gone wrong or to contemplate decades – centuries – of political failure in Ireland. Instead British policy switched to reorganise what was left. In 1922 they gave the million or so inhabitants of Northern Ireland their own grand parliament at Stormont. The result of what many Irish people called a 'gerrymander', was generations of discrimination against British citizens who happened to be Catholic and for that reason were significantly disadvantaged in jobs, housing and other matters. This was tolerated or at least unremarked by British politicians at Westminster until 1968 when civil rights marches and ultimately IRA violence literally exploded in Northern Ireland and beyond. As the rise of Sinn Féin demonstrates, British political failures since Brexit may yet lead to a united Ireland and Sinn Féin may also secure its position as the largest party in the Irish Republic too.

During a 1934 debate in the imposing new parliament at Stormont, on the outskirts of Belfast, the Ulster Unionist prime minister, James Craig, was clear about his vision of the future. One sentence from his speech is often remembered: 'All I boast of is that we are a Protestant Parliament and a Protestant State.' The next sentence is often forgotten: 'It would be rather interesting for historians of the future to compare a Catholic State launched in the South with a Protestant State launched in the North and to see which gets on the better and prospers the more.' In the 2020s those 'future historians', economic commentators, politicians, journalists and statisticians, will note that the GDP per capita of the Irish Republic (Craig's 'Catholic State') within the European Union is considerably higher than the GDP per capita not just of Northern Ireland (the Protestant State) but higher than the GDP per capita of *the whole United Kingdom*. If we are to be prepared to face the challenges of the future, it will be necessary to remind ourselves of these challenges from the past. Constitutional historians may also have cause to pay attention to the consequences that rankle already in the 2020s and the views of unionists in all parts of the United Kingdom that the union itself is in trouble.

In February 2022 the DUP's Ian Paisley told the House of Commons that unionists in Northern Ireland were fearful that their allies in what was once called the Conservative and Unionist party were losing their commitment to the union in order to concentrate on winning 'Red Wall' Labour Party areas of the north of England. Paisley said:

> There is a fear that the Conservative and Unionist Party, which governs this nation, is actually a nationalist party. An English nationalist party, that it is not concerned about a border in the Irish Sea but is concerned about a Red Wall on this island, the mainland island, and that's what keeps them up every single day. If that is their only concern then that government is betraying the union and the unionist people.[6]

The Conservative peer and former Hong Kong Governor Lord (Chris) Patten agreed with Ian Paisley. He said that he fears for the unity of his country, because

> I don't think that Mr Johnson is a Conservative. I think he is an English nationalist. And all the things that Conservatives used to believe in – like standing up for the union, like not attacking

our institutions, like the judges, like believing in international co-operation – seem to have gone out of the window.[7]

The former Conservative Chancellor of the Exchequer George Osborne also seemed troubled that the UKIP/ERG English nationalist streak had taken over his party. Writing in the *Evening Standard*, Osborne suggested that Boris Johnson would go down in history as 'the worst British prime minister' ever – worse than Lord North who lost the American colonies in the eighteenth century – by contributing not just to the decline of the United Kingdom but potentially to its decease. By 'unleashing English nationalism', Osborne says, Brexit means that

Northern Ireland is already heading for the exit door... [and] the rest of the world would instantly see that we were no longer a front-rank power, or even in the second row. We would instead be one of the great majority of countries who are on the receiving end of the decisions made by a few, subject to the values of others. We would become another historically interesting case study in how successful nations can perform unexpected acts of national suicide.[8]

In Wales, the sense of Westminster arrogantly refusing even to consult with the democratically elected Welsh government is just one of many underreported sores within the British body politic. Wales' First Minister, Mark Drakeford – a Labour politician and a supporter of the Union – told the parliamentary Welsh Affairs Committee:

What we have to do... is we have to recognise that the union as it is, is over. We have to create a new union. We have to demonstrate to people how we can re-craft the UK in a way that recognises it as a voluntary association of four nations, in which we choose to pool our sovereignty for common purposes and for common benefits.[9]

Drakeford added that the 'relatively random basis' on which the UK government engages with the devolved Welsh, Scottish and Northern Ireland administrations 'is not a satisfactory basis to sustain the future of the United Kingdom'. His sentiments were echoed more succinctly by former Labour prime minister Gordon Brown, who said 'I believe the choice is now between a reformed state and a failed state.'[10]

Brown, Drakeford, Patten, Osborne, Paisley – are all unionists of different kinds, a Scotsman, Welshman, two Englishmen and Ulsterman. As if in a bad joke, they go into a room and agree that the union of the United Kingdom is in trouble. Then they head off in different directions, their worst fears realised in the innovations that threaten the dissolution of the state, the constitutional tinkering that has become the aesthetics of a deranged democracy. Nationalists – Sinn Féin, the SNP, Plaid Cymru – are unlikely to disagree with the analysis of their unionist counterparts.

An Institute for Government report explained why all these existential problems for the British state are linked to Brexit and agreed that the United Kingdom's haphazard constitutional arrangements mean we may be sleepwalking towards oblivion:

'What the EU referendum result and its aftermath revealed is that the UK lacks a shared understanding of the rules of the constitutional game... Brexit is less amenable to resolution via Britain's "make do and mend" approach to the constitution.'[11]

Anthony King understood all this earlier than most. Back in 2009 he argued that 'the long era of constitutional continuity portrayed in the old textbooks is now ended, that continuity and gradual evolution have given way to radical discontinuity and that the traditional British constitution... no longer exists'.[12]

King's 'radical discontinuity' is the real innovation of our times. There is no one 'system' of government in the United Kingdom, and certainly not one which 'just evolves' or which is agreed upon. There are several systems, all in contention. The traditional fantasies about the British constitution are simply that – fantasies. King was also correct in prophesying that haphazard and piecemeal attempts at devolution designed to pull the United Kingdom together would most likely have the opposite effect. England has lost out most because it is the most centralised part of the union, and the most lopsided. London dominates everything and the sense of English grievance outside the capital and its hinterland is profound.

Constitutional complacency has given way to constitutional failure and political fragmentation. The tectonic plates of the United Kingdom have moved in different directions for more than twenty years. They continue to do so, and it is unionist politicians who are sounding the alarm. Nationalists see the opportunities.

The philosopher George Santayana famously remarked that those who cannot remember the past are condemned to repeat it. Those who have forgotten how a large chunk of the British state seceded in the early twentieth century are currently demonstrating similar difficulties in grappling with Northern Ireland, the unresolved Scottish question, and growing nationalism in Wales. Scotland is a third of the UK's current land mass. Scottish waters – stretching from Shetland to Rockall and into the North Sea, account for two-thirds of the UK's total maritime area. Managing the post-1921 land border between the UK and the Republic of Ireland has never been easy. Managing that same border now that the UK is out of the European Union and the Irish Republic remains part of the EU is fraught with difficulty. It therefore takes no predictive genius to conclude that managing a potential land border between England and Scotland, especially when post-independence Scotland aspires to EU membership, will be what British civil servants euphemistically describe as a 'challenge'.

It is not just electoral systems or competing nationalisms that signal differences between the different parts of the UK. It is election results. Voters in Northern Ireland do not vote directly for a Conservative or Labour government at Westminster. The Northern Ireland Conservative Party does exist, but barely. It describes itself on its website as 'the modern, positive & compassionate centre-right alternative for the people of Northern Ireland'. Possibly, but Northern Ireland's 'positive and compassionate' Conservatives won just 0.03 per cent of the vote in the 2022 NI Assembly elections and 0.07 per cent of the vote in the 2019 UK General Election. The party is all but invisible, even if it claims around 500 members.

In Scotland a majority of voters have not voted for a Conservative government since 1955 – three generations ago. In the 2019 General Election the Scottish Labour Party lost all but one of its Westminster seats, and the SNP won 48 out of the 59 seats that were contested. Unionist parties, in other words, cannot claim to speak for Scotland, even if the independence referendum was lost in 2014. Since 2022, the Conservative and Unionist Party, as it used to be called, runs no local councils at all in Scotland, nor any in Wales, and it has never run any councils in Northern Ireland. The political preferences, electoral methods, political cultures and priorities of the different nations are quite distinct.

Zeitenwende

Taken together, all these institutional idiosyncrasies in post-Brexit and post-Elizabethan Britain – the quasi-dictatorial possibilities of the office of prime minister, changes to our cabinet form of government, parliament, the union, the judiciary, the monarchy, the norms of behaviour in our public life – should encourage a degree of national stock-taking. The next few years will force the British people to ask ourselves who we are, who we want to be and what we demand for ourselves and our country.

The former National Security Adviser and Ambassador to France Lord (Peter) Ricketts, when I spoke with him at a meeting of foreign policy specialists in Brussels in 2022, argued that Brexit had not only caused domestic tensions, it also significantly diminished Britain's standing in the world. Ricketts said it made us less important as an ally to the United States *because* we are no longer a significant player in the European Union. Commonwealth member nations are considering the removal of the British monarch as head of state. Some may use the passing of Elizabeth II as the trigger for change. Barbados has already decided to become a republic. Jamaica, other Caribbean countries, and Australia and Canada may follow. Australia decided not to put the face of King Charles III on its new $5 bill but to feature indigenous Australian art instead. Scotland will continue to seek independence. Northern Ireland may eventually establish a new relationship with the Irish Republic. As the US magazine the *Atlantic* noted, 'The grim reality for Britain... is that no other major power on Earth stands quite as close to its own dissolution.'[13] That would be the most significant innovation of all. Even if disunion does not occur, opinion polls suggest a majority of British people believe that the United Kingdom, as currently constructed, needs to be rebooted and reformed.

At this, our *Zeitenwende*, if Scotland leaves the union, England, or England and Wales, will be forced to consider their own, much-diminished role in the world, outside the European Union, less significant as an ally to the United States, poorer in GDP per capita than Ireland, and probably no longer one of the five permanent members of the United Nations Security Council. I put such a scenario to the leading British diplomat and former ambassador Sir Nick Browne a few years ago. 'If we were faced with an attempt to remove our veto as a member of the permanent five on the United Nations Security Council', Sir Nick joked with me, 'well, then,... we would veto it.'

Vetoing the loss of a veto is a very English-mandarin style of relaxed humour. But as Browne himself recognised, there is a serious problem with this analysis. If Scotland does leave the United Kingdom then 'we' are no longer the 'we' we once were. The United Kingdom which after 1945 was granted permanent five UN Security Council status and a veto will, as George Osborne prophesied, have passed into history. England, perhaps along with Wales, would then have to reapply for the UK's Security Council seat. Would France object? Would China? Russia? Even the United States? Nobody knows. Either way, the transition from Great Britain to Little England would be confirmed.

Before speculating further about the future it's time instead to explain why all this has happened, and why it has been so sudden and so damaging. In the most basic terms we have lost trust in British institutions. That's because we have also lost trust that people in public life are telling us the truth. Trust and truth are necessary for democracy to survive.

PART TWO

Ideals – Truth, Trust, Tropes and Tradition

And the parson made it his text that week, and he said likewise,
That a lie which is half a truth is ever the blackest of lies;
That a lie which is all a lie may be met and fought with
   outright;
But a lie which is part a truth is a harder matter to fight.

Alfred, Lord Tennyson, *The Grandmother*, Stanza VIII

I deas about the importance of truth, trust and tradition are universal, but all three concepts have been damaged in the twenty-first century, and not just in the United Kingdom. In a BBC interview broadcast at the end of January 2023 Boris Johnson told the world that when he was prime minister during the invasion of Ukraine the President of Russia threatened to kill him in a missile strike. Johnson claimed Vladimir Putin said: 'I don't want to hurt you, but with a missile, it would only take a minute.' Dmitry Peskov, the Kremlin spokesman, responded immediately to Johnson's comment and insisted it was 'a lie'. In the past almost any British citizen would immediately believe the word of a former British prime minister but… Boris Johnson? One definition of our democratic recession is that commentators on social media, in newspaper columns and comedians on TV and radio wondered aloud whether the liar in this case was the former prime minister of one of the world's oldest democracies or the leader of the Kremlin kleptocracy which had invaded its neighbour.

Doubts about truth in public office ultimately signal death for democracy. The response to the Johnson–Putin story was similar to Samuel Johnson's quip about trying to choose between two bad actors: 'There is no settling the point of precedency between a louse and a flea.' Unfairly, many conclude that 'all politicians lie' or 'they are all the same'. That isn't true. Most – and I have met hundreds of politicians – really do try to tell the truth and do believe that honesty in public life is essential to the workings of democracy. But the subversion of truth and the loss of our traditional expectation of a degree of honesty is part of a worldwide decline of trust in democratic institutions. Traditional norms of behaviour, of which truth-telling is a part, are necessary to make democratic systems work. These norms of behaviour have also been comprehensively undermined. The damaging results are not confined to the United Kingdom and the United States, but Boris Johnson and Donald Trump feature prominently in the next two chapters because they are two of the best-known examples of a successful truth-busting and trust-destroying leadership style. This is not intended as a rehearsal of the well-known weaknesses of these two leaders, but rather of something often overlooked – their strengths. Johnson and Trump share a peculiar genius that made their rise to the top unstoppable despite their obvious flaws. Both distorted the truth, yet while their serial dishonesty was well known, both *at the same time* built trust with millions of voters. That is a remarkable kind of genius. It rests upon modern democracy's dark arts, three techniques which have done most to undermine truth, trust and democratic traditions in the twenty-first century. These techniques will be defined in detail in the next chapter, but in brief they are a tactic, a strategy and an objective. The tactic is Dead Catting or 'throwing a dead cat on the table' to distract public opinion from more serious matters; this occurs as part of a strategy of repeated disinformation known as Strategic Lying; and finally there is a result or objective, called Truth Decay, by the RAND Corporation and others. Truth Decay in essence is a state in which the general public is unsure what or whose 'truth' to believe. You believe Putin? How about Johnson? One of them has to be lying, surely? Could it be both?

Donald Trump and Boris Johnson are masters of these dark arts, overturning the norms of behaviour usually expected in a democracy. Both promoted their actions by referencing versions of their different national traditions. For Trump this was to 'Make America Great Again'. For Johnson it was a similarly nostalgic: 'Take Back Control'. What follows, then, uses the familiar failings of both leaders to provide insight into something much bigger and even more damaging, the common systemic weaknesses of these two democracies on either side of the Atlantic, with particular emphasis on the UK.

Britain and the United States have often been political echoes of each other in our virtues and vices. Prime Minister Margaret Thatcher and President Ronald Reagan were conservative soulmates. Tony Blair and Bill Clinton presented themselves as 'New' Labour and 'New' Democrats at the peak of democratic hubris in the 1990s. By the second decade of the twenty-first century Boris Johnson and Donald Trump rose to prominence simultaneously as the poster boys of post-truth politics, masters of what one Trump acolyte called 'alternative facts'. They proved themselves to be accomplished manipulators of the opportunities afforded by the so-called Information Age. Trump even called his own competitor to Twitter '*Truth* Social' and had the Twitter handle @*real*donaldtrump. At his peak he had 88 million Twitter followers. When you are in the lying and fakery business, branding yourself as the arbiter of reality and the speaker of truth is always a good idea. The damage to both democracies has been immense.

5

Truth Decay: Strategic Lying, Dead Cats and Our Democratic Recession

The term 'democratic recession' was coined by the Stanford University political scientist Larry Diamond in 2008. In his book *The Spirit of Democracy* Diamond observed the undermining of democratic principles worldwide, and noted that it came as a shock after the hubris of the 1990s. I lived in Washington DC throughout the 90s and there was an inescapable sense of western triumphalism following the rise of Mikhail Gorbachev to power in Moscow, the collapse of communism, the dismantling of the Soviet Union, the end of the Warsaw Pact, and new democracies rising in Eastern Europe and elsewhere. Under Deng Xiaoping even China abandoned the shackles of Maoism. Western politicians and Washington intellectuals showed astonishing degrees of self-congratulation. Some spoke of a 'unipolar world' revolving around the United States and allied democratic countries. It was 'the end of history' according to Francis Fukuyama's striking but misleading phrase. There was certainly plenty of good news after five decades of the Cold War. The Varieties of Democracy project calculated that:

> Over the course of the second half of the twentieth century, large numbers of people gained democratic political rights. In 1950, more than 200 million people – mostly in Western Europe – lived in liberal democracies, and another 240 million lived in electoral democracies in Western Europe and the Americas. This number increased in the next decades, and by the late 1990s the majority of the world's population – around 3 billion people – lived in electoral and liberal democracies.[1]

What happened next was tracked by the Washington DC based thinktank Freedom House. Their *Freedom in the World 2022* report warned that:

> Withering blows marked the 15th consecutive year of decline in global freedom. The countries experiencing deterioration outnumbered those with improvements by the largest margin recorded since the negative trend began in 2006. The long

democratic recession is deepening. The impact of the long-term democratic decline has become increasingly global in nature, broad enough to be felt by those living under the cruelest dictatorships, as well as by citizens of long-standing democracies.[2]

So what went wrong? Within that global pattern the 'long-standing democracies' of the US and UK saw clear evidence of democratic decline, while continuing to celebrate their shared virtues and democratic traditions. Both celebrated Magna Carta's 800th anniversary in 2015. I chaired an Anglo-American celebration in the Palace of Westminster at which Law Lords and other constitutional experts paid tribute to our shared democratic values as a gift to the world. But by that time both the United States and United Kingdom had already begun to display a particularly acute trust problem in public life. This was rooted in a truth problem that was eroding the very thing we were celebrating, democracy itself. Back in the glory days for the West in the 1990s, I had spent a year of my life on one lie. That one lie was American, and we will get to it in a moment. This one American lie a generation ago illuminates what has changed in the acceptance of lying on both sides of the Atlantic. It enables us to contrast the past with the ability of leaders in the twenty-first century to exploit industrial scale lying without obvious penalty.

To begin by stating the obvious, lying is a significant cause of loss of trust. Some lies in our personal lives – 'I love your new hairstyle' or 'that meal was delicious' – may be forgivable. Others – 'I love you' – are almost certainly not. The same, as we will see, is true of lying in public life. The pattern of deliberate Strategic Lying that we have witnessed in recent years has a central place in the collapse of trust in democratic and other institutions – government, big business, the media and even NGOs. Lying as a deliberate strategy plays a key role in the British national malaise.

So, take a deep breath. Are *you* a liar? Unless you are a saint or someone prepared to lie even about lying then you, like me, will admit to telling lies occasionally. Would you also accept that in the past twenty years lying, falsehoods, deliberate misstatements of fact, have become more obvious and more tolerated in our lives? Consider, for example, the box that pops up when you order something online. You are required to state that you have 'read and understood the Terms and Conditions'. Do you immediately read the T&Cs? Or do you just tick the box and proceed? Have you *ever* read the T&Cs? I haven't, although I have used a wordcount to discover that some T&Cs are 30,000 words long. This is longer than *Hamlet,* and a lot less fun. When you tick the box, you lie. But this chapter is not about the human frailty of box ticking or insincerely praising someone's new clothes or hairstyle. Nor is it about getting things wrong and occasionally misstating the facts. This is about a political choice and the consequences of the deliberate use of distractions and lying as a strategy for political and personal advancement. Lying has gone from being a sin to becoming a policy option. Frequent and deliberate falsehoods in public life destroy public confidence. Can we ever now know for sure the difference between truth and falsehood or fact and fiction? And that's the point. The truth about lying is – it works.

'Throw in a Dead Cat'

The Dead Cat tactic is defined as a distraction technique involving the use of a shocking announcement to change the course of a conversation. It has long been associated with Lynton Crosby, a Britain-based Australian communications specialist who has worked on Conservative Party campaigns and for the party's prominent candidates. One of those was Boris Johnson. Johnson became an expert in the Dead Cat technique. He has used it repeatedly as a diversionary tactic throughout his political career to change the subject when confronted with difficult conversations. This became a pattern of distraction amounting to Strategic Lying, which we will define in detail in a moment. Given Johnson's success and prominence, his Strategic Lying has been a significant contribution to Truth Decay in British public life. This is not accidental. It is a well-thought-out programme of deceit and it has become embedded in the British political system. To find out how it works, we have an expert view. It comes from Boris Johnson himself.

In 2008 Johnson secured, with help from Lynton Crosby, what turned out to be his part-time job as Mayor of London. It was part-time because Johnson continued his other career in journalism, mainly writing newspaper columns for the *Daily Telegraph*. His *Telegraph* salary amounted to £275,000 a year. Johnson occasionally suggested the paper was his main employer. Crosby's advice was not cheap. It was reported that the Conservative Party paid his company £140,000 for four months' work with Johnson. In a 2013 *Daily Telegraph* column Johnson wrote about an 'Australian friend' and that friend's advice about how to handle a discussion when 'the facts are overwhelmingly against you' by changing the subject dramatically and theatrically. Crosby's name was not mentioned in the article, but the advice was consonant with his style. The 'Australian friend' suggested that a political candidate should shockingly disrupt any argument to escape from uncomfortable facts. It was, he said, rather like walking into a room where a serious discussion was taking place and throwing a dead cat on the table. Johnson wrote:

> There is one thing that is absolutely certain about throwing a dead cat on the dining room table – and I don't mean that people will be outraged, alarmed, disgusted. That is true, but irrelevant. The key point, says my Australian friend, is that everyone will shout, 'Jeez, mate, there's a dead cat on the table!' In other words, they will be talking about the dead cat – the thing you want them to talk about – and they will not be talking about the issue that has been causing you so much grief.[3]

Boris Johnson (and Donald Trump and many other populists) made a career for themselves by repeatedly using Crosby's tactic. In Trump's case, he could change America's conversation through just one tweet. He did it with a bizarre and possibly accidental tweet one morning. It said simply 'Despite the constant negative press covfefe'. It went viral. Was the president of the United States asking for coffee? Was it a weird code? Whatever the point, the national – and in this case international – conversation was changed by seven presumably mistyped letters of the alphabet. It is a perverse kind of genius, but it works.

In Johnson's case, the examples of the Dead Cat technique are legion. In one bizarre episode, when Johnson was the main contender to replace Theresa May as prime minister in the summer of 2019 he was dogged by uncomfortable allegations of lying both as a politician and as a journalist. There were lurid, awkward, and true stories about Johnson's private life, and lies he told about sexual affairs. He was challenged about his affair with an American businesswoman, Jennifer Arcuri, and asked repeatedly about the lie blazoned on the Brexit bus – famously it claimed that the UK gave £350 million a week to the European Union, and that this would become available on leaving the EU to make the lives of British citizens easier. Everyone knew the figure was wrong, including those who travelled in the bus and were repeatedly challenged by journalists about it, as Johnson was.

On the verge of becoming prime minister Boris Johnson used the Dead Cat technique to change the narrative. He stole newspaper headlines by giving an interview to someone called Ross Kempsell. Johnson claimed that his hobby (hitherto unknown) was to make model buses out of wooden crates and then paint them. If you Googled Boris Johnson and the word 'bus', instead of being dominated by the Brexit bus lie, up popped the more recent ludicrous tale of Johnson spending his leisure hours sticking bits of wood together to make model double-decker buses. Here's one newspaper's take:

The internet has been scratching its collective head after Boris Johnson's bizarre comment in an interview that to relax he crafts and paints model buses, an answer one political scientist called *'so bizarre that it's mesmerising.'* Speaking on Talk Radio on Tuesday, the frontrunner to replace Theresa May was asked

by an interviewer called Ross Kempsell, what he did to relax.
Johnson replied: 'I like to paint. Or I make things. I have a
thing where I make models of buses. What I make is, I get old,
I don't know, wooden crates, and I paint them. It's a box that's
been used to contain two wine bottles, right, and it will have
a dividing thing. And I turn it into a bus. So I put passengers
– I paint the passengers enjoying themselves on a wonderful
bus – low carbon, of the kind that we brought to the streets
of London, reducing CO_2, reducing nitrous oxide, reducing
pollution.'[4] [my italics]

Kempsell turned out to be Boris Johnson's tennis partner and a
friend of Johnson's then-fiancée, Carrie Symonds. But – and this
is the key point – the Dead Cat story worked. Does Boris Johnson
really have a hobby painting old wine crates? Did Vladimir Putin
really threaten to nuke him? I have no idea. It doesn't matter.
The important phrase in the newspaper report is that of the
anonymous political scientist who called the bus story 'so bizarre
it's mesmerising'. That was the point. It was – like the Putin tale –
just one strikingly successful example of Johnson's use of the Dead
Cat technique to steal headlines by making weird comments as
part of a deliberate strategy to refocus conversations away from
inconvenient publicity back in the real world. To be a successful
distraction, it doesn't matter whether the story is true or false, or
even idiotic. What matters is that it breaks through the information
blizzard and gets noticed. It is the messaging that is important,
not the content or veracity of the message. And Johnson mastered
the art.

He talked about his fondness for the children's cartoon *Peppa Pig*
in a speech to the CBI business group. He tried a Kermit the Frog
joke at the United Nations. He repeatedly offers allusions to Ancient
Greece or Rome, once comparing himself to Cincinnatus, a Roman
leader who left power only to return. Cincinnatus, incidentally, was
a nasty piece of work, a dictator who claimed he 'returned to the
plough'. He had slaves to do the ploughing.

By 2022 the largely unknown-to-the-public Ross Kempsell appeared on Johnson's list for a resignation honours life peerage in the House of Lords. He was then aged thirty. Kempsell was therefore tipped by Johnson to become one of the youngest life peers in history, possibly serving in the Upper Chamber of the British parliament for the next fifty years thanks to whatever service he provided to B. Johnson.

At other times Johnson's political distractions were more subtle. He was challenged robustly by the Labour MP Chris Bryant on the Brexit bus '£350 million for the EU' lie in the parliamentary liaison committee:

'When a minister lies, they should correct the record – I assume you agree?' Bryant asked. 'It seems that you very rarely correct the record? Why is that?'

Faced with a rigorous interlocutor like Bryant, even Johnson could not seek solace in *Peppa Pig* or painting boxes. He used a different distraction technique – shamelessness. He suggested that if the £350 million figure was wrong, it should have been higher:

It is commonly asserted for instance, that when we put the figure of £350 million a week on the side of a bus which went round this country causing a great deal of hoo-ha, this was a figure that related to the gross sum that the UK gave to the EU budget... actually it turned out to be if anything *a slight under-estimate.*[5] [my italics]

This was not an attempt to correct the record. It was an attempt to magnify the falsehood. Once there is a deluge of bizarre, 'mesmerising' and shamelessly invented stories in public life, in newspapers, TV, radio and social media, then it is easy for readers, voters, journalists and commentators to become baffled or misled to the point at which no one can readily tell fact from fiction. That is not an accident. It is the objective. The German philosopher Hannah Arendt did not use phrases like Dead Catting, Strategic Lying or Truth Decay back in

1951, but she understood the phenomenon perfectly. In *The Origins of Totalitarianism* Arendt observed that a pattern of deliberate lying was useful to totalitarian leaders to confuse and control millions of ordinary people. Arendt declared:

> The ideal subject of totalitarian rule is not the convinced Nazi or the convinced Communist, but people for whom the distinction between fact and fiction (i.e. the reality of experience) and the distinction between the true and the false (i.e. the standards of thought) no longer exist.

The United Kingdom is of course not on the verge of 'totalitarian rule'. But we have already crossed the line in which the distinction between fact and fiction, truth and falsehood, has become difficult to discern. As with the difficulty of deciding between Johnson or Putin on the missile story, it is the *doubt* that matters. Doubt or confusion benefits the liar, not the rest of us. It not only works, but when lying becomes 'normal' there is often no immediate penalty. Most of us just shrug and move on. The lie on the Brexit bus did not destroy or even undermine the Brexit campaign. It did the opposite. It energised the advocates of Brexit. The leading Vote Leave strategist Dominic Cummings boasted about it, confirming that the lie was a Dead Cat story (though he did not use that phrase) designed to get people talking about the cost of EU membership. Reports saying that the figures were false did not matter, as Cummings accepted. They merely gave the story the oxygen of publicity. £350 million a week? £200 million? £500 million? Whatever the exact price tag, it sounded like a lot of money, and that was enough to capture the headlines and stir up the debate. While lies and liars have always been among us, the toleration of lying in public life to the extent we observe in the 2020s is something qualitatively new. That brings us back to the one lie which took up twelve months of my life more than twenty years ago. It runs as follows: 'I did not have sexual relations with that woman, Miss Lewinsky.'

The Big Lie

That one lie famously led to the impeachment of a US president and almost to his downfall. The Liar-in-Chief was William Jefferson Clinton. He had a well-deserved reputation of always finding ways to avoid blame. Clinton could charm his way out of checkmate. When his presidential campaign lost momentum in 1992 and he regained support in the New Hampshire primary, Clinton wrote the next day's newspaper headlines for journalists by nicknaming himself 'The Comeback Kid'. But when he lied about having sex with the White House intern Monica Lewinsky, I was sure – as was everyone in the White House press corps – that for Clinton this time the game was probably up. We were wrong.

I had met Bill Clinton even before he was formally running for the presidency. When he was Governor of Arkansas, I literally bumped into him early one morning when he had been out jogging in New Hampshire. We struck up a conversation and I interviewed him a few times, including (eventually) at the White House. When I followed his campaign for the presidency Clinton shrewdly used the presence of BBC cameras to suggest to audiences that since British broadcasters took him seriously, New Hampshire voters should too. He never missed a trick, but his reputation and appetites were well known in Democratic political circles. In the summer of 1991, before he formally announced his presidential bid, I was drinking beer in a bar in Iowa with a group of Democratic party operatives. I mentioned that I rated Clinton highly and said that he would make a great presidential candidate. My BBC producer, David Taylor, agreed. The response from the Democrat operatives was alarm. 'Oh, no!' one blurted out. 'Not... Governor Zipper Problem!'

Clinton's fondness for women was never a secret. The Clintons burst into the American political consciousness a few months later in a CBS *60 Minutes* interview after one of the biggest TV audiences of the year, the 1992 Superbowl. They talked about Bill's adultery, although the word was never used.

'I have acknowledged wrongdoing,' Clinton said, sitting side by side with his wife, Hillary, in a hotel suite in Boston. 'I have acknowledged causing pain in my marriage. I have said things to you tonight and to the American people from the beginning that no American politician ever has.'

That was true. And it cut through. Clinton introduced himself to tens of millions who had never even heard of him as a contrite sinner. Suddenly many voters found a future president, and a story, they could relate to. But when the Lewinsky scandal broke – the most powerful man in the world in a sexual relationship with a very junior employee – Clinton's staff and advisers were unanimously appalled, yet no White House staffers resigned. Several of them told me that Clinton's conduct was reprehensible, but the impeachment proceedings for a lie about something that had nothing to do with Clinton's presidential duties or the constitution was – they said – just the latest twist in the six-year-long Republican anti-Clinton witch hunt. Clinton's story features here, therefore, because it illuminates the ways in which things really have changed in the Information Age and the rise of social media since the 1990s.

High Crimes and Misdemeanours

Clinton was the first US president to be impeached for 130 years. At the end of the US Civil War in 1868 President Andrew Johnson was impeached under Article II Section 4 of the constitution for 'Treason, Bribery, or other High Crimes and Misdemeanors'. He was acquitted at his Senate trial by a narrow, partisan vote. A century later, in the 1970s, Richard Nixon was not impeached over Watergate. He resigned rather than face the inevitable impeachment trial. Clinton was impeached in 1998 and by the 2020s Donald Trump was impeached not just once but twice. Both times Trump narrowly survived a partisan vote. Things have sped up in US politics. After a gap of 130 years between the first and second impeachments of an American president, the United States endured three impeachments in three decades, all based on allegations of presidential dishonesty or lies.

In the UK we do not have impeachment proceedings like this, but we do have our own problems with mendacity. We have also witnessed how deceit has become normalised in our public life, even though the British often use euphemisms for lying, partly because a journalist calling someone a liar in print may result in legal action for defamation. We say, therefore, with a wink and a nudge, that someone is 'economical with the truth', telling 'porkie pies' or 'whoppers' or being 'less than completely honest'. But Boris Johnson's Stakhanovite lying, in parallel with events involving Donald Trump in the United States, broke the taboo. It resulted in numerous newspaper columns, magazine articles and even entire books about his serial falsehoods and reign of error. Google 'Boris Johnson lies' and you will be deluged by everything from the musician Johnny Marr's tweet of an ancient and feeble joke reworked: 'How do you know Boris Johnson is lying? – His lips are moving' – to *The Irish Post* offering Boris Johnson jokes including Johnson telling everyone 'down the pub' that he will 'buy them a drink'. The pub crowd are disappointed, because it's just one pint of beer to be shared by everyone in the pub – '*a*' drink. The joke is weak, but the perception is acute. Boris Johnson had an extraordinary ability deliberately to mislead people, and when caught out to pretend it was a joke or simply refuse to correct what he had said. He remained unpunished. Under the British system, it was Johnson's accusers who were not so lucky.

After his ludicrous suggestion to Chris Bryant that the Brexit bus lie had been an *under*-estimate of the cost of the EU to the British taxpayer, in the House of Commons chamber the Labour MP Dawn Butler claimed that Johnson 'lied to the House and the country over and over again'. Calling another 'Honourable' Member a liar is forbidden in the House of Commons. Butler was ejected. Johnson stayed. Outside the chamber the Labour leader Sir Keir Starmer agreed with Ms Butler: 'I think the prime minister is the master of untruths and half-truths, and Dawn was simply giving some examples of that.' Most parliamentarians accept that the convention not to call another MP a liar in the Commons' chamber is reasonable. Repeated name-calling would further diminish respect for parliament. But that means euphemisms have become essential inside the Commons while the word liar outside parliament can be attached to Johnson with impunity. The most famous House of Commons euphemism originated with Winston Churchill in 1906 when he suggested a fellow MP was guilty of 'terminological inexactitude'.

That other parliamentary euphemism – 'economical with the truth' – is usually sourced to Edmund Burke. He asserted that:

> Falsehood and delusion are allowed in no case whatever but, as in the exercise of all the virtues, there is an economy of truth. It is a sort of temperance, by which a man speaks truth with measure that he may speak it the longer.[6]

For Bill Clinton, that one lie about Monica Lewinsky led to some brutal consequences, even though he tried to wriggle out of responsibility by living up to his Arkansas nickname.

'Slick Willie'

When pressed about his affair with the then twenty-four-year-old Ms Lewinsky, President Clinton said, very carefully, that there 'is not a sexual relationship' with the White House intern. He then told a judge, 'There *is* no sex of any kind.' When finally caught out, Clinton defended these misleading statements by claiming it 'depends upon what the meaning of the word "is" is'. His use of the present tense was a dismal lawyerly way of trying to avoid impeachment. When I talked with Clinton's political opponents in his home state of Arkansas they explained that they had for years nicknamed him 'Slick Willie', for this kind of slippery splitting of hairs. Clinton was impeached by the US House of Representatives on 19 December 1998 on charges of perjury, obstruction of justice and malfeasance in office. After months of prolonged scandal, in early 1999 Clinton was tried, as the US constitution demands, before the Senate. He survived by the narrowest of margins. The chief prosecutor Congressman Henry Hyde argued that:

> A failure to convict will make the statement that lying under oath, while unpleasant and to be avoided, is not all that serious... We have reduced lying under oath to a breach of etiquette, but only if you are the President.

The counterargument from Democrats was that Clinton had indeed lied about sex but this was not an impeachable matter since it did not meet the constitutional test of 'high crimes and misdemeanours'. American democracy was most certainly not in peril. Clinton's press secretary Joe Lockhart assured me personally that he was just as appalled as everyone else by the conduct of his boss but the lie about sex had been weaponised to stage a Republican coup against a man twice elected to the highest political office by tens of millions of the American people, and whose personal weaknesses were well known and hardly unique. During the Clinton impeachment process two key Republicans – House Speaker Newt Gingrich and the chief prosecutor Congressman Henry Hyde – were themselves outed as having had extramarital affairs. Not being entirely honest about sexual activities turned out to be a bipartisan habit.

Clinton survived. He ended his presidency in January 2001 even *more* popular than when he was first inaugurated eight years earlier. And that's why the Clinton story remains relevant to the current normalisation of lying in public life on both sides of the Atlantic. What has changed in just twenty or so years is that lying is now much more frequent, more brazen and not confined to matters which – at least arguably – are private, like sex. Lying in public life *about* public life has now been tolerated to such an extent it is expected. In the past leaders who lied have – like Clinton – sometimes been forgiven, either because the lie was seen essentially as a private matter, or a common human failing, or for reasons of state. Winston Churchill argued that in wartime truth is so precious 'she must always be attended by a bodyguard of lies'. The former US Navy Secretary John Lehman once told me – I'd almost say he boasted to me – that during the Cold War he had deliberately misled Congress and the American people when he was berated about how much better and faster Russian submarines were than their US equivalents. Lehman (whom I admired immensely) took the heat, knowing all the while that this was a phoney row. Russian submarines were indeed faster, but their noisy engines made them much easier to detect. American submarines were – and are – much better. That's why submariners think of themselves as 'the Silent Service'.

When it comes to lying in public life, things have greatly changed between Bill Clinton's impeachment in 1998 and Donald Trump's impeachments some twenty years later. Trump didn't tell one lie. He told thousands. Trump survived because he was, in his way, a master communicator absolutely perfect for the era of the Politics of Distraction. And, as we will see, so is Boris Johnson.

How Lying Has Changed and Why It Matters in the UK

Donald Trump was first impeached in 2019, then again in 2021. During his presidency Trump told so many lies and falsehoods, and made so many misleading statements, that the *Washington Post* began to keep a tally. At the end of the Trump presidency in January 2021 they put the total at 30,000. This was an average of more than twenty falsehoods a day, almost one an hour, every day, including Sundays and public holidays, for four years. Some falsehoods appeared trivial yet obvious. Trump and his public relations staff lied literally from Day One about massive crowds at his January 2017 inauguration. I've been to several presidential inaugurations – Clinton, George W. Bush, Obama – and even a casual television viewer could see that the Trump inauguration was poorly attended.

The District of Columbia Metro figures showed public transport was used by far fewer people than at Barack Obama's inaugurations four and eight years previously. Trump's spokesman Sean Spicer could have used a bit of 'spin' and said (truthfully) that Trump's voters loathed Washington's 'inside-the-beltway' culture so wouldn't want to attend. Instead Spicer brazenly disagreed with the evidence before the eyes of TV viewers by claiming that Trump had the '*largest* audience to ever witness an inauguration – period – both in person and around the globe'. When the challenges continued, another Trump apologist, Kellyanne Conway, spoke of Spicer's use of 'alternative facts'. The lies never stopped. Trump even lied about being hard at work in the White House when he was playing golf.

The *Post* study noted that the lies increased in frequency and significance towards the end of Trump's time in office. His presidency ended with the biggest and most damaging lie in American constitutional history when he claimed that he had won the 2020 election but it was 'stolen' by Joe Biden. It led to far-right groups intent on violence marching on the US Capitol in January 2021 chanting 'Stop the Steal'. For the first time in US history, an outgoing president appeared actively to encourage a coup to keep himself in power by overturning the clear verdict of the American people. This was a strategic lie par excellence. The Trump presidency was reminiscent of the famous line from the 1933 Marx Brothers comedy *Duck Soup* when Chico is caught out in an obvious deception and responds, 'Who are you gonna believe – me, or your own eyes?' Tens of millions of Americans believed Donald Trump over the evidence of their own eyes.

This, obviously, is where lying in public office becomes a grave constitutional issue, even though there is no clause of the US constitution that asserts a losing candidate should concede defeat. A graceful concession is merely the accepted norm of behaviour. That is why Trump's lie still casts a long shadow over American democracy. One year after the Stop the Steal insurrection, more than 40 per cent of Americans still refused to believe that Joe Biden had won fairly and 37 per cent said they had lost faith in American democracy as a result. That figure included 48 per cent of Republicans. Another 10 per cent said they had never had faith in the system anyway. Just under half (49 per cent) said they did still have faith.[7]

Trust in democracy was the ultimate casualty of Trump's strategic lies. It was a glimpse of Hannah Arendt's 'totalitarian mindset', the inability of ordinary people to separate fact from fiction and truth from lies. By September 2022, resentment was still festering. President Joe Biden therefore came to the city where American democracy began, Philadelphia, to excoriate Donald Trump and the MAGA (Make America Great Again) Republicans for the lies which undermined democracy. As he put it:

'Donald Trump and the MAGA Republicans represent an extremism that threatens the very foundations of our Republic. For a long time, we've reassured ourselves that American democracy is guaranteed. But it is not. We have to defend it. Protect it. Stand up for it. Each and every one of us.' Biden then claimed that Trump Republicans, 'thrive on chaos... don't respect the constitution' or the rule of law and 'you can't love your country when only you win.'[8]

These American political convulsions are instructive for the United Kingdom and elsewhere in our worldwide democratic recession. Just one lie tarnished Clinton's reputation. It was a lie that had no lasting impact on trust in, or the functioning of, American democracy or governance. It merely turned on the flaws of one powerful individual. Donald Trump's lie, about a stolen election, was very different. It came after a torrent of falsehoods exposed repeatedly over four years, but without the Liar-in-Chief suffering any obvious consequences among his supporters. MAGA Republicans continued to believe Trump not despite his lies, but *because* his lies were in some way what they wanted to hear rather than – for them – the unpleasant truth. The Stop the Steal campaign was the ultimate in Strategic Lying, the point at which a lie ensures Truth Decay.

The United Kingdom is not quite there yet, but we've been walking along the same road towards the same dismal destination.

Definitions: Strategic Lying and Truth Decay

Strategic Lying has been defined as 'a priming device to set the news agenda'. It is an effective way of campaigning that 'represents a development of political spin – first evident in the mass media era – that has been intensified by the increasing professionalisation of political communications and the rise of social media'.[9]

Strategic Lying may also involve boasting about political plans and great projects. Beyond claiming the biggest crowds ever at his inauguration, Donald Trump frequently spoke of his intention to 'build a wall and make Mexico pay for it'. Some bits of a border wall were constructed. Mexico paid for none of it. Boris Johnson never built a tunnel or bridge to Northern Ireland, a Garden Bridge across the Thames, an airport in the Thames estuary, the forty new hospitals he promised, nor did he secure £350 million a week extra for the NHS. But one sign of the effectiveness of Strategic Lying is that failure to deliver any or all of those projects does not seem to matter. The British and American public have become so jaded by empty promises that it is fair to speculate that nobody really believed that any of those great projects would ever become a reality anyway.

'"Strategic Lying": The Case of Brexit and the 2019 U.K. Election', the 2021 paper by Ivor Gaber and Caroline Fisher quoted above, repeats a 1971 observation of Hannah Arendt that in one sense there is nothing new in leaders who lie: 'The deliberate falsehood and the outright lie used as legitimate means to achieve political ends, have been with us since the beginning of recorded history.'[10] That's true. But Gaber and Fisher did note that a significant recent change came with the more organised pattern of lying. It is no longer merely an occasional use of deception. It has become a deliberate strategy of political communication. In both the US and UK this strategy could be connected to 'recent electoral successes, the 2016 Brexit

Referendum and the 2019 General Election in the United Kingdom, and Trump's victory in 2016 and his increased electoral support in 2020'. Gaber and Fisher concluded that Strategic Lying in recent years differs significantly from the past because the more recent events 'point to an apparent growing tendency for politicians caught lying *not* to be punished at the ballot box'. After the enormous publicity given to those 30,000 lies noted by the *Washington Post* over the previous four years, Donald Trump in the 2020 election actually received more votes (74 million) than he obtained in 2016 (almost 63 million). Boris Johnson's Brexit bus lie – despite endless media coverage of that and other falsehoods – did not prevent him becoming Conservative Party leader and winning the 2019 General Election. In both cases lies and liars were rewarded by millions of voters.

In a separate analysis Ivor Gaber explained why even when the lie is exposed, the liar is often unpunished. He described Strategic Lying as a process beginning with:

> Telling a blatant untruth in the full knowledge that within minutes of its dissemination it will be called out as a lie, but for a number of reasons this doesn't appear to matter... second... to ensure that the subject matter of the lie stays at the top of the news agenda... third... to sow confusion making audiences immune to messages from opponents that might cut through the misleading narrative – the post-truth environment incarnate.

In analysing Boris Johnson's victory in the December 2019 election, Gaber implicitly dissented from Hannah Arendt's observation that political lies and liars have always been with us. The volume and impact of lying had changed so much, historical comparisons were irrelevant:

> In covering and researching more election campaigns than I care to remember, this is the first one that the notion of

liars and lying has been so prominent. Nor can it simply be attributed to the particular character of Boris Johnson, whose relationship to the truth has been, to say the very least, casual. The lying in the 2019 election has been more systematic than in past campaigns where the problem was more one of voters trying to navigate a stream of spin rather than trying to swim through a torrent of lies. In fact the lies of 2019, particularly from the Conservative side had a particular character which I am describing as 'Strategic Lying' and can be traced back to the evolution of an environment in which politicians, who in the past if caught lying were obliged to resign, now appear to have gained a 'permission to lie'.[11]

In his analysis Gaber returned to 2016 and the Vote Leave campaign cofounder Dominic Cummings. The lie that the EU cost Britain £350 million a week, Gaber concluded, was indeed immediately debunked by journalists, politicians and academic experts. That did not matter. Cummings understood that in a political climate where lies and truth have become so intertwined refuting a falsehood simply gave more oxygen to the original lie. In a 2021 interview the BBC political editor Laura Kuenssberg challenged Cummings on precisely that point.

'You knew very well then, and you know very well now, that that figure didn't include the so-called rebate, the money that the UK got to keep,' Kuenssberg said.

'Yes,' Cummings replied, explaining that was precisely the point, to create a debate on the 'balance sheet' of Britain's EU membership, and to 'drive the Remain campaign and the people running it crazy'.

'So it was a deliberate trap for the other side?' Kuenssberg persisted.

'Yeah,' Cummings replied.

'But wasn't the important thing what you were saying to the public?' Kuenssberg persisted.

'No, I don't think so,' Cummings replied.

'It wasn't important what you were saying to the public?!' Kuenssberg responded. Then judging from the smirk on Cummings' face she added: 'I can see today you are almost laughing thinking about it.'

He still is. By the December 2019 General Election campaign, as Gaber noted:

> There were numerous other examples of this strategy in action – Mr. Johnson denying there would be any border checks between Great Britain and Northern Ireland, despite the Treasury and his own Brexit Secretary saying there would be. The Chancellor of the Exchequer Sajid Javid claiming that Labour's spending commitments amounted to an astronomical £1.3 trillion – a gross exaggeration, made to sound seemingly credible by the figure £1.3 trillion rather than a more general £1 trillion. The figure was demonstrably bogus but as the Chancellor toured the TV studios rebutting the rebuttals, Labour's claimed overspending stayed in the headlines.

Gaber concluded that Strategic Lying works, at least in the short term of an election campaign, even if in the long term it undermines trust in democracy itself:

> First, because correcting inaccurate statements, by either journalists or fact checkers, might persuade the uncommitted, but those sympathetic to the original message will reject the correction. Indeed it can *actually increase the intensity of their belief in the original lie as a means of avoiding cognitive dissonance.* Second, for those sympathetic to, or neutral about, the original message, the memory of the correction fades rapidly but *the memory of the original lie remains.* Third, because of the tried and tested power of repetition, if a lie is repeated often enough its content becomes easier to process and subsequently regarded as more truthful than any new statements rebutting it. So, in an age of 'permission to lie', it appears that the benefits

of Strategic Lying far outweigh any costs which could well mean that soon enough all politicians will be doing it and the quality of our democracy will further decline. [my italics]

Strategic Lying, then, does work. Loss of trust in truth itself is the objective of the overall strategy, and the attention-grabbing tactic of throwing dead cats on the table. That objective is sometimes called Truth Decay.

The phrase was coined by the US think tank the RAND Corporation in 2018. RAND define it as a phenomenon that 'has taken hold over the last two decades, eroding civil discourse, causing political paralysis, and leading to public uncertainty and disengagement'. We are surrounded by Truth Decay and its synonyms – fake news, fake science (most recently about coronavirus and global warming), fake history (including Holocaust denial), 'alternative facts', and even the sense that what we are reading on social media is the product of fake accounts, or people with fake 'followers'. Truth Decay will be made more intense, and more difficult to spot, as we enter into the world of Artificial Intelligence (AI) and 'deepfakes'. These involve the manipulation of images and voices to make it look as if real people are doing or saying things which in reality they did not do or say.

On a recent podcast for journalists I was asked what the news media can do about deepfakes. I responded that unfortunately newspaper, television and radio news broadcasts are even now often unable adequately to deal with 'shallow fakes' such as Donald Trump and Boris Johnson, and so the deepfakes problem may prove insurmountable. It is a gloomy prognosis.

The RAND definition of Truth Decay focuses on the United States although there are obvious parallels with the United Kingdom and elsewhere. The Putin regime in Russia is based on the principles of Strategic Lying and Truth Decay. So are a number of other totalitarian or authoritarian regimes. In January 2023 in Brazil Jair Bolsonaro supporters rioted against his loss in the presidential election of the previous year. They were in thrall to a series of strategic lies and self-serving distortions which were a Brazilian echo of Donald Trump two years previously. The 2018 RAND report noted that Truth Decay is a distinctly twenty-first-century phenomenon. It leads to the undermining of democracy and to 'public uncertainty and disengagement' from the democratic process. A third of the voting age population not bothering to vote would be one obvious and irrefutable symptom in Britain.

Truth Decay is defined by RAND as:

A set of four interrelated trends: an increasing disagreement about facts and analytical interpretations of facts and data; a blurring of the line between opinion and fact; an increase in the relative volume, and resulting influence, of opinion and personal experience over fact; and lowered trust in formerly respected sources of factual information.

The RAND report then focuses on four characteristics:

Human cognitive processing, such as cognitive bias; changes in the information system, including social media and the 24-hour news cycle; competing demands on the education system that diminish time spent on media literacy and critical thinking; and polarisation, both political and demographic. The most damaging consequences of Truth Decay include the erosion of civil discourse, political paralysis, alienation and disengagement of individuals from political and civic institutions, and uncertainty over national policy.

RAND also compared the twenty-first century with three historical eras – the 1890s, 1920s, and 1960s – and found evidence of two of the four trends in these earlier periods, but concluded that 'declining trust in institutions, while evident in previous eras, is more severe today. No evidence of an increase in disagreement about facts and analytical interpretations of facts and data was seen in the earlier periods.'[12]

The final sentences here are worth considering in detail since they are directly relevant to the loss of trust in institutions in the next chapter. The RAND report asserts that there is nothing new in the blurring of opinions and facts, or indeed in our dearly held opinions trumping disagreeable facts. But what has changed is that we are experiencing much greater 'disagreement about facts' and how they are interpreted. This has led to a 'more severe' decline in trust in institutions. The Russian chess grandmaster and pro-democracy campaigner Garry Kasparov understood this very clearly in comments directed at Vladimir Putin's Russia, but with resonance in post-Trump America (where Kasparov now lives) and Brexit Britain. Echoing Hannah Arendt, he wrote: 'The point of modern propaganda isn't only to misinform or push an agenda. It is to exhaust your critical thinking, to annihilate truth.'[13]

For those who believe Trump won an election 'stolen' by Joe Biden, truth has indeed been annihilated. And one further twist to Truth Decay is worth exploring. We have repeatedly noted how those who stand up for truth – academics, journalists, economists, fact-checkers, some politicians – may be ignored, while those who promote falsehoods – Dominic Cummings, Donald Trump, Boris Johnson – not merely survive, they may thrive, at least for a time. Dawn Butler MP was, as we saw, expelled from the House of Commons chamber for calling Boris Johnson a liar. Johnson remained in the House. And then there is the peculiar tale of the world's best-known liar, Donald Trump, securing the resignation of a distinguished British diplomat. Kim Darroch's crime was to tell the truth... about a liar.

Lies Rewarded, Truth Penalised

What happened to the former ambassador to the United States Sir Kim (now Lord) Darroch links Strategic Lying on one side of the Atlantic with Truth Decay on the British side. Darroch's CV reads like the best of British. He rose from humble beginnings – council house; scholarship boy at a good school; often in trouble as a result of what he calls 'a lifelong resistance to authority'; and unable for a long time to settle on a clear career path – yet he eventually became British ambassador in Washington and ultimately Baron Darroch of Kew, KCMG (Kindly Call Me God, as the mandarin wits have it). Darroch served as British Ambassador to the United States from January 2016 to December 2019. Before that he had been British National Security Adviser and the UK Permanent Representative to the European Union. His distinguished career came to an abrupt end in 2019. Private messages Darroch wrote to the Foreign Office in London back in 2017, seven months after the start of Trump's presidency, were made public in *The Mail on Sunday*. It is not clear how the newspaper came by them, but you may form your own conclusions from what happened next. In the extracts Darroch described Donald Trump's White House as 'inept' and 'deeply dysfunctional'. He observed that the president 'radiated insecurity' in a presidency potentially in a downward spiral leading to disgrace. He assessed that Trump was unlikely to become 'more normal; less dysfunctional; less unpredictable; less faction riven; less diplomatically clumsy and inept'.[14] Writing a private and robust message to colleagues in the Foreign Office is exactly what we pay diplomats to do. Anyone who has ever read a newspaper report about Donald Trump might also understand that Darroch was not a crazed outlier. He merely pointed out obvious deficiencies at the heart of the government of the United Kingdom's most important ally. These deficiencies were not a secret. They were observable to anyone with a pulse.

Darroch's private communication was leaked in the year of Trump's first impeachment for abuse of power and obstruction of Congress. The US movie star Mia Farrow tweeted sympathetically: 'The (UK) Ambassador is only saying what everybody knows.' But Trump was furious and said he would 'no longer deal with him'. The *coup de grâce* came from Boris Johnson, then Foreign Secretary and just a few days away from becoming prime minister. The man who had outlined the Dead Cat theory in his newspaper columns and who had employed it throughout his career, including on his pathway to Downing Street, was repeatedly asked by reporters if he supported Darroch. Johnson failed to defend Our Man in Washington. This led to newspaper headlines that Johnson was throwing Darroch 'under a bus'. (Buses play strongly in Johnson's career advancement. I have no idea why.) A striking cartoon in *The Times* showed Darroch literally under a bus and The future prime minister with blood on his hands.

Senior Conservatives tried to rally round Darroch. Tom Tugendhat, the chair of the foreign affairs select committee, commented rhetorically that, 'If you do not support those you put into very difficult positions, what do you think is going to happen?' The outgoing prime minister Theresa May offered an implicit rebuke of Johnson. She told the Commons: 'I hope the House will reflect on the importance of defending our values and principles, particularly when they are under pressure.' In his autobiography Darroch is generous towards Johnson, merely noting that in a phone call the Foreign Secretary said, 'But why did you resign? Wouldn't it all have blown over in a few weeks?' Johnson then asked Darroch if his own failure to back the ambassador had sealed Darroch's fate. The top diplomat responded – you may conclude – diplomatically. He told Johnson that there were several factors behind his decision to resign and the soon-to-be prime minister's words (or lack thereof) 'were one of them'.[15] Darroch's wife was less circumspect. She thought Johnson's conduct was 'unforgivable'.

As an example of Truth Decay, the situation was stark. A highly regarded British public servant was forced to resign from the best diplomatic posting in the world because he told the truth about a president who was the most consistent liar ever to hold the presidency of the United States. The truth-teller was then undermined by the refusal of a British politician to support him – a politician who himself frequently employed Strategic Lying.

But slowly, very slowly, the British public was beginning to wake up to the Politics of Distraction and deliberate deceit. The shock of discovering that while the UK was in coronavirus lockdown and we avoided seeing even close relatives and friends, law-breaking parties were being held in Downing Street began the process of discovery. Lying in public office was now the enemy within:

> New polling from YouGov/*The Times* reveals more than three-quarters of Britons (78 per cent) think Boris Johnson has lied in his response to the issue of parties being held at Downing Street during lockdown. Just 8 per cent think he has not lied, and 14 per cent are unsure.[16]

And there was this:

> A poll by JLPartners found that just 16 per cent of people would use positive language to describe the prime minister (Johnson) with more than 70 per cent characterising him in negative terms. Voters were asked to describe the prime minister, with the most frequent description being that he is a 'liar' – followed by 'incompetent' and 'untrustworthy'.[17]

And this from the polling expert, Professor John Curtice:

> According to Savanta ComRes, 65 per cent feel that throughout the furore [of his time in office] the Prime Minister has either 'only told lies' or at least that he has 'lied more than he has told the truth.' In contrast, just 13 per cent take the view that he has 'only told the truth' or 'has told the truth more than he has lied.' Even among 2019 Conservative voters, only 23 per cent believe he has largely been truthful.[18]

By August 2022, as Johnson ended his scandal-filled time in office, the truth gap in our public life had led to a measurable trust gap, with Boris Johnson now distrusted by 76 per cent of voters and trusted by only 11 per cent.[19] Even Conservative MPs had had enough. They got rid of the Liar-in-Chief they had tolerated, supported and venerated as a vote winner for years.

You may wonder why it took them, and us, so long.

What changed was that the facts about Boris Johnson's years of practised lying finally became politically salient. Why it took so long goes to the heart of why Dead Catting, Strategic Lying and Truth Decay have become so insidious and so effective. Countless newspaper and magazine articles, book-length publications and illustrations by cartoonists showed Johnson's 'pants on fire', or the prime minister with an extendable Pinocchio nose. But for years before he became prime minister these character flaws were public knowledge. In the 1980s Johnson was fired from *The Times* for making up quotes. In 2004 he was fired by the then Tory leader, Michael Howard, from positions as Shadow Arts Minister and Conservative Party vice-chairman. He had lied – as we noted earlier – about his extramarital affair with *Spectator* columnist Petronella Wyatt – the supposed 'inverted pyramid of piffle'. One well-known journalist who worked with Johnson told me bluntly that no one could trust him. He would brazenly lie to your face, laugh and add a few yo-ho-hos, treating his frequent indiscretions as a great joke. And it did not matter. Some forty years before his political career developed even his housemaster at Eton noted that Johnson appeared 'free of the network of obligation which binds everyone else'. Yet as late as July 2019 British public life tolerated losing a Kim Darroch at the same time as promoting a Boris Johnson to the office once held by Churchill, Disraeli and Gladstone. Three years after his 2019 resignation, I bumped into Lord Darroch. In a brief conversation he told me that one of the consequences of the changes to public life in the United Kingdom was that civil servants can 'no longer speak truth to power'. I have put that comment to other former senior civil servants and they broadly agree. These non-partisan senior advisers to British government ministers have now accepted that they cannot always tell their bosses inconvenient truths. They risk their careers if they do so. That makes it difficult to tell a minister that he or she risks breaching public trust, or the law itself, through relying on falsehoods. Examples where British civil servants, advisers and other insiders have mentioned to me that they have found it difficult to engage ministers in the factual, practical, ethical or legal basis of their decisions include the proposal to send asylum seekers to Rwanda; the 'push back' of migrant boats in the Channel; the obvious economic and political damage caused to the UK by Brexit and its lost opportunities; misinformation about the Northern Ireland Protocol; potentially corrupt relations with Russian and other political donors; the insistence that the UK government is building more than forty new hospitals despite clear evidence to the contrary; the notion that the slogan 'Levelling Up' is not doing what the words suggest; and the idea that the UK is employing 20,000 more police officers, when after cuts made by Conservative governments that is precisely the number of posts lost since 2010.

By this point perhaps we should recall another insight into lying. It comes from Bill Clinton. It is a bit of Arkansas wisdom he had been told as a child and he often quoted it: 'Fool me once, shame on you. Fool me twice, shame on *me*.'

We have all been fooled, on both sides of the Atlantic, many more times than once or twice. By February 2022 the *Guardian* published what it called a 'Truth-O-Meter' column asking 'How many lies has Boris Johnson told this week?' A website, Boris Johnson Lies,[20] began an extensive compilation. Books on systemic truth denial appeared, including Peter Oborne's *The Assault on Truth*. By 2022 it was clear the UK was suffering from an advanced case of Truth Decay and that Boris Johnson had to go. But the damage has been done and Johnson is not the real problem. The real problem is the system which produced, tolerated and promoted him. The veteran political commentator Steve Richards summed up the Johnson years and the destruction of trust in British public life that persists even now by focusing on Johnson's 'absurd narrative' of political martyrdom and his self-pitying fiction that being forced from office was the 'betrayal of greatness'. This fairy tale was aided by Johnson's

wilfully selective memory. He forgets conveniently that he could not form a government before he resigned. Potential ministers refused to serve. They walked away because even this group of subservient mediocrities, willing to accept humiliation after humiliation in order to keep their place in Johnson's administration, could continue no further. Belatedly they made the right call. I have no doubt that... historians across the political spectrum will judge Johnson's premiership to have been a calamity. For all my wider reservations about the claim, I judge him without qualification to be the worst prime minister in the UK's history, the least suited for office.[21]

The fate of Boris Johnson was, in the end, not in the hands of the British people. It was decided by a group of Conservative MPs, those whom Richards characterises as 'subservient mediocrities' who 'belatedly' made the right call. But what if they did not? What if instead of getting rid of Johnson, those who tolerated his mendacity for years persisted in thinking he was still fit to be prime minister or at least a potential vote winner enabling them to hold on to their seats in parliament? Why, in other words, is the British political system dependent on the judgement of parliamentary colleagues – mediocre or otherwise – from the same political party to keep in check 'the worst prime minister in the UK's history'? Constitutionally, with the support of enough 'subservient mediocrities', Johnson could have survived in office because there exists no clear constitutional imperative that demands otherwise. A prime minister and MPs in his or her own party exist in a symbiotic relationship. This can be a dark power in the hands of a populist 'rule breaking' politician. A future rule breaker may eventually arise who is more ruthless, more ideological and less indolent than Boris Johnson. The British constitution and system of government in that sense is an accident waiting to happen. Donald Trump retained the public support of almost all Republican members of Congress to the (very) bitter end. In Britain it is not far-fetched to assume that party loyalty could cohere around a similarly rule-breaking British prime minister in future. That person would be largely immune from the checks and balances of the kind found in the American system, because such checks and balances in Britain are generally dependent upon the good behaviour of the person in charge. That is the prime minister himself.

As these events unfolded I had a conversation with Dr Hannah White of the Institute for Government. Dr White suggested to me that the lessons of Boris Johnson's reign of error go well beyond his own personal failings:

> What we should learn is how vulnerable the constitution would be to someone with a real agenda. Boris Johnson's main objective in government was to be Boris Johnson in government. But if you had someone actively malevolent, you could end up in real trouble because the guard rails aren't there.[22]

The guard rails truly are not there. And when truth is the first casualty of politics, trust is next in line. To answer my original questioner Elizabeth, our loss of trust in the institutions at the heart of British democracy is the principal reason why things are 'so... so shit'.[23]

6

Trust and the Suspicious Century

B ritain has a trust problem. British people do not trust the institutions of our democracy, and we are not alone. We live in a suspicious century in which a loss of trust in institutions is a rational, national and international response to a lack of certainty about truth in public life. The combination of being attention poor, surrounded by a blizzard of information at our fingertips as a result of new technologies, and being unable to separate fact from falsehood rests at the heart of both the worldwide democratic recession and our own political turbulence. The most obvious historical parallel is the cultural, social and political upheaval following the impact of an earlier new information technology. The printing press was invented in 1436 by a German goldsmith, Johannes Gutenberg and powered the information revolution of its day. Printing on paper meant that books became more readily available, literacy increased and citizens in largely illiterate societies across Europe began to read. When they encountered all this new information for themselves, especially through reading the Bible in their own language, and independently produced religious tracts, the world opened up to interpretations of Christianity subversively different to rulings from Rome and the Papal hierarchy. Unsurprisingly, faced with very different views and insights from those outside 'official' sources, many ordinary people in Germany and across Europe decided that what they were being told by those in authority was self-serving and false. The disruption we now call the Reformation later led to the Thirty Years War and other conflicts with echoes today in Northern Ireland and elsewhere. Our own information revolution may – we can hope – prove not to have such bloody consequences, but it is at least as disruptive. It enables and accelerates our Culture Wars. It may even provoke our own reformation.

The biggest library in the world is the US Library of Congress. It claims 1.3 kilometres of shelving holding 170 million documents in 483 different languages. But even that is tiny compared to the production cycle in our twenty-first-century information revolution. In 2016, the year of Britain's Brexit vote and of Donald Trump's election to the presidency, it was calculated that humans were creating the information equivalent of more than 250,000 US Libraries of Congress *every single day*. By 2021 there were two trillion Google searches and 347,222 stories posted on Instagram *every minute*; 1.134 megabytes of data created every minute; 3 million emails sent every second, two-thirds of which were spam. That meant there were 2.5 quintillion bites of data created every day.[1] A quintillion is a number followed by 18 zeros. Every week the world saw an explosion of superabundant information roughly equivalent to 2 million copies of the biggest library in the world. Superabundant information transforms what we know, or think we know, how we live, and how little we may truly trust our sources of information in an age when almost anyone can research – or make up – almost anything, anywhere, all the time. Our unprecedented dilemma is no longer a lack of information. It is a lack of assuredly reliable sources and information we can definitively trust. Much of this data can only loosely be called 'information' at all: it is an outpouring of opinions and trivia. As with the problems facing the Church in Rome from the fifteenth century on, a deluge of new information sources inevitably diminishes trust in traditional institutions. Human nature means we realise that we need to search for trusted guides to cut through the tide of information and assist us, yet the dilemma persists. Who are these trusted guides?

In terms of our British malaise in the twenty-first century, where there are new risks there are also new opportunities, and new kinds of communicators. These are people who have the skill to cut through the information blizzard to connect with us personally to speak to our hopes and fears. In politics this kind of person is sometimes called a populist. It is undeniable that prominent people who do cut through and build trust in our increasingly suspicious century often share some very odd characteristics. One of the peculiarities of such people is their obvious character flaws. Flaws that would have disqualified leaders from being trusted in the past, may – perversely – help them build trust in the twenty-first century. That's because successful leaders in the era of information overload are often people who represent a refreshing break from 'politics as usual'. Donald Trump and Boris Johnson are joined by other new wave practitioners of 'Politics as Un-usual' – Jair Bolsonaro in Brazil, Viktor Orbán in Hungary, Giorgia Meloni in Italy, Rodrigo Duterte in the Philippines, Narendra Modi in India and others. Hundreds of millions of voters in democracies put their trust in leaders like these, at least for a time. This is a phenomenon which perplexes, even outrages, what we might describe as Establishment politicians, academics, commentators, and journalists in mainstream media organisations. These are people who often see themselves representing Enlightenment values demanding evidence, facts, and verifiable truths. The outrage of the Enlightened Establishment is, of course, exactly what the Politics-as-Unusual mould breakers seek to achieve. It brings to them the oxygen of publicity and controversy, amplifying their core message – that they are different.

Understanding why these changes have taken place involves another paradox. The Trust Paradox is that a measurable decline in trust in the institutions of democracy has provided an opportunity for what may appear to be untrustworthy leaders to reach positions of power and responsibility within those same democratic institutions. These less-than-trustworthy leaders succeed not despite their eccentricities, odd behaviour and even lies but as a result of them. Prominent trust builders in our suspicious century turn out to be skilled manipulators of pictures, photo opportunities, humour and memorable phrases. Whether any of what they say is true is largely irrelevant. What matters is that they cut through the information blizzard. As one self-confessed media manipulator put it, 'In an age of images and entertainment, in an age of instant emotional gratification, we neither seek nor want honesty or reality. Reality is complicated. Reality is boring. We are incapable or unwilling to handle its confusion.'[2]

The Enlightened Establishment – Hillary Clinton is a good example, as we will see in a moment – may be more careful in their respect for facts and truth, but their weakness is that they often fail to connect. Their 'reality is boring'. They may not even get noticed in the information deluge. Donald Trump had numerous catchphrases

– Make America Great Again, Lock Her Up, Stop the Steal – that could and did fit on a baseball hat, coffee mug or tee-shirt. What three- or four-word catchphrase from Hillary Clinton broke through to resonate across America? Does anything come to mind? Boris Johnson also had his own glib word arsenal – Get Brexit Done, Take Our Country Back, Levelling Up, Global Britain and so on – all memorable; all vacuous. His opponents? Not so much. So here's how trust may be built – and lost – in the Information Age. And here's why it matters, especially in the United Kingdom where our loss of trust in institutions is both measurable and particularly acute. We begin once more in the United States however, because the parallels with the UK are illuminating, and concerning.

The Authenticity Delusion

In 2013, *Reader's Digest* asked US subscribers to vote for those they trusted most in public life. No American political leader, no Obama, Bush or Clinton, came near top of the poll. The most trusted person in America was Tom Hanks. Sandra Bullock came second, Denzel Washington third, Meryl Streep fourth. Americans placed their trust in actors. An actor's key professional skill is to pretend through convincing story-telling to be something they are not. They fake it. That's the job. We believe them, or at least we engage in what Samuel Taylor Coleridge called the 'willing suspension of disbelief'. Tom Hanks is not Forrest Gump. Meryl Streep is not Margaret Thatcher. Denzel Washington is not Malcolm X or Macbeth. All three credibly and brilliantly impersonated those characters in their film performances. Coleridge noted that trusting a performance by suspending our disbelief requires 'a human interest and a semblance of truth'. Trust used to be talked about in terms of artistic 'sincerity'. Nowadays we tend to talk of skilful fakery in public performances requiring a 'semblance of truth' as 'authenticity', but sincerity and authenticity are very different things. Sincerity is a relationship with other people. Authenticity is a relationship with oneself or one's own public image. It is possible to be authentically duplicitous, authentically incompetent and authentically unethical and still succeed, as we will see. As the old George Burns joke goes, if you can fake authenticity, you've got it made.

Three years after the American *Reader's Digest* poll, a successfully 'authentic' reality TV performer secured sufficient levels of trust from tens of millions of Americans to become president of the United States. Reality TV, of course, is fake. It is not reality. It's television. And it is authentic only in the sense that everyone knows the situations are confected and unreal, although the details are often largely unscripted. Viewers 'suspend disbelief' because we are in on the joke. If you can fake your performance on *Love Island*, *The Apprentice*, *Survivor*, *Big Brother*, and in Boris Johnson's case on the comedy show *Have I Got News For You*, then George Burns was correct. You really have got it made. You enter into viewers' living rooms and they may come to feel that they 'know' you.

Despite (or, once again, because of) his chequered past, Donald Trump had a history of 'authentic' story-telling. There was a 'semblance of truth' in the claim that he was a self-made successful New York businessman. It was boosted significantly across the United States by his appearances on the TV show *The Apprentice* where, rather like George W. Bush's description of the presidency, Trump was 'The Decider'. In fact Trump inherited his wealth from his father, at least $413 million (in 2018 dollars) according to the *New York Times*. Trump's own businesses were often far from successful. Nevertheless, his story was 'authentic' enough for 'reality' TV and for tens of millions of viewers. Having personally observed Trump on a box in their living rooms, viewers-as-voters gave Trump his entry level job in politics, trusting him enough to make him the most powerful elected person in the world. Trump's unique political success was often reported in Enlightened Establishment newspapers such as the *New York Times* as coming about despite never having held or even run for any political office at any time, anywhere. But it was precisely because he was untainted by any contact with politics-as-usual or any experience in any public office that he succeeded.

Like Boris Johnson, Trump's vices were both plentiful and obvious to anyone who paid attention. And again like Johnson, these vices were broadly accepted because 'in an age of images and entertainment, in an age of instant emotional gratification' such vices were themselves part of the entertainment. What follows is not, then, a recitation of familiar moral failings. It is instead a recognition of the skill with which both Johnson and Trump turned their very public failings into trust-building advantages. They successfully cut through the information blizzard. They play a starring role in our Information Age Reformation, whether we like it or not.

Trust Me, I'm Faking It

'The Donald', as one commentator called him, was undoubtedly one of a kind. We learned about his glamorous wives, his endless boasting about how successful he was, and his reputation for supposedly straight talking. We also learned about crude bullying, bad manners and recorded comments about 'pussy grabbing'. When these emerged during Trump's 2016 election campaign it was obvious that any previous presidential contender would have been immediately destroyed, yet Trump was the Teflon candidate. Nothing stuck. The rules had changed. On BBC News I interviewed a prominent Republican campaigner, a self-described conservative woman in her sixties. I asked whether she was shocked by Trump's lewd comments. She responded that 'pussy grabbing' was just typical of men's 'locker room talk' and so no big deal. For her, and for millions of Trump voters, it was genuinely, authentically, Trump. (For me, as someone who has spent a lifetime in locker rooms, from rugby, squash and golf clubs to swimming pools, tennis clubs and gyms, I have never encountered such comments from other men. I must lead a sheltered existence.)

While Hillary Clinton produced endless detailed policy papers to show she was ready for the highest political office, Trump said that 'everything is negotiable'. The *Atlantic* in May 2016 described him as a political chameleon, meaning it as a criticism. For potential Trump voters, it was an asset. Trump's only ideology was self-love and his narcissistic skill was recognised by David Axelrod, President Obama's former top strategist, who tweeted during the 2016 election campaign: 'This is what makes @realdonaldtrump an elusive target. He believes in himself. Everything else is fungible.'

Trump's slipperiness was a characteristic shared by his British political soulmate, Boris Johnson. Trump called Johnson 'Britain Trump' (sic), his trans-Atlantic Mini-Me. Johnson, like Trump, eventually gained the trust of the political right, far right and politically homeless because Johnson's 'authentic' performances as a 'rule breaker' meant he too was able to move beyond 'politics as usual' without the encumbrance of an ideology or even a coherent policy programme. Johnson was authentically just 'Boris'. In April 2012 on the website Conservative Home, writer Tim Montgomerie nicknamed him the 'Heineken Tory' after a famous beer advert. Johnson was 'the Tory that reaches parts of the electorate that other Conservatives struggle to reach'. Ideologically, if anything so grand could be attached to Johnson's thinking, he appeared to be a liberal or centrist when he was Mayor of London. He was proud to announce eye-catching plans that involved (as he would put it) 'spaffing' billions of public money on various grand projects, none of which ever came into existence. He was happy to play the right-wing English nationalist when it became necessary to suck up the Brexit votes that in the 2015 General Election had gone to Nigel Farage's UKIP party. Johnson successfully replaced ideology with charismatic 'human interest' narcissism. And like Trump, he proved that those who do not believe in something may come to believe in almost anything. Johnson quipped that he had only one serious conviction – for speeding. He was even in two minds about the biggest decision taken by British voters in decades, leaving the European Union, writing two newspaper columns, one in favour of Leave, the other in favour of Remain. Everything was negotiable except his own best interests. Johnson therefore published the pro-Brexit article, calculating that the Leave campaign would lose but that he personally would gain support from Conservative right-wingers, those who called themselves the European Research Group and who functioned like a party within the Conservative Party. Johnson was proved wrong in his belief that Leave would lose the Brexit vote, but right on the latter part of that calculation. Right-wing English nationalist support enabled him to become prime minister.

His one-time key aide in the Leave campaign Dominic Cummings described Johnson's 'everything is negotiable' activities as being the zigzag manoeuvring of a broken shopping trolley. But Johnson's real genius, like that of Trump, was his entertainment value. It enabled him to break through the norms of 'politics as usual', to build and maintain trust with millions of people. The Enlightened Establishment responded with books, opinion columns and vicious TV commentaries that Johnson was demonstrably, publicly and irrevocably untrustworthy and a liar, but he too was coated in Teflon. His ludicrous promises and stunts were astonishingly successful nonsense, designed to dominate the next day's newspaper headlines. He was filmed in a suit on a high-wire waving Union Jack flags. He promised to lie down in front of diggers extending Heathrow airport. As the Enlightened Establishment pointed out, he did lie – but not in front of any diggers. He was frequently filmed cosplaying a role in various uniforms, police officer's jackets, hi vis costumes, or jogging in mismatched and ancient-looking sports gear. He and his wife had a dog, Dilyn, which Johnson occasionally walked awkwardly on a lead as if he had never walked a dog before. Perhaps he hadn't. For dog lovers (like me) this was where the cosplay clearly failed, especially when a friend in southwest London reported that Dilyn the dog was often resident with Boris Johnson's mother-in-law, rather than in Downing Street. I hope for Dilyn's sake that is true. Either way, 'in an age of instant emotional gratification', when 'we neither seek nor want honesty or reality' Johnson's entertainment value, his political performance art, kept him constantly in the headlines with or without the dog.

The point of rehearsing these familiar stories is not moral censure. It is to marvel that simultaneously on both sides of the Atlantic in the twenty-first century two notorious ethically challenged liars rose to power because they managed to display, boast about and profit from a pattern of behaviour which would have destroyed politicians in earlier decades. Trump and Johnson have many flaws, but they were never boring. Their key skill was to break through our collective information overload to build a degree of trust with, and retain the support of, tens of millions of viewers-and-voters in a century full of suspicion, doubt and dispiriting facts. Their political programmes were not based on research and thoroughly costed ideas. Instead they began – and often ended – with memorable soundbites and photo opportunities, the slogans that could fit on a baseball hat or on a Brexit bus.

And it worked, even if the policies that followed usually didn't.

The core policy promise of the Trump presidency was to secure US borders against migrants from Latin America: 'I will build a great, great wall on our southern border and I'll have Mexico pay for that wall.' Some bits of a wall were constructed but of course Mexico didn't pay and the border problems continued. Boris Johnson's great projects did not come to anything either. Brexit was always a process and not an event. 'Global Britain' was a delusion which exploded when the United States summarily withdrew from Afghanistan and British troops had no option but to leave. We were 'global' only with American permission. 'Levelling Up' was similarly a slogan without a policy. As the Institute for Fiscal Studies reported in November 2022:

> The UK is not alone amongst developed countries in having experienced an increase in income inequality over the last 60 years. But income inequality in the UK has grown more than in most OECD countries. Today the level of UK income inequality is high by international standards.[3]

The *Financial Times* noted that while the wealthiest people in the UK were doing extremely well, 'last year (2021) the lowest-earning bracket of British households had a standard of living that was 20 per cent weaker than their counterparts in Slovenia'.[4]

The important point is not serial policy failures but the fact that to supporters none of this seemed to matter. The negativity of the Enlightened Establishment came from those who simply could not comprehend that the real skills of the two leaders was that they knew how to 'speak human', to connect and entertain us with 'human interest and a semblance of truth'. As Ivor Gaber noted, the outrage of establishment politicians and journalists often merely acted as the unwitting megaphone aiding the very politicians and political views they despised. One example is the inability of some mainstream commentators to understand Donald Trump's great skill as an orator – and in this I am not being sarcastic.

Jerkish Trumps English

At rallies and news conferences supporters were often entertained by repetitive slogans mixed with Trump's own vindictive and rambling brand of personal abuse against opponents. They were also treated to a very simple speaking style. The American writer Philip Roth was revolted by this. He described America's 45th president as 'ignorant of government, of history, of science, of philosophy, of art, incapable of expressing or recognising subtlety or nuance, destitute of all decency, and wielding a vocabulary of 77 words that is better called Jerkish than English'.[5] American analysts from Factbase also studied Trump's speaking style and concluded that his vocabulary and grammatical structure were those of the average third- to seventh-grader, a child aged eight to thirteen. They claimed he had the lowest level of linguistic skill of any president since Herbert Hoover.[6]

Both Roth and Factbase may be correct, but they were profoundly wrong on the consequences.

For his potential audience in the twenty-first century Donald Trump built trust one simplistic sentence at a time in an era when trust in democratic institutions and norms of behaviour worldwide was in short supply. When newspapers, notably the *Washington Post*, called out Trump's lies, it did not matter. The *Post* has 2.5 million subscribers, mostly inside the Washington beltway – the heartland of the Enlightened Establishment. Around the greater Washington area, Trump voters are thin on the ground. In 2020 the United States had some 170 million registered voters many of whom saw journalistic fact-checking in the 'mainstream media' as domination by 'the "Inside the Beltway" crowd' designed to undermine 'an outsider' like Trump who bravely refused to follow the traditional and unwritten rules of 'politics as usual'. Put simply, Donald Trump communicated with millions of Americans in language they could understand. He exploited the division between the *bien pensant* few who read the *New Yorker* and the *Washington Post* and the tens of millions who didn't and never would. This played perfectly into a long-established American tradition, summed up by the 1972 presidential candidate George Wallace, who once blamed America's woes on 'pointy headed intellectuals' who couldn't even ride a bicycle straight. Or maybe it's a reminder of the bitter American proverb sometimes assumed to have been coined by the humorist H. L. Mencken, 'Nobody ever went broke underestimating the intelligence of the American public.' Even when Trump was caught out lying, it didn't matter. He deftly used Enlightened Establishment outrage to his own advantage. A Trump tweet from 2017 was repeated with variations throughout his presidency every time he was caught telling a particularly egregious untruth. The tweet said his critics were spreading 'FAKE NEWS' about the presumed lies and that the US media were 'the enemy of the American people', more or less the same phrase that was used by the *Daily Mail* in Britain about inconvenient judges. It was also a Stalinist trope, as well as the phrase that appeared in Nazi newspapers in the 1930s. The language of totalitarianism had become part of the routine political vocabulary in these two great bastions of democracy, the UK and the US. The anger these Trump tweets caused meant they were re-tweeted millions of times, enlightened outrage magnifying the effect. On both sides of the Atlantic intellectuals like Roth and mainstream journalists underestimated how far great communicators like Trump and Johnson could build trust in themselves with an 'authentically' mould-breaking style that diminished trust in almost everything else. They connected with millions by offending the sensibilities of Enlightened Establishment figures who were never going to vote for them anyway. To Trump and Johnson supporters, mainstream media criticisms simply proved that the mainstream media was out of touch. The Enlightened Establishment was denigrating leaders whose entertaining speaking style resonated warmly with the concerns of ordinary folk. By the 2020s, loss of trust in the veracity of information and supposed facts had become the most significant part of our worldwide democratic recession. This was to prove particularly damaging in the United Kingdom. Our democracy was itself losing the people's trust.

Britain's Trust Deficit

As the name suggests, the American thinktank Freedom International specialises in monitoring democratic freedoms everywhere. It reported in 2022 that from 2006 onwards:

> The long democratic recession is deepening... democracies are being harmed from within by illiberal forces, including unscrupulous politicians willing to corrupt and shatter the very institutions that brought them to power. This was arguably most visible last year in the United States, where rioters stormed the Capitol on January 6 (2021) as part of an organised attempt to overturn the results of the presidential election. But freely elected leaders from Brazil to India have also taken or threatened a variety of anti-democratic actions, and the resulting breakdown in shared values among democracies has led to a weakening of these values on the international stage.[7]

The US National Intelligence Council was equally bleak in its prognosis. The Washington DC based NIC is extremely well informed. It describes itself as serving as 'a bridge between the [US] intelligence and policy communities, a source of deep substantive expertise on intelligence issues, and a facilitator of Intelligence Community collaboration and outreach'.[8] The NIC predicted that the worldwide democratic recession would deepen in the 2020s, and that the post-Trump United States and the post-Johnson United Kingdom, supposedly secure, or perhaps complacent, in our own democratic traditions, would be part of that inexorable decline:

> The challenges governments face suggest there is a high risk that an ongoing trend in erosion of democratic governance will continue during at least the next decade and perhaps longer. This trend has been widespread – seen in established, wealthy, liberal democracies as well as less mature partial democracies. Key democratic traits, including freedom of expression and the press, judicial independence, and protections for minorities, are deteriorating globally with countries sliding in the direction of greater authoritarianism.[9]

Within this worldwide picture of democratic recession and loss of trust in institutions of democracy, Britain lived up to the idea of 'British exceptionalism' only in the sense of being exceptionally complacent and exceptionally damaged. The Edelman Trust Barometer annually surveys public opinion in twenty-eight rich countries. In 2020 it placed the UK twenty-seventh out of twenty-eight OECD nations for trust in the four key types of democratic institutions – government, business, the media and NGOs, including charities and other non-governmental organisations. Only Russians showed less trust in their institutions. You may see this reflected in the difficulty some British commentators had in deciding whether Johnson or Putin was lying about the supposed Putin threat to take out Johnson with a missile.

In 2021 Edelman summed up the negative, highly sceptical and distrustful British national mood. British people are not stupid. We know we are being lied to:

> Alarmingly, some 53 per cent of those in the UK believe that government leaders are purposely trying to mislead them, whilst 52 per cent subscribe to the idea that business leaders are purposely trying to mislead by saying things they know are false or gross exaggerations.[10]

The rapid acceptance of the normalisation of lying in British public life and the related collapse in trust is astonishing. The phrase 'purposely trying to mislead' is important here. A majority of the British population assumes that the British government deliberately lies to us, implying that British people intuitively understand the concept of Strategic Lying even if the term itself is not in common use. There is no shortage of examples. Coronavirus, a national and international struggle against a common enemy, a pandemic, failed to unite the United Kingdom in trusting the official (Westminster) response. On the contrary. Edelman's 2021 British survey found that: 'trust in government "to do the right thing" collapsed 16 points from 60 per cent at the height of the first (coronavirus) lockdown (in April 2020) to 44 per cent at the height of the third lockdown this February (2021)'. The coronavirus epidemic coincided with scandals about favoured government cronies receiving lucrative PPE contracts worth millions of pounds; large numbers of potentially avoidable covid related deaths, especially in care homes; and revelations about parties taking place in Downing Street while the country was supposedly in lockdown. The Edelman survey was just one of many such surveys. A Commons Library Research Paper entitled 'Political Disengagement in the UK' noted that 'the proportion of people who trusted the government to put the needs of the nation first decreased from 38 per cent in 1986 to 17 per cent in 2013. Trust in politicians has been fluctuating around 9 per cent.'[11]

This pattern of distrust was made even worse by the failures of what Americans, and increasingly the British, call Boosterism.

The American definition of Boosterism is the 'keen promotion of a person, organisation, or cause'. The *Oxford English Dictionary* characterises Boosterism more negatively as 'the expression of chauvinism'. Either way, Boosterism was one of Boris Johnson's key rhetorical skills for cutting through when 'reality is complicated' and 'we are incapable or unwilling to handle its confusion'. The most authentic characteristic of Boris Johnson is that he is honest in his duplicity. As we saw in the previous chapter, he wrote an entire newspaper column praising the Politics of Distraction, of throwing a dead cat on the table.

He has used that tactic endlessly. He even used the word 'Boosterism' publicly when questioned about what his economic strategy as prime minister would entail. 'Boosterism!' Johnson responded, then added that he wanted to put 'rocket boosters' on the British economy, as a way of 'turbocharging' it.

Shouting loudly about how great things are going to be is a rhetorical strategy. It is not a policy, nor does it offer clues as to how precisely to attach which rocket boosters to which parts of the economy. The turbocharging remained imaginary. Nevertheless, in July 2019 in his first speech to parliament as prime minister Johnson came out with more verbal rocket boosters, attached to everything: 'Our mission is to deliver Brexit on the 31st of October for the purpose of uniting and re-energising our great United Kingdom and making this country the greatest place on earth.' He then promised that the UK would overtake Germany as the biggest economy in Europe by 2050. British children and grandchildren 'will be living longer, happier, healthier, wealthier lives' while the country would in some unexplained way be 'Levelled Up', so that poorer areas, especially in the North of England would catch up with richer regions.

What happened next is well known. The longer, happier, healthier, wealthier lives proved elusive. Health care outcomes went into reverse. Excess deaths caused mortality rates to rise way above what might have been expected. The 'greatest place on earth' endured a cost of living crisis. Workers engaged in a series of strikes stretching from health care to education to trains and transport services, airport baggage handlers and Border Force, along with the worst health care performance and outcomes in NHS history. 'Boosterism' is not boring. It can be entertaining. But it is always a clash between promises and reality that is guaranteed to disappoint in the end. When that occurs, the inevitable consequence is a collapse of trust in both the once-entertaining 'rule breaker' and in the system that allows the Booster-in-Chief to get to the top. Of course, external factors including the war in Ukraine, escalating energy prices, and the lingering effects of coronavirus are beyond any one government's control. British people since the 2016 vote have been encouraged to hold two vastly contradictory ideas simultaneously. First, we live in the 'greatest place on earth', and will enjoy 'sunlit uplands' if we can only free ourselves of the shackles of the European Union and, in Johnson's famous phrase, 'have our cake and eat it'. But there is no cake. All available metrics show that the British economy has been performing worse than comparable major European countries. Brexit, along with other Boosterish ideas, promised unlimited cake and delivered at best a few crumbs.

Even when the facts began to poke through, by the time of his 2022 resignation speech and with the Brexit agreement being relitigated in respect of Northern Ireland, Boris Johnson was still claiming his unachieved promises were his proudest achievement – 'Getting Brexit done, settling our relations with the continent after half a century and reclaiming the power for this country to make its own laws in parliament.' By early 2023 and the third anniversary of Brexit, Johnson's successor Rishi Sunak was still trying to begin constructive discussions with our nearest trading partners to limit the damage, especially to the economy and to Britain's reputation for honest dealing. The political analyst Peter Kellner pointed out that Johnson's repeated assertion that he had 'got Brexit done' was undermined because 'most voters reject his claim'. Kellner quoted a Deltapoll that only one in three British voters thought Johnson had kept his promise. Almost two-thirds – 60 per cent – believed the opposite, agreeing that 'Boris Johnson has not really fulfilled his promise as Brexit is not going well and many problems in our relationship with the EU have yet to be solved.'[12]

Dissatisfaction extended to both Leave voters (46 per cent) and to those who voted Conservative in 2019 (41 per cent.) By 2023 a significant majority of voters told successive polls that they thought Brexit was a mistake. And as for Johnson's (entertaining) claim that Brexit was 're-energising' the UK, the chairman of the independent OBR, Richard Hughes reported that Brexit had reduced the UK's GDP by about 4 per cent in the long term, and that it would be a much worse blow for Britain than even the coronavirus pandemic. Covid shrank the economy 'by a further 2 per cent'.[13]

In terms of the destruction of public trust in governance in the UK, the strongly anti-Brexit newspaper the *New European* (November 2022) went on to list political leaders from Jeremy Corbyn and Theresa May to Boris Johnson, Rishi Sunak and others who all repeated the mantra 'I'll Make Brexit Work' and then failed to do so. The newspaper argued that there was no logical way Britain could be improved by worsening our relationship with our closest neighbours and that all Brexit had been good for was to act as the 'graveyard of political careers'. The hapless 'Brexit Opportunities Minister' Jacob Rees-Mogg, became so desperate for good news that he appealed to readers of the tabloid newspaper, *The Sun*, asking if they had discovered 'ANY petty old EU regulation that should be abolished.' He reminded *Sun* leaders of Lord Kitchener's Great War appeal 'Your Country Needs You', and followed up with a cry for help:

I implore you all to write to me with the regulations you want abolished – those which make life harder for small businesses, which shut out competition, or simply increase the cost of operating. Through thousands of small changes, we can enact real economic change – which means *The Sun*'s readers will feel a real Brexit bonus in their pockets and in their lives every day.[14]

A few months later the cost of living crisis pushed inflation into double figures and the Brexit bonus 'in their pockets' never appeared. A similar fate awaited that other Johnson break-through slogan and another unfortunate ministerial rebranding. In September 2021 the Department for Housing, Communities and Local Government was rebranded the Department for Levelling Up. By 2022 focus groups found that the phrase 'Levelling Up' was increasingly distrusted by voters. The Conservative MP Jake Berry admitted 'No one really knows what "Levelling up" means but when we see it, we'll all know.' One might say the same about the Second Coming of Christ.

Certainly the idea of attaching boosters to everything had – in that old advertising phrase – become more like trying to put lipstick on a pig. By January 2023 Conservative MPs were advised to avoid the Levelling Up term because it had gone from being meaningless to toxic and distrusted. The idea that Boris Johnson had 'got Brexit done' followed a similar pattern. Clever salesmanship that fails to deliver the goods is a marketing disaster. There were numerous and predictable suggestions that the Johnson premiership was a re-channelling of George Orwell's *1984*, especially this short passage:

The Ministry of Peace concerns itself with war, the Ministry of Truth with lies, the Ministry of Love with torture and the Ministry of Plenty with starvation. These contradictions are not accidental, nor do they result from ordinary hypocrisy: they are deliberate exercises in doublethink.

As the Ministry of Brexit Opportunities faded slowly into history, so did trust in the workings of British democracy.

Who Do British People Trust?

At the time of Boris Johnson's rise to political prominence and power, the top five most trusted people in the UK were, in order: the maker of natural history documentaries, David Attenborough;

Tom Hanks (again); Michelle Obama (but not her husband Barack); Prince William and the Queen.[15] The two least trustworthy people in Britain at that time were Boris Johnson himself and the journalist and broadcaster Piers Morgan. Around the same time a Hansard Society report pointed out just how desperate so many British people had become with what they saw then as the failures of British democracy. This report gives a clue why Johnson became prime minister. He fitted this rather desperate job description:

> Fifty-four per cent of the public say Britain needs a strong leader who is willing to break the rules; and four in ten people think that many of the country's problems could be dealt with more effectively if the government didn't have to worry so much about votes in Parliament. Although some of the core indicators of political engagement – certainty to vote, and knowledge of, and interest, in politics – remain stable, pessimism about the country's future combines worryingly with anti-system sentiment. Seventy-two per cent of the public say the system of governing needs 'quite a lot' or 'a great deal' of improvement. This measure has risen five points in a year and now stands at its highest level in the 15-year Audit series. Well over half the public are downbeat about the state of Britain. Fifty-six per cent think Britain is in decline, six in ten people think our system of governing is rigged to advantage the rich and powerful, and two-thirds of us think there are no clear solutions to the big issues facing the country today.[16]

That same year, just one year after being voted one of the least trustworthy people in the country, Conservative Party members elected Boris Johnson to succeed Theresa May as party leader and thus the United Kingdom's prime minister. He was, in the words of the Hansard Society survey, 'willing to break the rules' although whether he was a 'strong leader' remains debatable. What is certain is that by the time Johnson left office three years later, in 2022, a YouGov poll showed he was emphatically distrusted by 75 per cent of British voters. An investigation by the *Independent* and Full Fact calculated that as his term in office unravelled in 2022 Johnson and his ministers 'have made at least 27 false statements to parliament since the 2019 General Election – and have failed to correct them'.[17]

A misleading statement (without correction) to parliament by an MP and government minister in Britain traditionally leads to resignation. Lying in public office undermines trust in parliament. It therefore discredits democratic government. Boris Johnson's skill was to survive all this, Houdini-like, for several years by employing survival techniques that are 'authentically' part of his character. He was a joker, and entertainer. Novelists of an earlier age would have called him a bounder. He employed archaic language, the distractions of classical references to Ancient Greece and Rome, sloppy dress and scurrilous behaviour. The scruffy toff image cut through in part because it was remarkably different from the smart suits and suave manners of the traditional British political class. Johnson was an 'authentically' overweight man in tune with the 68 per cent of British men and 59 per cent of women who are overweight or obese.[18] He made the most of being strikingly different in his crushed ill-fitting suits, his carefully messed-up hair, woefully uncool sports kit and even a wooden tennis racquet. Numerous British TV makeup artists told me they 'fixed' Johnson's hair, shirt and tie, only to watch him deliberately distress his appearance before walking on set for an interview. Johnson, again like Trump, built trust not despite his career as a faker and liar. He built his career precisely because such fakery became an entertaining virtue for many people in a way that helped him stand out from the crowd. Some saw an English archetype of nastiness, a Flashman, the fictional Rugby School bully, the cad who posed as a hero. More endearingly, Johnson's speech mannerisms and scruffiness – for me at least – had echoes of the much-loved 1920s children's books by Richmal Crompton, the *Just William* stories. Just William (even the title reeks of 'authenticity' – he was authentically Just Boris as one biographer, Sonia Purnell, called him) – was famous for having 'scrapes' and 'adventures' yet would return home for tea in which there was cake and jelly with lashings of ginger beer.

It's worth noting that in the same year that his own Conservative Party MPs decided they had enough of Johnson's japes, *UK Press Gazette* reported that the other supposedly 'least trustworthy' person in Britain, Piers Morgan, signed a contract to write for *The Sun* newspaper and to present TV programmes for Rupert Murdoch's new channel. The salary was put at £50 million over three years.[19] How people regarded by the public as untrustworthy may survive and thrive in positions of power and influence where trust – one might think – is a requirement, clearly demands further study. But the facts speak for themselves. One of the two people voted the most untrustworthy in the UK in 2018 became the country's most powerful political figure; the other emerged as the UK's highest paid journalist. We cannot blame them for exploiting the system which allows this to happen. We can blame ourselves for permitting that system to continue.

Trust for the untrustworthy and success for those who are distrusted can in part be explained by the use of distraction techniques and deliberate mendacity. But that is not enough. Johnson and Trump, in their way, are communications geniuses. They have a remarkable ability to take advantage of the information reformation which began several decades ago.

How They Do It

In the 1960s, the era of John F. Kennedy and Richard Nixon, a US presidential candidate could expect a lengthy clip of a speech – up to a minute – to make it on to the evening news and the three big US networks of the time, ABC, NBC and CBS. These clips are called 'soundbites' by TV producers. By the twenty-first century our media and information landscape had changed beyond recognition. Viewers were faced with the choice of several hundred competing TV channels and streaming services, countless news sources and the rise of the information Wild West of social media, blogs, podcasts and the rest of the media blizzard. Traditional organisations coped by speeding things up. They shortened news reports, put clips on social media for instant access, focused on photo opportunities and cut back on the length of soundbites, even from important world leaders. Journalists were often slow to understand the significance of these changes. By the 1980s, one well-known US TV reporter, Lesley Stahl of CBS, delivered what she thought was a damning and lengthy (five-minute-long) report on CBS news about President Ronald Reagan during his 1984 re-election campaign. Stahl expected the White House to complain about the negative content.

'I worried that my sources at the White House would be angry and freeze me out,' she said. Instead they congratulated her.

'Way to go, kiddo,' a Reagan staffer told her. 'What a great piece. We loved it.'

'Didn't you hear what I said?' Stahl responded.

The senior staffer replied, 'Nobody heard what you said. You guys in Televisionland haven't figured it out, have you? When pictures are powerful and emotional, they override if not completely drown out the sound. I mean it, Lesley. Nobody heard you.'[20]

American academic researchers were among the first to note that the dominance of pictures over words and the decline in the attention span of viewers was changing the mainstream media long before any of us had heard of Twitter or TikTok:

In 1968, the average soundbite in presidential election news coverage was more than 43 seconds long. In 1972, it dropped to 25 seconds. In 1976, it was 18 seconds; in 1980, 12 seconds; in 1984, just 10 seconds. By the time the 1988 election season rolled around, the size of the average soundbite had been reduced to less than 9 seconds... By the end of the 1980s... the time and space allotted to political oratory in the American mainstream media had already been incrementally eroded.[21]

Richard Nordquist, professor emeritus of rhetoric and English at Georgia Southern University, recognised that media organisations were not leading but following what customers or viewers wanted: 'What defines a soundbite has changed through the years with the culture of communications. Consumers today want messages and information delivered to them more quickly than ever, and this is reflected in the media's use of sound grabs.'[22]

Nordquist traced the demand for shorter communications in the United Kingdom back to the pre-social-media days of the early 1990s. He noted that in the satirical British magazine *Punch*, the columnist Michael Bywater produced a parodic account of the growing demand for simplicity and brevity a decade before Twitter and Trump's clipped soundbite style. Bywater wrote:

> I am even told that you like your reading in short bursts now. Little chunks. Soundbites. Like that. Because you are busy. In a rush. Like to graze. Like cows. A bite here. A bite there. Too much to do. No time to spare. Under pressure. Bollocks. Lazy. Stupid. Finger out. Socks up. It was not always thus. Time was when an Englishman could happily gawp at a single sentence for an hour at a time. The ideal magazine essay took roughly as long to read as it took your umbrella to dry.[23]

Punch, with its 'ideal magazine essay' style was out of time. It folded in 1992.

Rather like Bywater's complaint or Lesley Stahl's attempted evisceration of Ronald Reagan's down-home simplicities, the communication styles of Trump and Johnson were derided by political opponents, commentators, academics and journalists. But Trump and Johnson were on the right side of communications history. Both had very different speaking styles from each other and were addressing very different audiences on opposite sides of the Atlantic. Yet both had the same basic characteristics, including a language that was often juvenile, simplistic, and riddled with falsehoods, but almost always entertaining, surprising and attention grabbing even when – or especially when – it was ridiculous. As British prime minister, occupying the office once held by great orators such as Disraeli, Gladstone and Churchill, when Boris Johnson quoted the children's cartoon character Peppa Pig to senior business executives and Kermit the Frog to the United Nations General Assembly neither audience was impressed but both speeches went viral to a much wider audience on social media and were widely reported in mainstream media. Time after time Trump and Johnson solved the two key problems facing a twenty-first-century politician. First, how do you grab attention in a noisy world? Solution: by being shocking, scurrilous, memorable and brief – and always entertaining. Second, how do you build trust with enough voters to win power in an era when trust is much diminished? Solution: by playing on the 'authenticity' of your public character, the character that the public 'knows' from television – and, once more, always being entertaining. In Trump's case, he was 'authentically' the decisive businessman; for Johnson the eccentric, comic Old Etonian who must be clever because he can quote Virgil and Catullus and still make you laugh.

This was not a matter of the political Left or Right. This was a matter only of the right communications strategy for the twenty-first century. Enlightened Establishment politicians like Hillary Clinton and many British political leaders remained marooned in the twentieth century, and nobody heard them because the audience was not really listening.

To take another British example, I worked for many years as a BBC journalist and presenter on live election coverage during General Elections. In his campaign in 2019 the Labour leader Jeremy Corbyn delivered speeches that he and his team knew the BBC and other broadcasters were going to transmit live. Instead of seizing the platform to build trust with a widening audience by following the new rules of effective communication in the manner of a Johnson or Trump – be brief, entertaining, audience-grabbing – Corbyn had the style of a politician of the 1950s, the era of mass meetings and black and white TV. Day after day Corbyn would visit a city, meet adoring crowds of Labour voters, trades unionists and party members – the already-faithful – and speak to them at great length. He would begin with long, sometimes ten-minute-long, votes of thanks to local individuals, praise for trades union organisers and namechecks for faithful supporters. You may applaud his good manners, but I confess I was so bored that I timed these perorations wondering if we would ever get to Corbyn cutting through to make a striking point. I suspect that beyond a few hundred attendees at Corbyn rallies, millions of potential voters and TV viewers simply turned off. I did, and my job was to pay attention. Supporters say Jeremy Corbyn was a decent chap much loved by those who knew him. They should remember that Boris Johnson was much loved by the millions who clearly did not know him. That's how political campaigning works, especially for the Heineken politician who could touch the parts others could not reach. Images and soundbites, whether authentic or authentically faked, will always triumph over the long, detailed speech that no one has time to listen to.

In the United States the contrast between Trump and Hillary Clinton was even more brutal. Trump mastered the two- or three-second soundbite – 'Lock Her Up'. Clinton was incapable of seizing the opportunities of the twenty-first-century media environment, or even that of the late twentieth century. In the 1990s Mrs Clinton produced a 1,300-page bill on health care reform. It may have been worthy but it was dead on arrival on Capitol Hill. Working as a White House correspondent as I then did, I never managed to find any politician in Washington DC who had read the Clinton health care bill. Why would they? After the bill was rejected by the US Congress, I challenged Senate Minority leader Bob Dole that he had campaigned against something he had never even read. Senator Dole laughed out loud. Of course he hadn't read the Clinton bill. 'I couldn't even lift it,' he told me.

The derision directed towards Donald Trump in 2016 by mainstream politicians and commentators was simply a replay of Lesley Stahl back in 1984, an Enlightened Establishment failing to understand what worked for various upstarts like Trump to build trust with modern audiences. As a member of that Enlightened Establishment, Hillary Clinton notoriously fell into an even worse trap. She referred to half of Trump's supporters as a 'basket of deplorables', probably the only three-word phrase of her entire campaign that anyone now recalls. Since 63 million Americans voted for Donald Trump, Mrs Clinton implied that more than 30 million Americans were 'racist, sexist, homophobic, xenophobic, Islamophobic' and ultimately deplorable. She regretted her remarks. Trump didn't need to regret anything. He could trumpet Clinton's contempt back to his supporters – 'this is what Crooked Hillary thinks of you' – and he went on to win the presidency. Such attacks confirmed to millions of Americans that 'the Donald' was indeed the change they needed to break away from politics as usual, the Washington they loathed, the Clintons and their pointy-headed intellectual friends. Trump built trust with Americans who 'knew' him as 'authentic' from personal experience – at least as 'personal' as you can get from watching the decisive, godlike figure who appeared deus ex machina in *The Apprentice* to tell contestants that they were Hired or Fired, 'The Decider'. As a former Labour Party leader, Neil Kinnock, once instructed me, unlike politicians and commentators in the Enlightened Establishment, most voters are too busy getting on with their lives and 'have better things to do with their time than to think constantly about politics'. Kinnock argued that a politician's job is to get through to voters where they are, not wait for voters to make the journey to where the politician is. Boris Johnson got it. Trump got it. Their opponents, notably Corbyn and Clinton, didn't. Truth and trust were damaged in the process. And that wasn't the only damage.

Distrust Abroad: Accounting the Cost

Accountants, to steal a phrase from China's great economic reformer Deng Xiaoping, do not care if the cat is black or white so long as it catches the mouse. Post-Brexit Britain in the 2020s failed to catch the mouse. The accountants of the International Accounting Bulletin

(IAB) added up the supposed Brexit Opportunities and found them to be just another delusion. The IAB is published in Britain but, as the name suggests, it is aimed at accountants worldwide. On the eve of the Brexit result the pound was trading at US$1.49. By September 2022 it was at US$1.15, declining to its lowest level against the US dollar for four decades. You might have thought that Britain would therefore prove to be a bargain for foreign investors in terms of foreign direct investment (FDI). Quite the reverse. Losing trust was – and remains – profoundly damaging. The loss of trust in Britain worldwide, the IAB reported, meant loss of investment and ultimately slower economic growth:

> Despite all his boosterism, UK investment performance has gone backwards under Johnson's leadership. While the UK managed a small increase in inward FDI in 2022 as global investment recovered from the injuries of covid, the country's FDI performance has lagged behind all other countries in the G7 since Johnson came to power in 2019. Johnson has damaged the reputation of UK plc and the effects of this will be felt long after he is gone.

The accountant's bulletin went on to explain why:

> Investors crave reliability and predictability. They hate partners they cannot trust. Johnson's leadership has not only eroded the trust in him but also trust in the UK. During each scandal that has unfolded around him, Johnson and his backers have relied on distortions, distractions and downright lies to cover up his misdeeds. Central to his legacy will be a reputation for dishonesty.

The Enlightened Establishment were piling on the facts and facts had begun to matter, as they always do eventually. The IAB report then focused on the other trust-busting part of the British malaise – lies, broken promises and ultimately failure:

Johnson's leadership was mocked abroad and ineffective at home. Johnson loved to make promises to the UK electorate but was incapable of keeping them. His central domestic project was to level up the UK, reducing economic inequality between London and the rest of the country. Yet research suggests that by the government's own metrics, most parts of the UK have fallen further behind London since this policy was launched... Two years on from Brexit, UK growth is lagging behind EU member states, exports have fallen by 46 per cent, and foreign direct investment flows remain far lower than they were in 2016. Where does all this leave the UK? Seemingly on the verge of a recession, with trust in politics in the gutter, and political institutions that have been pushed to the point of destruction.[24]

The wisdom or otherwise of Brexit is not the key point here. It is the significance and yet fragility of trust in public life when 'trust in politics is in the gutter'. Trust depends upon the ability of governments to try to keep promises. Respect for honesty lies at the heart of the public's trust in democracy. This accountant's profit and loss report comes down to two very simple observations.

- When you destroy truth, you lose trust.
- When you lose trust, ultimately you lose democracy.

Edelman's Trust Barometer found that by 2021 trust in the British government to 'do the right thing' collapsed by sixteen points and that the UK was 'fracturing':

The study suggests the integrity of the United Kingdom may now be under threat, with... widespread concern about the future of the union between England, Wales, Scotland, and Northern Ireland. Three in four people (75 per cent) say that the nations that make up the UK are becoming more divided, while 44 per cent of Brits believe that the Brexit deal was a bad deal for the UK, compared to 31 per cent of people who say it was a good deal and 25 per cent who are undecided.

Trust in the Westminster system also fell significantly, especially outside England:

Trust in the Prime Minister sits at relatively low levels within the devolved nations – 32 per cent in Wales, 34 per cent in Scotland, and 32 per cent in Northern Ireland. In England the figure is higher at 41 per cent. The leaders of the devolved governments in Scotland and Wales both enjoy considerably higher levels of trust among their populations than Boris Johnson.[25]

And it wasn't just Johnson. He features prominently here because his numerous political car crashes and key role in the Brexit failure ensured worldwide scrutiny. More important is the systemic problem which helped Johnson to rise to prominence and kept him there for several years. That systemic problem continued after he had been forced out of office.

A few years ago I was due to travel to report on the unrest in a country notorious for lawlessness and was asked to take a defensive driving course to avoid 'K&R' – kidnap and ransom. It all seemed a bit melodramatic but the most interesting part of the course was a question from my instructor.

'When your car has an accident with another car, how many accidents take place?' he said.

'Er... one?' I suggested.

'The answer is three,' the instructor said.

First, your car hits the other car. Second, your body hits the steering wheel, if there's no airbag. Third the internal organs in your body hit your ribs, and the internal damage is usually the bit that will kill you. In car crashes the deaths often come from severe internal bleeding, he said, and in war zones a lot of people are killed by careless traffic accidents as well as gunfire. The instructor's lesson was that everyone should wear a seatbelt. But the lesson that struck me was the one about internal damage.

In January 2023 Boris Johnson's successor (but one) as British prime minister Rishi Sunak was filmed for a social media video, explaining government policy while sitting in the back seat of a car and not wearing a seatbelt. Sunak received a penalty from police, and a fine reported to be a modest £100. That was the least of his troubles. It was the internal damage from a rapid series of political car crashes that caused the real problem. A few days after the seatbelt incident the first collision came when the chairman of the Conservative Party Nadhim Zahawi – a former Chancellor of the Exchequer and friend of Sunak – was forced to admit that he paid several million pounds in back taxes, plus a penalty. The figure of the repayment was put at £5 million. It was revealed that Zahawi had discussions with the tax collectors of His Majesty's Revenue and Customs (HMRC) about his back taxes when he was technically their boss as Chancellor of the Exchequer in charge of the Treasury. British newspapers recited with glee that Zahawi had also in the past attempted to claim parliamentary expenses to heat the stables in which he kept his horses.

The next crash came on 22 January, when the *Sunday Times* revealed that a successful businessman, Richard Sharp, helped facilitate meetings which led to a loan of £800,000 for Boris Johnson. This happened weeks before Johnson, as prime minister, recommended Sharp for the role of chairman of the BBC. Mr Sharp was a hugely successful businessman at Goldman Sachs. There he was the boss of a bright young lad called Rishi Sunak. Sharp also donated £400,000 to the Conservative Party. Everyone was at great pains to point out that there was no wrongdoing in any of this which, obviously, is a relief. Sunak and his wife Akshata Murthy, incidentally, entered the *Sunday Times* Rich List in May 2022 at number 222 with a reported net worth of $837 million, making Sunak the richest prime minister in British history.

We then learned that the cash-strapped Boris Johnson in January 2023 declared earnings of almost a million pounds in one month including more than £500,000 as an advance for an upcoming book, around £200,000 for a speech to an Indian conglomerate and nearly £250,000 for a speech in Singapore, along with his (part-time) job, as an MP on a salary of £84,000 plus expenses. In yet another remarkable coincidence, at this point we also learned that the inquiry into the Boris Johnson loan was to be led by William Shawcross, the Commissioner for Public Appointments, a person I have met a few times and whom I believe has impeccable qualifications for the job. But his daughter Eleanor was simultaneously head of the policy unit for Rishi Sunak in Downing Street. Mr Shawcross wisely (and with a view to making sure the process would be above suspicion) decided to step back and let someone else supervise the inquiry.

Now – all these people – Zahawi, Sunak, Sharp, Johnson, Mr Shawcross and Ms Shawcross – are undoubtedly among the brightest people in Britain. All of them repeatedly insisted that there was never any wrongdoing, although Zahawi was fired by Sunak from his post as chair of the Conservative Party. But it doesn't take Sherlock Holmes to work out that even if everyone at all times acted impeccably, as they insist, then the United Kingdom in the 2020s appears to be led by a small group of people who know each other, work with each other, work for each other and are supposed to act as checks and balances on the conduct of each other. The problem in Britain is not that any of this is considered a major scandal. The problem in Britain – once more – is that all this is too easily considered normal. And as the defensive driving instructor pointed out, the internal damage is always the worst.

Trust in the institutions of government, media and big business, politicians, the BBC and high finance, has been seriously diminished over the years. This story brought them all together. And there is one minor point which is worth noting. Do these people even trust each other? Mr and Ms Shawcross acted impeccably, but someone leaked the stories about all the others to newspapers. These stories were aimed at damaging Johnson, Zahawi, Sharp and Sunak, as were other unconnected stories around the same time aimed at destroying the career of the Home Secretary Suella Braverman.

One theory came from Peter Jukes, CEO of the independent newspaper *Byline Times*, who on 21 January 2023 noted that, 'All these stories are coming out now because Johnson supporters are briefing against Zahawi and Braverman, so Sunak supporters are dumping their info on Johnson.'

If that theory is correct then various factions at the top of British politics appear to be unable to trust each other, causing internal damage from a continuing series of political car crashes. The real casualty is trust in democracy itself. Even if no one did anything wrong, in a time when truth is much diminished and trust in British public life seriously damaged, you can see why voters in Britain sense there is something deeply rotten in politics as usual and why they yearned for a 'rule breaker' to shake things up. The superficial problem is that the 'rules' – as we will see – are very easy to break. But the systemic problem is that when it comes to the British constitution no one really knows what the rules actually are.

7
Tropes and How Others See Us

Poor old John Bull. Remember him? Whatever happened to that decent, jolly, traditionally implacable chap, the one you could trust with your wallet, the type of Englishman who – as Elizabeth suggested at our meeting at Dartington Hall – preferred to solve problems rather than create them? How's John Bull doing these days? W. H. Auden wrote him off years ago. He was a casualty of the First World War.

Auden's Letter to Byron (1937) suggested John Bull had died in the fields of Ypres and Passchendaele in World War One, but reports of his demise turned out to be premature.

In the British imagination he may be immortal, if not always likeable, especially when seen from outside the United Kingdom. John Bull certainly doesn't travel well, yet at home in England his stoical solidity is still in demand in times of trouble. The character made a recent public appearance on the cover of the news and current affairs magazine *The Week* on 3 September 2022 as part of their assessment of the British malaise in the 2020s. The cover artist's rendition was the 'traditional' John Bull. He had a Union Jack waistcoat tight across his generous belly; a top hat of a middle-class rather than upper-class variety; stout leather boots, ruddy of face, implacable of visage, but in preparation for hard times and the modern cost of living crisis, John Bull was clutching a hot water bottle. The great cartoon symbol of Britishness (or rather, Englishness) was freezing in a room with icicles dangling from the central heating radiator, an unpaid fuel bill on the table, and nothing in his pocket. The headline read: 'Hard Times Ahead – Britain braces for a bleak winter'. *The Week*'s editors, struggling for a visually striking image of hardship in Britain in the twenty-first century, reverted to a resonant national image more than 200 years old, a character invented by a satirical Scot, yet more notable within the English than the wider British imagination. It's an odd tradition. It's an even odder trope, symbol or metaphor for Britishness and the United Kingdom in the twenty-first century unless you agree that the country can be imagined as a swaggering, corpulent Englishman dressed in eighteenth-century fashions and brought low by inexorable decline.

In 2021 Tate Britain announced a new exhibition to try to put Britishness in a different frame. 'Hogarth and Europe' was designed in post-Brexit Britain to place William Hogarth, one of England's greatest artists, a painter, engraver, satirist and 'grandfather of the political cartoon', in the wider European rather than merely English tradition. Beyond the subtle political point – that leaving the European Union did not make British culture any less 'European' – the Tate Britain exhibition was seen as an attempt to rescue the artist from one of his greatest successes. In 1748 Hogarth was arrested as a spy by the French authorities for sketching, patriotically but unwisely, the English crest on the old gate of Calais. On his return to England he produced his revenge, *The Gate of Calais*, sometimes called *O the Roast Beef of Old England*. It shows a bunch of scrawny French people (and one very fat friar – anti-Catholicism was as strong as anti-French feeling) marvelling at a man struggling under a massive side of beef destined for Calais' English inn. It is unquestionably a symbol of England's confident growth in wealth and power as opposed to the miserable half-starved frog-eating French. The Tate Britain exhibition was designed at a time when rising English nationalism in the twenty-first century had become a John Bull-ish phenomenon noted in European capitals, especially Dublin, Berlin and Paris, but also in Edinburgh, Belfast and Cardiff. The idea, as *The Art Newspaper* put it, was to challenge 'the dominance of the "John Bull" nationalist cliché under which the artist's reputation has long laboured', because 'Hogarth is the victim of his own success, or at least the success of his most overtly xenophobic compositions, such as the Francophobic and anti-Catholic *The Gate of Calais* (1748)' which 'quickly defined, or consigned [Hogarth] to, the status of high priest of British (or English) gloating exceptionalism'.[1]

The Tate reimagining of Hogarth's genius was a worthy attempt to rescue a politically astute and brilliantly witty artist from a popular myth through which he became known around the world. But both the reimagining of Hogarth and the John Bull story – including *The Week*'s sketch of him freezing in an unheated modern room – are insights into the changing ways we see ourselves in the United Kingdom, and the very different ways others see us amid our current difficulties, 'gloating exceptionalism' included. As the Robert Burns poem has it:

> Oh wad some power the giftie gie us
> Tae see ourselves as ithers see us
> It wad frae mony a blunder free us,
> An' foolish notion.

'Ode to a Louse' (1786)

The poet is watching a louse on the neck of a beautiful young lady, while she herself is oblivious to the infestation. Perhaps if in Britain we could only see the John Bull in ourselves as others see us, or remove the louse from our otherwise elegant neck, this could also free us from blunders and foolish notions. It's certainly true that this difference in perspective has within it a long history of animosity and traditional suspicion. One of the reasons Sathnam Sanghera's *Empireland* or the writings of historian David Olusoga cause such a stir is that seeing the history of British colonialism from the viewpoint of the colonised is a lot different from the history written by the colonisers that many of us learned at school. Our current predicament, then, should remind us that we need to understand just how far Englishness or Britishness is not always seen positively abroad. Where Britishness is still seen positively, that often turns out to be more as a celebration of our past, our heritage and culture rather than an appreciation of the more troublesome here-and-now.

D'ye Ken John Bull?

John Bull began as satire. He first made his appearance in the golden age of bitter English political humour, the early eighteenth century, the time of Jonathan Swift and Alexander Pope, but it was a Scotsman who gave birth to this enduring figure of Englishness.

John Arbuthnot produced in 1712 *The History of John Bull*, a stolid Englishman who took on 'Louis Baboon' (Louis Bourbon, the king of France). He also attacked the corruption at the top in Britain, the money-men with political connections who made a profit out of a crisis, in this case the War of the Spanish Succession. Insider knowledge and well-connected people obtaining access to British public money in times of trouble is a trope that did not, obviously, begin with the coronavirus procurement scandals of the 2020s. Nor is it likely to end there.

Arbuthnot saw John Bull positively as an example of how many English people may see themselves today. He was at heart 'an honest plain-dealing fellow' but also 'choleric, bold, and of a very inconstant temper'.[2] The myth of John Bull as a decent but occasionally irascible chap lives on in some of the attitudes the Tate Britain show tried to correct. Arbuthnot's creation was not fully popularised until a generation after Hogarth. By then the dominant satirist was James Gillray, another great British artist, often described as the 'father of the political cartoon' to Hogarth's 'grandfather'. By Gillray's time England was under threat of invasion during the Napoleonic Wars, and John Bull became an unforgettable English national symbol of freedom against tyranny, loyalty to king and country, and resistance to foreign aggression. John Bull was the ordinary man in the British street with extraordinary resilience and stubbornness, determined to fight Napoleon with his bare hands if that was what it took. There was English pride in this English trope, yet how John Bull was seen in other countries is instructive. It mirrors past and current British delusions about 'greatness' and the idea that British institutions, especially the Westminster system, are somehow admired, trusted, free of corruption and the 'envy of the world'.

As Others See Us

By the 1760s Gillray and Sir John Tenniel had turned John Bull into the positive archetype of a freeborn Englishman that we recognise today, bluff, rosy cheeked, middle class, no-nonsense but undoubtedly trustworthy, full of good beef and a decent glass of ale. The contrast with Hogarth's portrayal of the French as skinny, etiolated figures reduced to eating frogs' legs roasted over open fires on their cutlasses, could not have been more obvious. Outsiders, however, rarely considered John Bull, the nation he represented, or the citizens of that nation they encountered, as particularly trustworthy. The phrase 'Perfidious Albion' was much used in France in the late eighteenth and early nineteenth centuries to describe Britain's longstanding reputation for duplicity, bad faith, and dodgy diplomatic dealings. To foreigners this was an unwelcome British tradition repeated in various one-sided treaties and agreements enforced on conquered lands by imperial Britain and then – when regarded as inconvenient – reneged upon. It was a characteristic that others, most notably the Irish, French and US administrations, saw repeated in the twenty-first century in the duplicitous manner in which Boris Johnson attempted to repudiate almost immediately an agreement his administration negotiated, agreed, recommended to parliament and declared 'excellent' – the Brexit deal and Northern Ireland Protocol.

As far back as the seventeenth century the French Catholic bishop and theologian Jacques-Bénigne Bossuet, wrote a poem attacking England in terms which resonate today, 'L'Angleterre, ah, la perfide Angleterre, / que le rempart de ses mers rendoit inaccessible aux Romains... ('England, oh perfidious England, / Shielded against the Romans by her ocean ramparts...')[3]

And there is the Irish ballad, 'The Foggy Dew':

Oh the night fell black and the rifles' crack
Made Perfidious Albion reel.
'Neath the leaden rail', seven tongues of flame
Did shine o'er the lines of steel.

Perfidious Albion traditionally was a phrase 'used by Irish Catholics to describe England's decision to renege on commitments to Catholic rights in Ireland made in the Treaty of Limerick in 1691... the provisions were reversed by the Penal Laws introduced in 1695'.[4] The expression was picked up again by French writers in the 1790s, when Britain opted to join the old, autocratic monarchies of Europe in fighting the new revolutionary French government and its successor Napoleon. More recently it was used by Ian Smith, prime minister of the white supremacist settler minority government in Southern Rhodesia from 1964–79. In his book, *The Great Betrayal*, Smith 'bewails Britain's supposed treachery towards the whites of Southern Rhodesia. And it is said he viewed the British Conservative foreign secretary as the embodiment of Perfidious Albion'.[5]

The idea of Perfidious Albion repeatedly betraying Ireland and the hopes of Irish Catholics in particular is a subject which stretches from the seventeenth century through the Great Famine and the many failed attempts at Irish Home Rule in the nineteenth and early twentieth century. It is not just Catholics or Irish nationalists who speak of betrayal and double dealing at Westminster. Rudyard Kipling wrote of the British government's 'betrayal' of unionists (mostly Protestants) in Ireland in his poem 'Ulster 1912'. Today the Democratic Unionist Party is also deeply distrustful of what leading members see as a resurgent English rather than British nationalism at Westminster. The Irish writer Fintan O'Toole – hardly a fan of the DUP – seemed to agree with the Ulster Protestant view that John Bull is in trouble, and for the same reason, writing in the *New York Times* in June 2017:

> The problem with English nationalism is not that it exists but that it is incoherent, inarticulate and immature. This underground torrent has always been there, but it was buried for centuries beneath two powerful constructs: the British Empire and the United Kingdom. With the empire gone and the union under strain from rival nationalist movements in Scotland and Northern Ireland, English nationalism has flooded to the surface with great destructive force.

O'Toole believed that this new English nationalist spirit could not be trusted because it was ultimately negative and 'you can't govern a modern democracy by defining only what it isn't'.

The Chief Minister of Gibraltar Fabian Picardo subtly used allusions to Perfidious Albion to describe the then UK government's 'nuanced' diplomacy in respect of Gibraltar and the UN Decolonisation Committee. Gibraltarians fear that the modern UK does not stand four-square behind Gibraltar's 'Britishness' in the face of Spanish determination to reclaim a strategically important land mass attached to their country. And it's not just the French, the Irish, Ulster Protestants, white Rhodesians, Gibraltarians and quite a few modern European governments who see John Bull as something less than the bluff fellow you could trust with your wallet. The Brexit-supporting Conservative MP Mark Francois even boasted about it when he trumpeted enthusiastically the prospect of deliberate Brexit duplicity in a speech to the anti-EU Bruges Group:

> My message to the European Council... [is] if you now try to hold on to us against our will, you will be facing Perfidious Albion on speed. It would therefore be much better for all our sakes if we were to pursue our separate destinies, in a spirit of mutual respect.[6]

The somewhat well-upholstered Mr Francois was soon to find himself compared directly to the negative image of the similarly well-fed John Bull after he wrote a book about the 'successes' of the Brexit campaign. Francois' book was scathingly reviewed by the writer Will Self who, after a very public televised argument with Mr Francois, saw the Conservative MP as a stunted John Bull manqué:

> But the really meaty beef between me and this pocket John Bull came when I asserted that the problem for the Brexiteers was that while not everyone who voted for Brexit was a racist or an antisemite, the odds were that just about every racist and

antisemite in the country did. Francois exploded, demanding I apologise.[7]

Self declined to apologise.

The idea of English perfidy stretches across the Atlantic too. The American writer Washington Irving, writing some fifty years after Hogarth's death rehearsed the clichés which formed part of John Bull's attraction among what he called 'the common orders of English'.

> They seem wonderfully captivated with the beau ideal which they have formed of John Bull, and endeavour to act up to the broad caricature that is perpetually before their eyes. Unluckily, they sometimes make their boasted Bullism an apology for their prejudice or grossness... If one of these should be a little uncouth in speech and apt to utter impertinent truths, he confesses that he is a real John Bull and always speaks his mind. If he now and then flies into an unreasonable burst of passion about trifles, he observes that John Bull is a choleric old blade, but then his passion is over in a moment and he bears no malice. If he betrays a coarseness of taste and an insensibility to foreign refinements, he thanks Heaven for his ignorance – he is a plain John Bull and has no relish for frippery and knick-knacks... Thus, under the name of John Bull he will contrive to argue every fault into a merit, and will frankly convict himself of being the honestest fellow in existence.[8]

Washington Irving could not have predicted the row between Will Self and Mark Francois, but he undoubtedly nodded in that direction. And it came again in the Belgian Liberal politician Guy Verhofstadt's characterisation of the former UKIP politician Nigel Farage during the time both served in the European parliament as MEPs. Verhofstadt suggested that far from being a symbol of positive Britishness the biggest waste of money in the EU was 'Nigel Farage's salary'. Farage and his party turned their backs when the European anthem, Beethoven's 'Ode to Joy', was played in the European parliament. Even John Bull was unlikely to have been so uninformed as to have done that. He was of an era when it was well known that that 'Ode to Joy', though written by a German, was commissioned by Englishmen of the Philharmonic Society of London in 1817. Verhofstadt compared Farage not to John Bull but to an uncaring and incompetent armchair general – a caricature from the TV show *Blackadder* of the First World War's Field Marshal Douglas Haig 'sitting safely in his office, while his people are walking in the cold and the rain'.

The Washington Irving analysis of Englishness and John Bull turns up repeatedly in different formulations in twenty-first-century European commentaries on post-Brexit Britain's political posturing. A *Süddeutsche Zeitung* editorial on Boris Johnson concluded that 'he's always been a seducer and a loudmouth; always lied when it's in his interest. He is the great illusionist of British politics' adding that

> Johnson has himself led Britain into an existential crisis, for which he bears full responsibility. He has not given up his frivolous, unserious nature. His fickleness is revealed in his government's absence of strategy. Snobbery explains his lack of interest in the state of the country. Boris Johnson doesn't govern, he plays at being prime minister.[9]

In France *Le Monde* noted that Johnson was defined by three qualities 'opportunism, no attention to detail, an elastic relationship with the truth' echoing Irving's observation that an Englishman's ignorance and coarseness could enable them to turn every fault into a merit. To complete the picture, a century after Irving another Irishman, George Bernard Shaw, took a similar tack in his satirical play which directly references the classic English trope, *John Bull's Other Island*. It features an Englishman who has so little self-awareness he goes to Ireland and insists Irish Home Rule will be wonderful 'under English supervision'. John Bull, to draw a modern comparison, often appears to Britain's critics abroad like a nastier version of Homer

Simpson rather than a symbol of the English as God's chosen people. (The idea of Englishmen as God's Chosen People/the Lost Tribe of Israel is a very deep rabbit hole that we will resist descending into.) But for many of Britain's European friends and allies in the twenty-first century, and for some in the United States and elsewhere too, it is Washington Irving's portrayal or George Bernard Shaw's decent but unthinkingly arrogant Englishman or Guy Verhofstadt's cack-handed general sitting in comfort while sacrificing others that is discernible today in the semi-comedic bluster of Boris Johnson, Nigel Farage and Mark Francois. To Brexit supporters like Francois the United Kingdom appears to be justified in using any ethically dubious behaviour to make a great success of Brexit. He is proud and boastful about being proud and boastful, because he sees himself as a no-nonsense Englishman defying the machinations of those who inherited the wickedness of 'Louis Baboon' and Napoleon; people, presumably, such as Verhofstadt, Ursula von der Leyen and the European Commission. To many of our European friends and allies and to significant numbers in the British population who now think Brexit is a mistake, the John Bull/Francois/Farage/Johnson trope is merely a group of old-fashioned English eccentrics blundering their way into a mess of their own making while contriving 'to argue every fault into a merit, and... frankly convict (themselves) of being the honestest fellow(s) in existence'. Despite the humour, this has serious consequences. Behind the bullish posturing, Britain's image in the world, our soft power as well as our hard power, has been seriously damaged.

Perfidious Albion and Decline

The lyricist of 'The Foggy Dew' may be permitted a chuckle from the grave that some 300 years after the unilateral abrogation of the Treaty of Limerick's provisions, Perfidious Albion was at it again. A treaty involving Ireland was being undermined. Within weeks of Brexit finally taking place in January 2020 the British government threatened to break or ignore the Northern Ireland Protocol. The Protocol was a hard-fought part of the Brexit deal designed to limit damage to the Good Friday Agreement. That agreement had brought peace and stability to Northern Ireland from 1998 by allowing the free flow of goods and services between Northern Ireland and the Irish Republic. In the past British customs posts on the Irish border had often been blown up or booby trapped by the IRA. People died to maintain – or to destroy – the Irish border. The Protocol recognised that one part of the island of Ireland was in the EU while the other part was not, but 'frictionless' trade should continue between both parts to help keep the peace. When the border that had caused so much violence and heartache on the island of Ireland since the 1920s was 'moved' by Boris Johnson into the Irish Sea, this was not some devious trick by the Irish or European malefactors. This was something Johnson himself suggested and agreed with the Irish prime minister Leo Varadkar. The trouble with Johnson's plan was obvious to anyone who had paid attention to the Troubles in Northern Ireland that had taken more than 3,000 lives since the 1960s. Separating Northern Ireland from the rest of the United Kingdom was regarded as an existential threat by Northern Ireland's unionist, mostly Protestant, community. The anger among unionists about Boris Johnson's agreement remains profound, since it plays into another damaging trope – that of a 'Lundy'. Robert Lundy was a Scottish Protestant army officer during the siege of Derry in 1717 who sabotaged the defence of the city and is regarded as a traitor to the Protestant cause. In the twenty-first century Lundy is burned annually in effigy in the city, which is still divided by those who call it Derry (in Irish Doire) and unionists who call it Londonderry (the city of London, Derry).

At a December 2021 meeting with former loyalist paramilitaries on the Protestant Shankill Road area of Belfast I was told repeatedly of their sense of post-Brexit betrayal by Perfidious Albion and its Lundys in the Westminster government. Young men in loyalist communities burned buses and attacked the police in street disturbances. These former loyalist 'combatants', including those who had served jail time for murder, said that they feared much worse violence could follow. In that, they were not alone.

A spokesman at the White House said President Biden was 'concerned by the violence' in Belfast and elsewhere. The spokesman reminded the British government of the dangers inherent in trying to renege on the Northern Ireland Protocol to appease the unionist community in a way which posed a threat to 'the gains of the hard-won peace'. French president Emmanuel Macron suggested the UK government's flirtation with a return to Perfidious Albion would turn the months of Brexit diplomacy into a sick joke: 'If after six months you say we cannot respect what was negotiated, then that says nothing can be respected. I believe in the weight of a treaty. I believe in taking a serious approach. Nothing is negotiable. Everything is applicable.' Britain's Channel 4 News was told scathingly by an aide to the EU Commission president that the Brexit agreement 'was written in English so that the British should have understood it'.

The attitude of the UK's chief Brexit negotiator Lord Frost, deserves special mention here. Frost and Boris Johnson together recommended to the Westminster parliament the cumbersome arrangements enshrined in the Northern Ireland Protocol. Both, as we have noted, described their Brexit agreement as 'excellent'. Both then announced just a few weeks later that they would demand changes to the Protocol or unilaterally ignore it. Frost appeared puzzled by accusations that the United Kingdom, and perhaps he himself, had acted perfidiously. He complained that, 'We constantly face generalised accusations that we can't be trusted and that we aren't a reasonable international actor.' Lord Frost's puzzlement about why the British government could not be trusted is, one might say, puzzling. The accusations were not 'generalised'. They were very specific. European politicians and the White House were telling the British government in straightforward language that the United Kingdom government could not unilaterally abrogate an international agreement that they had signed just a few weeks earlier without looking duplicitous. The EU foreign minister Josep Borrell, summed up the mess the British had inflicted upon themselves by commenting that 'with Brexit, nothing gets easier and a lot gets more complicated. How much more complicated depends on the choices that both sides will make.' Borrell then noted in diplomatic language that the choices from the British side indicated a rejection of 'old obligations' turning honest diplomacy into a transactional relationship that will be 'structurally adversarial for the foreseeable future'.[10] John Bull was beginning to look like a very dodgy character indeed.[11]

Very few British governments have managed, by a single act, to irritate or alienate both Protestant and Catholic communities in Northern Ireland, unionists and Irish nationalists, the president of the United States, the president of France, the Taoiseach of Ireland, and governments across the European Union. John Bull really does not travel well. In the United States there was a particularly damning analysis from one of those who could not understand the British inability to accept how negatively the world now regarded some of the decisions taken by the United Kingdom. Steven Erlanger was formerly the *New York Times* bureau chief in London. In 2017 he moved to where the power in Europe really lay, Brussels. In an article published in the *New York Times* on 4 November 2017, Erlanger saw the UK as not so much waving as drowning:

Many Britons see their country as a brave galleon, banners waving, cannons firing, trumpets blaring. That is how the country's voluble foreign secretary, Boris Johnson, likes to describe it. But Britain is now but a modest-size ship on the global ocean. Having voted to leave the European Union, it is unmoored, heading to nowhere, while on deck, fire has broken out…. I've lived and worked for nine years in Britain, first during the Thatcher years and then again for the last four politically chaotic ones. While much poorer in the 1980s, Britain mattered internationally. Now, with Brexit, it seems to be embracing an introverted irrelevance. The ambitious Mr Johnson was crucial to the victory of Brexit in the June 2016 referendum. But for many, the blusterings of Boris have lost their charm. The 'great ship' he loves to cite is a nationalist fantasy, a remnant of Britain's persistent post-imperial confusion about its proper place in the world, hanging on to expensive symbols like a nuclear deterrent while its once glorious navy is often incapable of patrolling its own coastline… Britain is undergoing a full-blown identity crisis.

Muddling Through and Splendid Isolation

Erlanger's description of John Bull's 'introverted irrelevance' could be interpreted as a return to another long, if not particularly glorious, British trope, the astonishing degree of complacency connected to the idea that Britain can always 'muddle through'. The usual dictionary definition of 'muddling through' is the idea that you can manage to do something despite not being organised and not actually knowing how to do it. The problem with this idea is that historically there is a wealth of evidence for the first word, 'muddling', and generally scant evidence for the second, 'through'. The idea persists in the British imagination that muddling through may be a virtue. It's as if statecraft is a game for gifted amateurs. The reality is that errors in behaviour in British public life often persist until there is a crisis so devastating that the need for profound change eventually permeates even John Bull's skull.

In international affairs a similarly contradictory trope about Britain also often emerges, that of 'splendid isolation'. The idea of Britain separating itself from foreign entanglements in Europe was a significant part of British foreign policy under the Conservative prime minister Lord Salisbury from 1885 to 1902. It had its admirers at the peak of empire. These included the Canadian politician, George Eulas Foster who spoke in 1896 of 'troublesome days when the great Mother Empire stands splendidly isolated in Europe'. Yet even then there was a catch. Splendid isolation was never splendid. Joseph Chamberlain, Britain's Colonial Secretary during this period (1895–1903) including the time of the Boer War, lamented that cutting the United Kingdom off from European nations and alliances meant that isolation was both unwise and ultimately dangerous:

'We have had no allies,' Chamberlain complained. 'I am afraid we have had no friends... We stand alone.'

This led back to yet another British trope, the age-old British dilemma of which way to face – towards Europe or to the rest of the world? The dilemma became more acute as the British Empire grew. Those determined that the United Kingdom should exploit the resources of a great empire all around the globe – Global Britain – often wished to disentangle the country from the future of an entire continent just 26 miles across the Channel. The Empire was a net gain in resources, the troubles on the continent were a net expenditure. But the problem with disentanglement from Europe – summed up in the jokey and probably apocryphal newspaper headline of 'Fog in Channel, Continent Cut Off', is that it is impossible. Geography and history always meant that whatever the profits of empire or global trade, conflict in Europe, and the threat of Europe cohering under one powerful ruler against British interests, has always presented an existential threat to the United Kingdom. It happened with France for centuries until Waterloo, with Germany in the decades before the First World War, then again in 1939, and also in the late 1940s with the creation of NATO as a pre-emptive measure against Soviet communism and the Warsaw Pact. It has happened once more with the possible contagion from the war in Ukraine.

Winston Churchill, in opposition in 1948, tried to think ahead to ensure that post-imperial Britain might in future still retain a pivotal place in the world and solve that geostrategic dilemma by being part of every important sphere of influence. In his speech to the Conservative Party conference in Llandudno Churchill told his party faithful that the United Kingdom was the crucial link between the 'three great circles among the free nations and democracies', by which he meant the British Commonwealth and Empire, the English-speaking world especially the United States, and what he called 'United Europe'. Britain stood, Churchill said, 'at the very point of junction, and here in this island at the centre of the seaways and perhaps of the airways also, we have the opportunity of joining them all together'.

Being the crucial link for the world was a grand ambition, but as the Empire faded and the British Commonwealth emerged as a useful forum for discussion (although hardly an international powerhouse), those three great circles became in reality just two – the pull of the 'English-speaking world', sometimes called the 'Anglosphere' with the United States as the key player, and the emerging 'United Europe' which became the European Union.

For British thinkers of the period, connecting the Anglosphere and Europe was seen as an opportunity rather than a dilemma. Lord Peter Ricketts was the UK's first National Security Adviser. He's also formerly chairman of the Joint Intelligence Committee (JIC), the UK's Permanent Representative to NATO and UK Ambassador to France. He usefully sums up the direction of British strategic thinking after 1945, and its current crisis:

Since the post-war years Britain's national strategy has been built on two pillars: influence on global affairs through a close partnership with the US, and a leading role in European affairs via involvement in the various schemes of European coordination and then integration. Both those pillars are crumbling... outside the EU Britain is less useful to the US and self-excluded from whatever direction European integration takes.[12]

The simultaneous crumbling of both pillars of Britain's post-war national strategy is not 'splendid isolation'. It is the incompetence of a self-inflicted wound. Ricketts sees the obvious conflict between the proud British self-image of competent governance, and our disruption of the long-term strategy taken very deliberately after the Second World War to make sure Britain played a big role in Europe as well as with the United States. We have diminished both.

In 1959 prime minister Harold Macmillan witnessed the invigoration of the European project after the founding of the European Economic Community in Belgium two years earlier. Those historic enemies Germany and France came together along with Italy, the Netherlands, Belgium and Luxembourg in an economic grouping designed to ensure there would never be another war fought in Western Europe. Macmillan decided that 'muddling through' had to end. He ordered a top-secret inquiry to be chaired by the Cabinet Secretary Norman Brook. Its remit was to 'try to forecast what the state of the world would be in 1970 and what role the United Kingdom would be able to play in it... which would allow us to continue to play a significant part in world affairs'. The findings of the 'Future Policy Study', as it was called, were delivered to Macmillan in February 1960. Those findings have a particular resonance in our current malaise. As Lord Ricketts notes, the study became the basis of a 'grand strategy' for most of the following six decades with the objective of maintaining the UK's worldwide influence even if in relative terms Britain was a declining power. The key point in this extraordinarily prescient piece of strategic thinking was the assumption that the (then) six countries of the EEC ('the Six') would in future bind more closely together through their trade links. In economic terms a newly united Europe might even become as strong as the United States. It would mean that

a new world power will come on to the scene... it would probably replace us as the second power in the North Atlantic alliance (NATO)... and if an economic division led to conflict, the United States with their traditional attachment to European unity might even feel obliged to support the Six against us, to the great detriment of Anglo-American cooperation.[13]

The original Six of the EEC became the twenty-seven democracies of the European Union. They embrace former communist countries of the Warsaw Pact, and former right-wing dictatorships in Spain, Greece and Portugal, in an organisation stretching from Limerick to Lublin. Britain has now opted out, doing precisely what the 1960 Future Policy Study warned against. Norman Brook's fifty-page document argues that:

> if disputes or tensions force the US to choose between their allies in Europe and the United Kingdom they are likely to throw their weight behind the ally for whom they have the most respect as an actively powerful opponent of Russian and Chinese expansionism... one basic rule of British policy is clear: we must not find ourselves in a position of having to make a final choice between the United States and Europe. It would not be compatible with our vital interests to reject either one or the other and the very fact that a choice was needed would mean the end of the Atlantic alliance.[14]

The Empire is long gone. The rejection of the European Union is now a fact. The United Kingdom has, in Lord Rickett's view, weakened its relationship with the United States precisely because we are weaker in Europe. If the United States has to 'throw their weight behind an ally for whom they have the most respect' they may prefer the 68 million people of the United Kingdom to the 450 million people of the European Union, but that is far from certain. The danger has been obvious since the 1960s. Actually it was obvious back in the 1560s and the era of Elizabeth I. The idea that the continent of Europe would unite in any kind of organisation with England on the outside was always regarded as an existential threat to, at that time, Protestant England. Nowadays the dangers of a different kind of European unit with England (or the UK in this case) again on the outside is obvious to former senior civil servants like Ricketts as well as to those still in the Whitehall bureaucracy, who cannot speak out openly.

One who can is the former permanent under-secretary in the Foreign and Commonwealth Office (FCO) Sir Simon Fraser. In a speech at the defence and foreign policy think tank Chatham House in London, Fraser was very outspoken.

'It is hard to call to mind a major foreign policy matter on which we have had decisive influence since the [Brexit] referendum,' he said. Then in what was clearly a dig at the rhetorical abilities of Boris Johnson, Fraser noted that those very successful communications techniques which brought Johnson to public attention and then power were disastrous in government.

'Successful foreign policy calls for careful analysis and sustained effort, not soundbites and wishful thinking,' Fraser said. Brexit was 'revealing fault lines in our society and animosity towards foreigners' while geography and history would ensure that 'our relationships with other European democracies will remain central to our foreign policy. To contemplate simply walking out and looking elsewhere is a simplistic fantasy'.

The result of serious political and geopolitical misjudgements, John Bull rhetoric and contempt for the views of friendly nations meant that 'our political establishment commands little respect abroad, and the negative economic consequences of Brexit are beginning to show'. That is because Brexit represents 'the biggest shock to [the UK's] method of international influencing and the biggest structural change to our place in the world since the end of World War Two'. Fraser went on to suggest that the United Kingdom's position as one of five permanent members of the United Nations Security Council might also be under threat since as a nation we had blundered into our own irrelevance:

Brexit weakens our hand on both sides of the Atlantic. For years we have exploited our role as what Tony Blair called 'the bridge', and William Hague calls 'the hinge', between

Europe and America. Now our purchase on both will be reduced. Washington will look to Berlin, because Germany will be strongest in Europe. Under President Macron, France is regaining momentum. Our bilateral relationships will be structurally weaker, not stronger, after Brexit, and France and Germany will be looking to work together through EU machinery.[15]

We have muddled but not muddled 'through'. We have isolated ourselves, though evidence that this is 'splendid' is hard to find. And we have overturned seven decades of British strategic thinking since Winston Churchill's suggestion that the UK could remain at the heart of Europe, working within the Anglosphere and in some post-imperial British Commonwealth of nations. That latter day John Bull Boris Johnson once argued that his own personal mission was

> to recover our natural role as an enterprising and outward looking and truly Global Britain, generous in temper and engaged in the world. No one in the last few centuries has succeeded in betting against the pluck and nerve and ambition of this country.[16]

That is, of course, simply not true. The Americans bet against Britain in 1776. The Afghans in 1842. The Boers in 1900. The Irish did so after 1916. The Mau Mau in Kenya, along with Malaysian insurgents, Aden rebels, the Irgun in what became Israel, the people of India, Pakistan and Bangladesh at the time of partition, to name some of the most obvious examples, all decided that they were better off without Britain, Global or otherwise. And many are betting against us now. Lord Ricketts points out that 'the British government finds itself advocating "Global Britain" just as globalisation is in retreat and the world is fracturing into spheres of influence dominated by the US and China'.[17] Above all, while the UK remains a member of NATO and has offered significant assistance to Ukraine, we have more will than wallet. While Boris

Johnson was speaking in fluent Boosterish of 'Global Britain', he announced (in March 2021) cuts to the British army that would reduce it to just 72,500 soldiers by 2025. The National Army Museum said the cuts meant the army would be at its lowest level since demobilisation at the end of the War of Spanish Succession in 1714, a time when the British population was estimated at a little over 8 million. As for the Navy, *Forbes* magazine put the idea that Britannia Rules the Waves into a modern context:

> If you aim to go to war with the Royal Navy, plan to fire the first shot in 2026 – the year the British fleet could be at its weakest. In five years under current projections the Royal Navy will have just 10 frigates – down from 13 today – as ageing Type 23 vessels decommission. The 10 frigates, plus the six Type 45 destroyers that should still be in service at the time, could struggle to meet the United Kingdom's naval needs.[18]

Even the Defence Secretary Ben Wallace was forced to accept the scale of the problem, admitting that the British army was now so 'hollowed out' by 2023 it is barely able to field one fully equipped combat division of 10,000 soldiers. The UK is 'deeply vulnerable' in some parts of its defences, and in a European war could run out of ammunition in a matter of days. As we noted earlier, Wallace's gloomy assessment concluded that, 'If we just want to stay at home and do a bit of tootling around, we've got an armed forces big enough.'[19] The great strategic dilemma faced by Macmillan in 1959 – how to live in the chaos of the moment with no time to pause and think about the longer-term consequences continues. Ricketts gives as an example Tony Blair failing to think through the implications of joining George W. Bush's ill-thought-out adventure in Iraq in 2002. We could add David Cameron not thinking through the consequences of losing the referendum on leaving the European Union in 2016, or the lack of interest in Britain's 2010 and 2015 National Security Strategies – examples of strategic thinking that warned about the eventual inevitability of a pandemic and suggested how the inevitable could be planned for. Their recommendations were ignored, until after coronavirus struck and the recriminations began.

The challenges of our own *Zeitenwende* therefore mean that even the 'head-of-oak' Englishman John Bull needs to begin to think strategically and realistically for the future. As Ricketts says:

> This is one of those periods as significant as the years after 1945, particularly for Britain. The decision to leave the EU was both a symptom and a cause of the wider upheaval and leaves the country facing a series of difficult decisions. Outside the EU, Britain is more dependent on its strategic partnership with the US, but less useful to Washington given its lack of leverage in Europe. Its foreign policy will necessarily be heavily weighted towards securing trade deals… Countries such as China and Saudi Arabia will not hesitate to use Britain's need for export contracts and investment to press for criticism of their wider policies to be muted.[20]

Muddling through is not an option. But there is hope. At a similar turning point in the past, the beginning of the Cold War, an American deep thinker, the Peter Ricketts or Simon Fraser of his day, wrote anonymously in an influential foreign affairs magazine an article which influenced American strategic thinking throughout the Cold War. George F. Kennan outlined the problems caused by Stalinism and the threats to world peace. He ended on a note of optimism. In his 'Sources of Soviet Conduct' published in *Foreign Affairs* in 1947 under the pseudonym 'X' Kennan outlined the reasons the United States should be alarmed by the communist threat, yet prepared and confident of its own strength:

> The issue of Soviet-American relations is in essence a test of the overall worth of the United States as a nation among nations. To avoid destruction the United States need only measure up to its own best traditions and prove itself worthy of preservation

as a great nation. Surely, there was never a fairer test of national quality than this.[21]

The issue facing the United Kingdom in the twenty-first century is the same. We can prove ourself worthy of preservation as a great nation if we live up to our 'own best traditions', and if we forget the delusions of being a 'great power'. But we are not living up to our own best traditions, especially not with our John Bull posturing and Perfidious Albion behaviour. We need to change the way we think and the way we act because 'there was never a fairer test of national quality than this'.

We have been failing that test.

8

Traditions: They're Not What They Used to Be

One evening in mid-December a few years ago, I stood nervously at the east end of the nave in Canterbury Cathedral, a place known as 'The Crossing'. I was invited to take part in a tradition, to read a passage from the Bible about the Christmas story in front of a thousand worshippers at a carol service. As the congregation arrived, I stared into this vast gothic cavern of Christianity with – as its builders intended – a profound sense of awe. The cathedral began as a church in AD 597, a year after St Augustine was sent by Pope Gregory the Great to convert the heathen Anglo-Saxons to Christianity. It was rebuilt in the 1070s following the Norman conquest. Given its vast size, Canterbury Cathedral remains a work in progress. The building is constantly being cleaned, rebuilt and renewed. I've been coming here since I was a teenager, and I do not remember a time when there has not been scaffolding somewhere on its vast structure. That December evening I was nervous because I was new to the honorary post of Chancellor of the University of Kent and I didn't want to make a fool of myself.

'What's my cue to start reading?' I asked the Dean, anxiously.

Several decades working in TV on my part met with puzzlement from the man embodying more than a millennium of the English Christian tradition.

'I mean, how do I know *when exactly* to go up to the lectern to start reading?'

He smiled, and explained patiently.

'We sing the first carol, light the candles and then the lights go out. That's when you go up to the lectern.'

'But,' I hesitated, 'when the lights go out in the cathedral, how will I see to read?'

The Dean smiled again.

'We've been doing it for a thousand years,' he said. 'It's a tradition. I expect you'll manage.'

We both laughed and I did manage. Reading by candlelight in one of the greatest buildings in the world on the spot where St Augustine founded the church in England, was one of the most memorable experiences of my life. Traditions are like that, a connection in the present to the past, offering a small gift to the future. 'Only connect' is the epigraph of E. M. Forster's novel *Howards End*. It sums up the strong links by which we connect to each other and different generations, in Forster's case, through the grand old English house which gives the novel its title. But there is another side to traditions. They can be out of date and stupid. In January 2023 *The Sun* newspaper reported that King Charles III had been told to 'Drop Your Breeches', ending the tradition of wearing knee breeches and silk stockings at his coronation in order to 'modernise' the monarchy, as *The Sun* put it. Modernising the monarchy will take a lot more effort than changing what the king wears on his legs, yet the story shows that traditions are always invented. They can – like breeches worn at a coronation – be dropped, dis-invented or rejected. They can also become resistant to change and evidence of a kind of cultural or political sclerosis. That, unfortunately, is part of our British disease. The British are good at inventing traditions but not so good at retiring those that are long past being useful. One powerful and long-lasting constitutional tradition is that Black Rod may hammer at the doors of the Commons but may not be admitted. The parliamentary website explains this – like so many of the customary practices in British public life – is about power; who has it and who doesn't:

> Black Rod is sent from the Lords Chamber to the Commons Chamber to summon MPs to hear the King's Speech. Traditionally the door of the Commons is slammed in Black Rod's face to symbolise the Commons independence. He or she then bangs three times on the door with the rod. The door to the Commons Chamber is then opened and all MPs – talking loudly – follow Black Rod back to the Lords to hear the King's Speech.[1]

Note the words 'he or she'. The tradition of where power lies retains its importance, but the vocabulary has changed to cope with a world in which gender equality has assumed its modern-day significance. Black Rod's uniform consists of black shoes with black buckles, silk stockings, black breeches, and black coat. It's easy to drop breeches. It's not so easy to drop other traditions in parliament and elsewhere, but it does happen. The once popular music hall tradition of 'black face' is now unacceptable. The BBC show, *The Black and White Minstrels* in which white men pretended to be black entertainers, was once popular and is now almost forgotten. As a journalist in Northern Ireland I recognised that the word 'tradition' was – and still is – used to cover all kinds of offensive practices. Every summer in Ulster's 'Marching Season', there were incendiary Orange Order parades of Protestant men through the Catholic area of Portadown known as the Garvaghy Road. This tradition was again about power – about who had it (the Protestant marchers) and who did not (the Catholic residents). Flute bands and marchers in Orange regalia were not welcomed by Catholic residents and there were outbreaks of violence. Residents told me how they felt trapped in their homes in the name of a 'tradition' they saw as sectarian and threatening. When I asked Orangemen why they felt it necessary to walk through an area where they did not live, had no friends and where they knew they were not welcome, the response was always variations of the following:

'We have a traditional right to march down the Garvaghy road …' Having a 'traditional right' to intimidate your neighbours is not a worthy customary practice. The invocation of tradition, in other words, may become an abuse or an entitlement to continue to do things which are long past their sell-by date. This is especially true when what is at stake is power. And since the British system of government is the heart of power you can see why, when power is abused, the recitation of the words 'it's a tradition' or 'it's in line with precedent' may seem a reasonable excuse to those in charge to justify their occasionally ludicrous practices. Even so, changes do happen. There was once a tradition for British monarchs to attend meetings of the cabinet in Downing Street. George I broke with that idea from 1717 onwards. George III chaired cabinet meetings for a time but he was the last monarch to do so regularly, stopping in 1781. That was the year General Charles Cornwallis and 8,000 British soldiers surrendered to George Washington at Yorktown, and the British colonies were lost. The historian Jane Ridley concluded it was more or less the end of the practice:

> I don't think there is any evidence that Queen Victoria sat in on cabinet or went near cabinet. She did occasionally get rather cross with her politicians and when that happened she would very occasionally write a furious letter to be read out in cabinet. George III went only very occasionally.[2]

Queen Elizabeth II did briefly attend David Cameron's cabinet meeting in December 2012 but only to celebrate her Diamond Jubilee. There was no question where the power lay in the room – with the prime minister.

The point of these anecdotes is to confirm that an event becomes a tradition when it happens repeatedly and any tradition can be abandoned when it is no longer useful. But traditions can also be employed as blocks on change. They can become a sign of what the American writer Jonathan Rauch calls 'demosclerosis', defined as a calcification of institutions rooted in a 'government's progressive loss of the ability to adapt'.[3] Demosclerosis is now a British tradition. As a nation we are slow to embrace positive change to institutions except when it is forced upon us.

Roy Lilley, a visiting fellow at Imperial College and the innovator who started the Health Management School at Nottingham University, has had a long career advising the NHS about modernisation. During the pandemic in late 2021 Lilley told me that the one discernible benefit of coronavirus had been to force a greater use of computers and information technology into the otherwise sclerotic NHS systems. He said that the pandemic in just two years had brought greater IT changes than he had been able to achieve by arguing for modernisation for more than twenty years. British demosclerosis is not however confined to one institution or government or one political party. It is endemic within the British system itself, extending from Jacob Rees-Mogg and his weaponised nostalgia for imperial weights and measures (which no one under the age of fifty can remember), to the 2016 Brexit battle cry of 'take our country back' (not forward), restoring a vague idea of 'lost sovereignty' (again, something from the past that's carelessly been mislaid), failure to tackle real reform within the NHS and in the peculiarities of the English school system as well as delusions of British grandeur as in some way a 'world leading' power. Being world leading as we noted, is not how the world sees the United Kingdom in the 2020s. But here's where tradition does play a role.

Britain as Historic Theme Park

To gauge what the world thinks of the United Kingdom the British Council conducts surveys in many countries. Repeated surveys found that the past is often Britain's greatest selling point: 'The United Kingdom is both loved and loathed for its traditions. The images most often associated with Great Britain in the survey are the Queen and the Royal Family, kilts, castles and rugby. This has implications for public diplomacy.' The survey then posed a question without any definitive answer: 'What can be done to close the gap between perceptions overseas and the reality of contemporary Britain without ignoring the strengths of our traditions for which we are respected?'[4]

By 2020 the British Council survey reported some qualified good news: 'This year's study finds that the UK is now considered to be the most attractive country overall among young people in the G20. The UK has risen three ranks since 2018 and now ranks above countries such as Canada, Italy and Australia,' although the survey also noted the reason. It wasn't because Britain was doing better. Others were doing worse: 'The UK's improved ranking is driven by drops in rating for Canada, Italy and Australia, while ratings for the UK have remained largely stable.' The survey did not explore precisely where the UK's attractions actually lie, but that happened in a detailed British Council investigation into American public opinion. This was an important survey because the United States was – and remains – a vital British interest as part of our 'soft power'. The survey was conducted at a time when political relations between London and Washington were strained by the peculiarities of the presidency of Donald Trump. He had been condescending towards the then British prime minister Theresa May and dismissive towards the US alliance with Britain and other European nations in NATO. Trump's daily tweets did not inspire confidence about future relations. The prospect of a massive new US–UK trade agreement – a post-Brexit British government fantasy – also finally died. The British Council opinion survey found positive responses in how the UK is seen by Americans, but yet again these involved traditions and the past, not creativity and the future. Nor did the survey answer the question posed two decades earlier, 'What can be done to close the gap between perceptions overseas and the reality of contemporary Britain?' Instead it confirmed the dilemma. Britain was seen as a historic theme park rather than as a modern forward-thinking partner in innovation and creativity:

> American views of the UK are driven more by cultural factors than political issues… pointing to a crucial role for culture in future relations between the two countries. The report… reveals that culture and history were the two top rated factors contributing to the UK's attractiveness among American respondents, with 43 per cent identifying 'cultural and historic attractions' as a major draw and 42 per cent identifying 'history'. The current and past actions of governments were only the 16th most important factor (at 17 per cent) in determining how attractive they found the UK.[5]

It's not only Americans who see the positive reality of Britain in the twenty-first century mostly in terms of our 'cultural and historic attractions' and 'history'. Many British people do so, or at least there must be a significant number who provide an audience for the way in which nostalgia continues to be weaponised by some British politicians. One clue about these visitations from the past is to watch out for the word 'back' and its synonyms in much of what follows, and in wider British public life. For example, to celebrate Queen Elizabeth II's Platinum Jubilee stories were put about Westminster that Boris Johnson was to make a commitment to go 'back' to the imperial weights and measures system in an announcement to celebrate the Jubilee. It never happened, of course. Flirting with restoring 'imperial' measures, as we saw with Jacob Rees-Mogg's supposed 'survey' of opinion on the subject, is just a traditional British political striptease, a metaphor for the restoration of a long-gone Empire. There was also an announcement that the crown symbol would be 'restored' to pint beer glasses. The government website explained why:

> For centuries British pint glasses intended for measuring and serving beer were marked with a crown stamp as a declaration that the glass accurately measured a pint. In 2006 the crown stamp was replaced by the CE mark, which was a new conformity marking required by EU legislation, and the crown stamp was no longer required as a conformity marking for pint glasses in the UK. The crown symbol is fondly remembered by many people as a symbol that they associate with traditional pint measures. In recognition of the heritage of the crown stamp, the Government is providing this guidance on how manufacturers can apply a crown symbol to beer glasses as a decorative mark on a voluntary basis.[6]

This was a classic Dead Cat story on the government website. That's because at no point was the crown symbol ever banned from pint glasses by the European Union or anyone else. The weasel words in the government 'guidance' are that the crown stamp was 'no longer required' after 2006. It was never forbidden. And at no point did the government 'announcement' insist that it must return, only telling 'manufacturers' that they 'can apply' it if they wanted to – restoring an ancient 'right' that was never lost. (And please at this point remember some people paid for government advisers to come up with this 'guidance' to fix yet another 'problem' that simply did not exist. These people are called British taxpayers.) That same month in 2022, as prime minister Boris Johnson was losing control of his own government, the British technology minister – the technology minister! – Chris Philp joined the never-ending campaign to 'return to' imperial weights and measures. This was now a plan to enshrine changes into law 'allowing a bit of our national heritage and culture back onto the shop shelf'. Greg Wood, from the British Measurement and Testing Association pointed out the obvious drawbacks of going back to a system that most British people were too young to remember – a system that included archaic measures like bushels, gills and hundredweights. It would entail the enormous expense of changing to a system British industry did not want or need and that no one else uses:

'The imperial measurement system has not been taught in UK state schools since 1974... common understanding of imperial measures is limited. It is unclear what the actual benefit of permitting the wider use of imperial measurement would be to anyone.'[7]

Once you start spotting the constant re-emergence of stultifying traditions and the political weaponising of nostalgia in British public life, it is difficult to know where to stop. The Brexit slogan was, of course, 'Take Our Country Back', not forward. There was the prime minister John Major's campaign in the 1990s to get 'Back to Basics'. Or Margaret Thatcher in the 1980s trumpeting the idea of getting back to 'Victorian values'. Presumably Mrs Thatcher did not mean putting young children up chimneys to clean them or bringing back workhouses or the tens of thousands of women believed to have been prostitutes in Victorian London, but perhaps for some that was a price worth paying for restoring our lost Victorian 'traditions'. Even as I am writing this I am distracted by a tweet from Lord Frost, responsible for, as Boris Johnson put it, the 'Titanic success' that is Brexit, boasting about his 27 January 2023 column in the *Daily*

Telegraph 'urging the government to get back to Tory tradition...' Or a month later, the newly appointed deputy chairman of the Conservative Party Lee Anderson insisting the United Kingdom should bring back capital punishment...

Once you spot the code words for demosclerosis within a significant section of British political life and newspaper reporting, it is the repetitive threnody of ancestor worship. Fortunately Britain really is better than this. We have an excellent tradition of strategic thinking about the future, usually in times of crisis. We could do so again – but only if we give as much prominence in British politics and journalism to thinking about the future as we do to moping sentimentally about the misremembered past. Norman Brook and Harold Macmillan did precisely that degree of strategic thinking in the late 1950s and 1960s. And so, at our turning point in the 2020s, if a top-level group of civil servants, defence and international relations strategists – a modern day equivalent of those assembled by Norman Brook in 1959 – were to consider Britain's world role in the future, what would they come up with? What political pressures would they face? What would they hear from British intellectuals?

Does Britain Have a World Role?

One possible version of Britain's role in the world has for years been regurgitated frequently in the public domain, given space in newspaper opinion pages and appeared in various forms in the speeches of politicians and English intellectuals. It comes in several variants but is often associated with the English historian Andrew Roberts, and supported by others on the Conservative right of British politics. They call it, with a nod to Winston Churchill's 1956 book *A History of the English-Speaking Peoples*, the 'Anglosphere'. It's yet another attempt to take us back to the future.

Roberts, writing as recently as 2020, defines it thus:

The Anglosphere is the name given to all those countries in the world where the majority of people speak English as their first language, almost all of which have similar outlooks and shared values. The four 'Canzuk' countries of Canada, Australia, New Zealand and the UK are a prominent historical subset of this larger group, and there is a mounting case that some form of federation among them – with free trade, free movement of people, a mutual defence organisation and combined military capabilities – would create a new global superpower and ally of the US, the great anchor of the Anglosphere.[8]

Oddly for a historian Roberts does not offer any evidence for his presumed 'mounting case' for an 'Anglosphere' creating 'a new global superpower', beyond his personal sentiment. The 'free trade, free movement of people' question is also problematic. The United Kingdom abandoned free trade and free movement with the European Union which starts 26 miles from England and is physically conjoined with the UK on the island of Ireland. The idea of a comprehensive free trade agreement with the United States – 'the great anchor of the Anglosphere' – on the far side of a great ocean is and is always likely to be a fantasy. While US presidents can negotiate trade deals, Congress is the arbiter of their suitability. Diplomats who have negotiated on behalf of British interests on trade in the past have admitted to me that a comprehensive US–UK trade deal is very unlikely. The United Kingdom did have better luck in finally negotiating a post-Brexit trade deal with Australia, some 9,400 miles away. Prime Minister Boris Johnson called it 'a new dawn' but like much of the prime minister's Boosterism, the dawn is false. The House of Commons bipartisan International Trade Committee was among those extremely unhappy with the result. They complained that the Australian deal has very significant negative consequences for British farmers, food standards, food producers and consumers – in other words, in the post-Brexit tradition, it is a woefully bad deal for the entire British population:

The cross-party Committee of MPs expressed disappointment that Australian food will not be required to meet core UK food production standards, for example regarding pesticide use, and argued that negotiating legal protection for the names of iconic UK food and drink exports – such as Melton Mowbray pork pies, Scotch whisky and Welsh lamb – should have been an easy win.

The 'easy win' turned into an own goal. The only minor benefit the committee noted was that the price of Australian wine might drop 'a few pence'.[9] The reaction from British farmers and the National Farmers Union was that the deal was simply terrible. It would significantly impact British food standards and undermine the farming industry. Supposed safeguards against hormone use in Australian livestock would be impossible to enforce. Even those who were party to the deal, including George Eustice, then the Environment Secretary, later admitted that we needed to learn serious lessons from this failure.

'The first step is to recognise that the Australia trade deal is not actually a very good deal for the UK,' Eustice said with considerable understatement, because 'the truth of the matter is that the UK gave away far too much for far too little in return' and what we gave away was 'not in our economic interests'.

Eustice was particularly scathing about the way the Trade Secretary at the time (and future prime minister) Liz Truss, handled negotiations. He said Truss insisted on a quick deal rather than a good one. The minutiae of this botch up are important because they demonstrate precisely where the ill-conceived nostalgia of the Anglosphere leads. Some things from the past – imperial preference? successful trade relations with the former colonies? – cannot be revived in the way they once were. The rest of the world has moved on. The Australia deal lacked strategic thinking and the patience necessary for a policy to produce beneficial results. It confirmed two recent unfortunate British traditions, the Johnson 'new dawn' Boosterism is detached from reality and in British public life instead of shaming those responsible for failure we promote them. Liz Truss negotiated what her own colleagues admitted was a shockingly bad deal for Britain, and within weeks became prime minister of the United Kingdom. All the systemic problems in the British political sclerosis are laid bare – nostalgia, lack of strategic planning, incompetence, arrogance and self-promotion followed by advancement to the most important job in British democracy.

A nostalgic view of the world assumes that a deal with a former colony 9,000 miles away will inevitably boost the British economy, or as Truss herself described it: 'Ambitious, wide-ranging free trade agreements with old friends like Australia and New Zealand are a powerful way for us to do that and make good on the promise of Brexit.' Second, an unseemly rush, similar to the rush to 'Get Brexit Done' without planning to decide what the thing to be 'done' might actually look like makes failure almost certain. Third, a refusal to listen to expert advice, especially from those within the British government itself. Civil servants and advisers argued for a slower and more methodical process. They were overruled by Truss, who was, unfortunately, clueless, yet in her effortless rise she appeared destined to live out the lines from Samuel Beckett's absurdist novella, *Worstward Ho*: 'Ever tried. Ever failed. No matter. Try again. Fail again. Fail better.'

Part of the problem is that those newsmaking and social media techniques described in Chapter 6 – rapid-fire announcements, headline-grabbing statements, Dead Cat distractions and endless photo opportunities – do succeed in enabling politicians like Johnson and Truss to rise to the top. But these are precisely the kinds of techniques which can never succeed to produce coherent policies or successful negotiations. It is also revealing that only after he left the government did George Eustice feel he could be honest about the mess with which he had been associated. What is it about being in government that often makes good people unable to admit responsibility for failure until they are liberated by leaving? In terms of the Anglosphere there's worse to come.

It has never been clear – beyond post-imperial longing – why Andrew Roberts' hope for the 'free movement of people' would create a new global superpower, while free movement within the European Union's 450 million people in contiguous states would not do the same and be much more advantageous to the United Kingdom. People can, even now, move relatively freely between Auckland and Saskatoon or New South Wales and Cardiff. Generally they don't. That's not because of bureaucratic restrictions, but because most of us tend to look for opportunities closer to home. A mobile European workforce has been a feature of European – and British – life for years, encouraged by the EU. Polish builders in London, East European fruit pickers in Kent, Spanish and other EU hospitality workers in the Scottish highlands and the more than 90 per cent of vets in British abattoirs who were EU citizens, were all welcomed. They enriched our country. Those who left are often missed during our continuing skilled and unskilled labour shortages. But the idea of seasonal workers coming from Adelaide or Vancouver to the Kent orchards near Ashford or a meat packing factory in Devon is in several senses a bit of a stretch. Perhaps the Anglosphere idea can most charitably be seen to stand in the tradition of Winston Churchill's famous 1946 speech on the post-war order at Fulton, Missouri, when he declared:

> We must never cease to proclaim in fearless tones the great principles of freedom and the rights of man which are the joint inheritance of the English-speaking world and which through Magna Carta, the Bill of Rights, habeas corpus, trial by jury, and the English Common Law find their most famous expression in the American Declaration of Independence.[10]

It's true that Winston Churchill almost eighty years ago did see some kind of Anglospheric unity as a potential counterweight to 'the United States of Europe', yet that notion was rapidly eclipsed by events. A little more than a decade later his Conservative successor Harold Macmillan recognised that Britain in Europe was an essential part of British influence. Subsequent political leaders agreed that Britain could be Tony Blair's 'bridge' or William Hague's 'hinge' between Europe and the US. It's also true that friendly and familial relations have always existed between 'CANZUK' countries, Canada, Australia, New Zealand and the UK. Shared democratic values mean there are already strong and significant cooperation agreements in defence, intelligence matters and national security, including 'Five Eyes' intelligence cooperation. But however Roberts and others may try to revive the Anglosphere idea with the United Kingdom at the centre of a new relationship, geography tells a stubbornly different story. Not about the United Kingdom, this time, but about Canada, New Zealand, Australia and the United States. They have something in common that the UK does not have. They are all Pacific nations.

The United Kingdom may send a gunboat to the Pacific (our only serviceable aircraft carrier, HMS *Queen Elizabeth*, did fly the flag briefly in that direction) but the rise of China and the strategic importance of the Pacific is inevitably more of a concern to those other putative Anglosphere countries who live on its shores than to us. President Barack Obama even formalised this by announcing a 'strategic tilt' away from Europe to the Pacific, though that has been moderated since the war in Ukraine. But Canada, the US and Mexico are already in an important trading relationship with each other. Australia and New Zealand inevitably have the closest of relationships and also ties with countries in east, southeast and south Asia. Rather than a closer relationship with Britain, and beyond the trade deal that significantly favours Australia, Australians increasingly seem inclined to ditch the British monarch in the post-Elizabethan age. For years there have been moves to become a republic, even when affection for Queen Elizabeth was a strong counterargument. In 2023 the Australian government decided not to put the face of King Charles III on its new issue of $5 bills, and go with an Australian first nations' design instead. Australia's Foreign Minister, Penny Wong, a Labour Party politician born in Malaysia, appeared to bury the last vestiges of the Anglosphere delusion when she said that the

UK needed to confront its 'uncomfortable' imperial past. She told an audience at King's College London that the relationship between the two countries had changed profoundly: 'Today, as a modern, multicultural country, home to people of more than 300 ancestries and the oldest continuing culture on Earth, Australia sees itself as being in the Indo-Pacific and being of the Indo-Pacific.'[11]

The Anglosphere would also create significant domestic problems for Canada's government in Ottawa since 'French is the first official language spoken by 22.8 per cent of the population.'[12] It doesn't take much for Andrew Roberts' perennial revival of the Anglosphere delusion to shrink back to nothing more than Little England and the unrestricted joy that we can continue to look at the imperial crown etched on pint glasses of warm beer while we drown our sorrows.

There is one curious omission before we leave the vacuous Anglosphere nostalgia. Roberts speaks of countries in which 'the majority of people speak English as their first language'. He then focuses on what he calls 'a prominent historical subset of this larger group'. This group manages to avoid Caribbean and other nations where most people are not white. There may be some important reason for this choice of that 'prominent historical subset' although it is not clear what it is. Perhaps it is some idea of what was once referred to as British 'patriality'. Whatever the reasoning, like Jacob Rees-Mogg's attempts to turn back the clock on metrication, we are dealing with nostalgia pretending to be forward planning and the sclerotic mindset which lies behind it. It's the tradition of Britain celebrating itself as a historic theme park through talk of ending metrication, rebranding the white colonial past, plus Brexit and all the flummery and mummery that camouflages our constitutional weakness. The result – perhaps the intention – is to prevent rational thought about the future by trying to breathe life into a post-imperial corpse.

The Special Relationship or A Special Relationship?

Beyond distractions like the 'Anglosphere', Britain does have other options in terms of a world role. There is a strong yet peculiar relationship with the United States. In 1943, the British prime minister Harold Macmillan is said to have told the Labour politician Richard Crossman:

> We, my dear Crossman, are Greeks in this American Empire. You will find the Americans much as the Greeks found the Romans – great big vulgar, bustling people, more vigorous than we are and also more idle, with more unspoiled virtues, but also more corrupt.

Macmillan thought Britain could teach the Americans how to run 'their empire' just as Emperor Claudius relied on Greeks to run the Roman Empire, although the parallel is less fortunate than he may have believed. The Greeks running the Roman Empire were slaves. There is clearly yet another strange British tradition of Old Etonian prime ministers, including Boris Johnson and Macmillan, making classical allusions in the hope that less privileged listeners will be impressed, even if those allusions do not truly serve the purposes they intend.

Two further phrases from Winston Churchill's 1946 Fulton, Missouri speech, have echoed for generations. One was the idea that an 'Iron Curtain' had descended on Europe as a result of the Soviet Union partitioning the continent into two blocs. The other was the existence of the 'special relationship' between the United Kingdom and United States. There was also a third idea that should have resonance today even if it has generally been forgotten. Churchill concluded that, 'The safety of the world, ladies and gentlemen, requires a new unity in Europe from which no nation should be permanently outcast.' This comment was interpreted as a reference to Eastern Europe at the time, and the need for Europe to find a way to unite in order to prevent another war on the most bloody continent on earth. The idea that no nation should be permanently outcast from Europe may have resonance for post-Brexit Britain, a subject to which we will return later.

For now, the US–UK 'special relationship' was and remains 'special' even if it was always a relationship of unequals. An American diplomat once told me that the phrase is now itself part of a tradition. It is deliberately inserted into every American president's speech about the UK, he said, to 'tickle the belly of the Brits'. Successive British ambassadors in Washington were cautious about all this. They warned British journalists never to refer to 'the' special relationship between the US and UK, but always to 'a' special relationship. When Sir Christopher Meyer was ambassador he reminded British visitors that the US has a special relationship with countries all over the world. There are shared borders and special relationships with Mexico and Canada, and other special relationships with Israel, Ireland and Japan (having dropped two atomic bombs on the country and the stationing of strategically significant armed forces there); with Germany, having troops there since 1945; with South Korea as a potential flashpoint with the North and home to US troops since the 1950s; and many other nations – including, one might say, with Panama, Cuba, and much of Latin America. Since 40 million US citizens speak Spanish, the US could be described as part of the Hispano-sphere, as well as the Anglosphere. The former US Secretary of State Henry Kissinger once asked: 'Who do I call when I want to call Europe?' If Britain ever truly had a role as America's diplomatic telephone exchange, Brexit pulled that plug. Shortly after his election victory in November 2020, at a time of deepening rows between the Irish government and Boris Johnson, US president-elect Joe Biden was asked if he had any words for the BBC. 'I'm Irish,' he laughed. This two-word corrective to British delusions about American affections was tinged with humour. It remains a corrective nevertheless.

Britain in the 2020s is an important US ally, but a diminishingly important one, even if the belly of the Brits is always worth tickling. In 2011 a resolution of the US Congress noted that 'the United

Kingdom remains and will forever be an important and irreplaceable ally to the United States'. In 2016 Hillary Clinton (when she still believed she could be president) said that Washington should 'make clear America's steadfast commitment to the special relationship with Britain' but added, significantly, 'and the transatlantic alliance with Europe'. American diplomats I have spoken with over the years repeatedly told me that Britain was a useful voice of sanity within the European Union but – as Lord Ricketts understood – leaving the EU has, in the eyes of many in the US policy establishment, brought an abrupt end to that role as well as, in the eyes of some US commentators, raised questions about our sanity too.

Even so, the US–UK relationship remains 'special' in some ways. During the lead up to the 2003 Iraq war a senior State Department diplomat told me that, 'When we say something is "multilateral", we mean getting the Brits on board.' George W. Bush got Tony Blair on board. They worked together through the United Nations, where the British provided a degree of diplomatic cover in the overthrow of Saddam Hussein. But the 2003 Iraq invasion, to continue the Churchill allusions, was not anyone's finest hour. Encouraging though it may be that Americans in the twenty-first century have warm feelings towards the UK, the British Council research about this affection being rooted in traditional soft power areas of culture and history is sobering. Our economic, diplomatic, technological, military, political and other hard power capabilities have been replaced by the admiration one might express towards the upmarket semi-factual royal soap opera, *The Crown*, or the fact that three of the most successful Hollywood movie series are based on the works of British writers, J. R. R. Tolkien, J. K. Rowling and Ian Fleming, or admiration for Adele, Roxy Music and The Beatles. Our creative artists, musicians, film makers, movie stars and novelists are hits around the world, as are our universities – especially St Andrews, Oxford and Cambridge. But it is the sclerosis within the traditions of our political system that is our focus here, and one constitutional oddity. British prime ministers are not only very good at recitations of tradition but, when it suits them, in inventing completely new traditions of how to govern. They call this constitutional 'flexibility'. We even have a tradition of celebrating the failed seventeenth-century plot to destroy parliament, while often forgetting that the real destruction of parliament came about through our own carelessness, something we may be about to repeat, as we will see.

Blowing Up Parliament

The British tradition of burning Guy Fawkes on a November fifth bonfire has endured for more than four centuries. It's a celebration of the thwarting of the plot to blow up parliament and assassinate King James I in 1605. We teach our children to sing in commemoration:

> Remember, remember, the 5th of November,
> Gunpowder, treason and plot.
> I see no reason
> Why gunpowder treason
> Should ever be forgot.
> Guy Fawkes, Guy Fawkes, 'twas his intent
> To blow up the King and the Parliament
> Three score barrels of powder below
> Poor old England to overthrow
> By God's providence he was catch'd
> With a dark lantern and burning match
> Holler boys, holler boys, let the bells ring
> Holler boys, holler boys
> God save the King!

Guy Fawkes of course failed, but we have also invented peculiar and disruptive political traditions which may themselves blow up parliament, if not literally, then at least figuratively. They may also destroy some of our complacent ideas that we live in a competent modern democracy. The problem is not the significance of any particular constitutional innovation. The problem is the ease with which constitutional innovations of varying degrees of usefulness may be introduced into the British system. And so before we examine the potential destruction of parliament itself, here's a relatively benign example of constitutional change for administrative convenience. It demonstrates how an invented constitutional tradition can be created for the personal advantage of the chief executive (the prime minister) and driven through without significant scrutiny in parliament. We know, at times, the identity of the person who is the United Kingdom's deputy prime minister. But do we ever ask ourselves a more important question. What on earth is the United Kingdom's deputy prime minister for? The answer, as often in constitutional matters, is that nobody really knows. Yet the recently invented 'tradition' persists.

In 1942 Winston Churchill invented the then new role of 'deputy prime minister' for good reason. It was a reward for Labour's leader Clement Attlee and his support in the wartime coalition. The post then (as now) had a title but carried no salary, no formal duties, there is no official residence and no right to succeed the prime minister. It therefore makes no sense, except as a titular reward from a prime minister to a potential rival, disgruntled parliamentary colleague or in Attlee's case, recognition of a decent man bringing stability to a democratic government in time of war. After 1945, the title of deputy prime minister was often not formally applied. In the case of William Whitelaw, he was regarded as the 'de facto' deputy to prime minister Margaret Thatcher after her election victory in 1979. This was seen as a consolation prize, a non-job without a department. Lord Whitelaw was made a hereditary peer in 1983 and became a member of the House of Lords. That meant he could not succeed Mrs Thatcher (without renouncing his title and standing as an MP), nor could he deputise for her at Prime Minister's Questions in the Commons, nor was he ever likely to step in as prime minister in the event of some calamity. Mrs Thatcher famously and roguishly said that 'every prime minister needs a Willie', a comment that perhaps sums up a confusing attitude to the deputy prime minister's role in public life.

In 2021 Dominic Raab was declared Boris Johnson's deputy prime minister (again as a consolation prize) after being removed from the much more significant role (and real job) of Foreign Secretary. Back in 2020 Mr Raab, whose star at that time was rising, did actually fill in for the prime minister when Boris Johnson was struck down with coronavirus, but at the time Raab was not referred to as deputy prime minister. (Is any of this making sense? Not really. But – as we will see in detail in the next chapter – no one expects the British constitution to make sense.)

Like much at the higher reaches of British politics – and unlike, say, the role of vice president of the United States – the title of Britain's deputy prime minister exists if the prime minister says it exists. It is just another part of our political hocus pocus. Academics even disagree on who has actually been 'deputy prime minister', who has been called by that title, and who should be regarded as having fulfilled that role, even if they did not use the title. For Dominic Raab in 2020, it was a job without a title. For Raab in 2021 it was a title without a job. Looking for insight from some who have written scholarly works on the subject, it appears that politicians referred to as 'deputy prime minister' include those formally gazetted as such in Hansard; those in some other way 'officially' designated by the prime minister (whatever that means), and also those widely recognised by colleagues as deputy prime minister even if the title was not formally acknowledged; plus those second in ministerial ranking to the prime minister (although no one is entirely sure how that ranking is defined); and those who at some time chaired the cabinet and even those who (like Raab) took Prime Minister's Questions in the prime minister's absence. As the authors of a book on the subject put it: 'The post of deputy to the UK prime minister is perhaps the most mysterious in the British constitution, possessing "no set or binding role", "responsibility without power" and once not acknowledged to exist at all.'[13]

A category defined as 'the most mysterious in the British constitution' is like saying that an astronomical black hole has its own black hole. We are back to the mysteries of the eucharist, or if you prefer Schrödinger's politician – a person who constitutionally exists and who does not exist at the same time. The only thing that is truly clear – and some readers may find this charming – is that the invention of constitutional traditions like that of deputy prime minister remains one of Britain's oldest traditions. What is less charming is the incoherence such traditions bring to our public life. They enable a prime minister to change the United Kingdom's constitution in pursuit of personal political advantage – including side-lining a personal rival by assuaging his or her ego – with the prize of a non-job. Patronage is common to all political systems, but in Britain it is an expression of exceptionalism, the 'flexibility' that an 'unwritten' constitution offers a prime minister who has the authority of a healthy majority in parliament. This is not an 'elective dictatorship'. But it is a circular system, mutual backscratching. British prime ministers owe their authority to supportive Members of Parliament. Those supportive Members of Parliament owe their possibilities of promotion to the patronage of the prime minister. This is not the checks and balances that you might expect in a mature democracy. It is political symbiosis in a British system in which the question asked by the Roman poet Juvenal in *Satires* 2,000 years ago has no clear answer: *quis custodiet ipsos custodes*? Who guards the guardians themselves? In modern Britain that is a question to which there is no easy answer.

Pure Gold, Paper Money and The Black Book

The Whig historian Lord Macaulay called the United Kingdom's unwritten constitution 'pure gold' compared to the 'paper money' of lesser nations with written constitutions, like the United States. In the age of credit cards, Apple Pay and cryptocurrency the tradition of paying for goods and services with 'pure gold' is unknown to most British citizens, and that has been true since the end of the Victorian era. Robust critiques of the British system are also a well-known tradition extending back decades, even before Lord Macaulay wrote his eulogy to our (supposedly glorious) constitution. One informative critique of the weaknesses of the British system, the corruption of people in power through patronage and their dishonest relationships with money, dates from the high point of Britain's triumphant defeat of Napoleon at Waterloo in 1815. The first edition of John Wade's *The Black Book or Corruption Unmasked: Being an Account of Persons, Places, and Sinecures* – was also known as the 'Bible of the Reformers'. It was first published in 1820 and was an immediate sensation selling 50,000 copies. *The Black Book* is a scathing account of the unchecked corruption of the major institutions in England. Wade painstakingly uncovered legal, electoral and ecclesiastical abuses. These range from the activities of the East India Company to the 'Robbery of Charitable Foundations', 'Press-Restriction Bills' and the profits of the Bank of England. Wade wrote for the *Spectator*, and was hugely impatient of the obscurantism and ritual that somehow sanctified the 'pure gold' of how we do things in Britain. Instead of honesty and good governance, Wade argued that

> pageantry and show, the parade of crowns and coronets, of gold keys, sticks, white wands and black rods; of ermine and lawn, maces and wigs, are ridiculous when men become enlightened, when they have learned that the real object of government is to confer the greatest happiness on the people at the least expense.[14]

Criticising the sclerotic British system, as the optimistic utilitarian Wade did, and believing Britain is better than this, as Wade did, is itself another British tradition. But attempts at bringing about real change, from those radical complaints of 200 years ago, have not resulted in Wade's prediction of 'enlightened' leaders conferring 'the greatest happiness on the people at the least expense'. As for the pageantry and show Wade ridiculed in 1820, it was despised during much of the Victorian period, a time when the imperial expansion of Britain was admired as a model of competence if not always of humanity. But pageantry and show really came into their own in the television age. All that 'culture and history' so admired by modern Americans was reinvented for viewers as a significant British tradition to mask decline and failure.

The historian David Cannadine, in an essay on changes in perceptions of the British monarchy from Wade's time in the 1820s to the 1970s, insisted that 'the secular magic of monarchy' did not die out as Wade predicted with the 'enlightened' education of greater numbers of British people. Instead, Cannadine writes, 'The situation is the exact reverse.' Commentators by the end of the twentieth century spoke enthusiastically (although inaccurately) of 'all the pageantry and grandeur of a thousand-year-old tradition' and promoted the historically inaccurate idea that 'the English are particularly good at ceremonial'. These comments, Cannadine says, would have astonished Victorians and astounded John Wade, who retained his belief in progress. The liberal Conservative politician Ian Gilmour, who was Defence Secretary in Edward Heath's government, understood better than most why the modern British enthusiasm for pageantry erupted. In part it was the television age, when the once distant monarch in London could – like Trump on *The Apprentice* or Johnson on *Have I Got News For You* – enter our homes and give us a glimpse of something that seemed almost fantastical, 'The lives of the Royals'. Gilmour suggested that, 'Modern societies still need myths and ritual. A monarch and his family supply it.'[15] Gilmour was correct. These 'myths and ritual' may include the peripheral naughtiness of *The Sun*'s story of the dropping of the King's breeches, and the various myths, dramas and soap operas, including the obsessive tracking of the doings of 'Harry and Meghan', or the sordid sex life of Prince Andrew. The myths and rituals sell newspapers and books. In the UK Prince Harry's autobiography *Spare* sold half a million copies in the week after publication. TV viewers around the world turn to events like the funeral of Queen Elizabeth II or the Coronation of King Charles III. They draw tourists to gawp at Buckingham Palace and are a mainstay of the tabloids, especially *The Sun* which claims a weekly reach of 38 million people, and the *Daily Mail* titles which give *The Sun* a close run in terms of circulation.[16]

Wade's era 'when men become enlightened' has been postponed. In some ways we appear to have become more infantile. When *The Sun* showcased the 2022 state opening of parliament, one of the few royal rituals of real constitutional significance, they printed a picture of Prince Charles, standing in for Queen Elizabeth, who had mobility difficulties and could not attend. The photograph showed the heir to the throne staring at a crown sitting beside him with a headline that read 'I Hope I Did You Proud, Mummy'. Prince Charles was then seventy-three years old. The empty crown travelled to parliament solemnly seated in its own car. A photo opportunity like no other.

To extend David Cannadine's argument, what is evident here is that the more 'Global Britain' has diminished as a world power, the more pomp and circumstance we appear to enjoy, or at least tolerate, spiced with cheeky irreverence. The irreverence was much more pronounced in the years when Britain was still rising to become the preeminent world power. *The Times* reported on the death of George IV in 1830 in a manner unlikely to be tolerated in our own time: 'There never was an individual less regretted by his fellow creatures than this deceased King. What eye has wept for him? What heart has heaved one sob of unmercenary sorrow?'

The British National Anthem, 'God Save the Queen', was not even sung at Queen Victoria's coronation; and the *Illustrated London Evening News* of 1852 was quite clear that for a time John Wade was correct in regarding British (or English) pomp and circumstance as both 'ridiculous' and not very British: 'The English are said to be a people who do not understand shows or celebrations or the proper mode of conducting them... unlike the French and other nations of the continent, they have no real taste for ceremonial.'[17]

Even Walter Bagehot's witty 1894 description of the significance of Queen Victoria and the Prince of Wales would in modern times be difficult to imagine if it were applied to Queen Elizabeth II and

Prince Charles as he served his long royal apprenticeship. Bagehot wrote:

> Most people when they read that the Queen (Victoria) walked on the slopes at Windsor – that the Prince of Wales went to the Derby – have imagined that too much thought and prominence were given to little things. But they have been in error; and it is nice to trace how the actions of a retired widow and an unemployed youth become of such importance.

What the English of the Victorian period most certainly did understand was something much more important than pomp and royal show. They knew how to fix things when they went wrong. Although in yet another British tradition, it sometimes took our nineteenth-century predecessors a very long time to notice that years of 'muddling through' often end in disaster.

Bonfire of the Vanities

On the night of 16 October 1834 the Palace of Westminster was incinerated in the most spectacular conflagration in London since the Great Fire of 1666. Guy Fawkes could not destroy Westminster, but the failure to recognise and correct longstanding problems at the heart of the British political system did the trick. That October night workmen were despatched to get rid of old tally sticks. These were a traditional and obsolete – yes, those words again – accounting system using pieces of wood as a receipt for government income. The system originated in the Middle Ages. It was abolished in 1826. Nothing was done about the old sticks until eight years later when the parliamentary authorities finally got around to some house cleaning. Two cartloads of tally sticks were burned. The geriatric furnaces overheated and – with the exception of the medieval Great Hall – most of the Palace of Westminster burned down.

At last, the rulers of Britain got a grip. And quickly. In 1835 politicians on all sides of the House of Commons and in the Lords decided to build a new parliament building suitable for modern times in the capital of the world's greatest empire. They held a design competition. Here's how the official parliamentary history records what happened next:

> The 1835 competition to redesign the Palace was won by the Westminster-born architect, 40-year-old Charles Barry. Barry turned for assistance in his drawings for the competition to Augustus Welby Pugin, a gifted 23-year-old Catholic architect and draughtsman who had devoted himself entirely to the pursuit of Gothic architecture... Pugin was nevertheless known to have been displeased with the result of the work. As he famously remarked to an acquaintance, 'All Grecian, sir; Tudor details on a classic body.' However, neither man would see their creation completed as they both worked long hours and endlessly worried about every detail of the design and building of the Palace. It was not until 10 years after Barry's death in 1860 that the new Palace was completed, with his son Edward taking over. Pugin's fragile health suffered greatly from his exertions. He was committed to Bedlam [an asylum for the insane which is now the site of the Imperial War Museum] for a short period and died soon after in 1852.[18]

It is instructive for the United Kingdom in the 2020s to remember that a tradition of British indolence brought about – eventually – a catastrophe, a fire at the heart of government that literally brought the House down. Insanity, untimely death, plus a demonstration of British architectural genius followed, and the seat of government was reconstructed, though it took more than three decades to do it. The Victorians, having exhausted the alternatives, got on with the job. The credit goes to Members of Parliament who – faced with the smoking ruins – seized upon a solution and found two talented young men to create the glorious building we know today. But history is repeating itself. The decay in the Palace of Westminster right now is a reminder of our own collective insanity in failing to tackle the obvious structural problems in the buildings, and also in the creakingly dilapidated government systems the buildings contain:

> The Palace of Westminster is falling down. Literally. In the decade from 2009 to 2019 there were 14 recorded instances of masonry falling from the nineteenth century buildings. In 2018 a chunk of a stone angel the size of a football fell 70 metres from the Victoria tower into a garden below... Between 2017 and 2019... 19 fires were found (and extinguished) in the Commons and three in the Lords.[19]

Decay in a great building and in a great democracy becomes much more expensive to fix with every year of inaction and denial. By 2007, the cost of renovation and repair of the Palace of Westminster was put at £30 million a year. By 2018, after a decade of nothing much being done, the cost rose to £127 million a year. Once again nothing of significance was decided, and more than 40,000 maintenance problems were reported between 2017 and 2020. Some cosmetic work was done to repair Big Ben, at the cost of £80 million, but the most recent estimate of renovations needed in the Palace of Westminster puts the cost at a staggering £12 billion to prevent, in the words of the Institute for Government's Hannah White, 'a Notre Dame style fire rampaging through parliament' thereby ensuring that the temple of British democracy would become a scandalous symbol of the failures of Global Britain. It is not yet clear what the modern equivalent of incompetent destruction of obsolete tally sticks might be, but the very traditional failure to act when the problem is literally staring parliamentarians in the face is already obvious. In March 2021 a strategic review found that 'the 150 year old building is falling apart faster than it can be'.[20] Hannah White also noted that the British constitutional system is similarly falling apart faster than it can be fixed, and for the same reason. In constitutional terms you could say that a 'conflagration' of the United Kingdom is only a matter of time. And that raises an obvious question. Why is nothing done? Here's a clue: it's not the money.

The answer can be found in large part in the lack of strategic thinking that bedevils British politics. Strategic thinking, like that of Macmillan and Norman Brook in 1959, means thinking about the next generation. In the 2020s, when politicians are consumed by the next news cycle, the next day's headlines, a commitment to any full scale modernisation of the Palace of Westminster would mean (at best) that the current generation of politicians would have to move out and work in a modern structure without the glamour or the history of the Mother of Parliaments and perhaps even – heaven forfend! – outside London. It will take years. Politicians who recognise that they may be Members of Parliament for no more than a decade tend to prefer things as they are. The genteel decay of the structure is less inconvenient than the long-term hassle of actually doing something about it. (Similar arguments apply to constitutional change too.) There's also a tricky political problem. How do MPs explain to constituents and taxpayers why their own workplace needs to be fixed at the cost of billions of pounds, when the constituents' own lives and homes may be blighted by high food and energy prices and inflation?

Several different renovation plans were put before the House of Commons Commission in February 2020. All of them demanded a lot of work. Beyond a fire literally bringing the House down none of the hugely expensive schemes ever looked as if they would result in rapid action. The cheapest plan was for all the MPs to vacate the building. This was called 'a full decant' and would take from twelve to twenty years, with work costing £7–13 billion. A partial decant could take nineteen to twenty-eight years. If MPs insisted on staying put while the rebuilding work took place around them, engineers in February 2022 reported that 'Work to restore the Palace of Westminster to its full glory could take up to 76 years to complete and cost as much as £22 bn.'[21]

It is therefore not surprising that nothing has been decided and nothing much has been done beyond applying a few sticking plasters. The Palace of Westminster's physical decay mirrors the deterioration of the democratic institutions which function in and around it. The failings and dangers of both have been obvious for years. It will almost certainly take a conflagration for something significant to be done both architecturally and constitutionally. And that, as we saw, is also a British tradition.

PART THREE

Institutions and Constitutions

9

The British Constitution

I f you are British and have American friends you will notice that trans-Atlantic differences go a lot further than how to pronounce the word 'tomato'. One big difference is that when Americans talk about almost any serious subject, they end up making references to the US constitution. Constitutional discussions feature repeatedly on American TV news programmes, from gun control and the right to bear arms to abortion, taxes, states' rights, the executive powers of the presidency and a host of other matters. I'd almost say that any American with whom I have ever had any serious conversation, from the halls of Congress to gun shooting ranges in Texas or blues bars in Memphis to Black Lives Matter protesters in South Central Los Angeles, had an opinion about something important to them backed up by what he or she thinks the US constitution has to say on the subject. Britain is very different. Have you ever had a discussion about the British constitution? You what? Do you remember being entranced by folk on *Question Time* or *Newsnight* engagingly discussing the British constitution? Me neither. No one has a clue. I can think of no conversation I have ever had with any British person outside journalism, academia and politics (and mostly even inside those fields of human endeavour) who, unprompted, mentions the British constitution as a guide on how to solve problems. Or a guide to anything else. At best the British constitution is considered boring. It's something for geeks, lawyers and a few university professors. It's not for ordinary folk. The eyes glaze over, because British constitutional matters are considered arcane, irrelevant to our normal lives. Or at least that's how they are often presented. But think for a moment about the question we have asked repeatedly. Who benefits from this? Who benefits from the impressively impenetrable tedium of the British constitution that not only prevents discussion but also prevents change? The logical answer must be that constitutional dullness and impenetrability is to the advantage of those for whom the status quo is just fine. It allows them to prevent scrutiny of how they do the things they do. It also means that troublesome British citizens cannot easily do as Americans do and demand our 'constitutional rights' because we haven't got a clue what those two words really mean.

The hollowness of the British system of governance is disguised by deliberately obfuscatory language and peculiar rituals usually involving fancy dress. But the most dangerous conceit is that constitutional change in Britain is only for experts, not for the rest of us. The subliminal message of so many books and official government documents about the British system of governance is that it's something for the Illuminati, a peculiar freemasonry, intelligible to the Constitutional Chosen. That's not you or me. So, as part of this attempt to answer Elizabeth's question, I have talked with experts and constitutional reform campaigners and also read scholarly accounts of the British and other constitutions, including those of the United States, Germany and Russia. The issues at stake in Britain are too important to leave to experts, and I have no pretensions towards any special constitutional expertise myself. What I have done is to approach British constitutional commentaries as a literary critic would do. That means looking at the words to see if they are helpful and even if they make any sense. Unfortunately, very often, they don't. Some writings on the British constitution seem to be little more than cheerleading – 'Aren't we British clever! We can work the government machine without an instruction manual!' Some are elegant and rather beautiful, like the circles or whorls of Celtic art, but they turn and turn until they disappear into tautologies.

The result is that I have one theory and one unshakeable belief about the British constitution. The theory is that much of the confusion about constitutional matters in Britain is only in part accidental. It is often deliberate. Constitutional hocus pocus exists in order to conceal the accretion of power and the capacity for self-serving abuse from those who rise to the top. The unshakeable belief is that – even if my theory is disputed – in an advanced modern democracy like that of the United Kingdom no citizen should be bored or confused by the way our country is run. We should instead be outraged by how badly the results have been in the twenty-first century. In that belief, at least, I am in good company.

In the aftermath of the 2016 Brexit referendum, the veteran Scottish journalist Neal Ascherson argued that the British constitution isn't just exceptional and impenetrable. It doesn't even exist. It's not only unfit for purpose, it's a myth. Ascherson wrote:

> Unlike most countries the UK has no constitution – and so through the centuries without a written constitution people sort of knew what was expected of them, and what was over the top. Why change that? The answer is: because our governments are growing lawless. The idiotic doctrine of parliamentary sovereignty – the late seventeenth-century transfer of absolutism from kings endowed with divine right to an elected assembly – excludes any firmly entrenched distribution of rights. Popular sovereignty in Britain is a metaphor, not an institution.[1]

Ascherson's claim that 'our governments are growing lawless' will be examined a little later, although perhaps the evidence of that is already clear. We will also explore the idea that 'people sort of knew what was expected of them' through what has been called by the constitutional historian Peter Hennessy the 'Good Chap' theory of government. Hennessy, somewhat tongue in cheek suggests the United Kingdom has traditionally been governed by Good Chaps who, if they step out of line, 'do the decent thing' and resign. The idea that the British government is 'growing lawless' means Good Chaps are in short supply. And if, as Ascherson contends, the United Kingdom's constitution is merely a 'metaphor' then the definition of a metaphor is something which is not literally applicable. If the Ten Commandments were metaphors they would not be a series of instructions about how to behave. If the Highway Code was a metaphor it wouldn't help us with our ability to drive safely. If the same is true about the UK constitution then it cannot be a useful rule book for British democracy. And it's not, of course, even a book. It's at best a few polite hints that perhaps those in power might occasionally bear in mind, if that's not too much trouble. Either way the evidence that constitutional matters are a tedious turn-off for most British people is abundantly clear.

In 2011, the referendum on something as significant as changing the Westminster FPTP voting procedures to a modern, fairer and more democratic system attracted considerably fewer than half of the 45 million registered British voters of that time. Of the 19 million who did vote, fewer than half of those wanted to change FPTP – a system which, it bears repeating, only one other national legislature in Europe uses, Belarus. Fewer than a quarter of British voters being interested in how their votes count (or don't count) in elections is not an endorsement of a healthy democracy. Yet judging from social media, TV and radio talk shows and letters to newspapers the urgency of constitutional failure is now slowly overcoming the traditional British somnolence and the glazed eyes that used to appear at the mention of the C-word. Perhaps we are beginning to recognise at last that constitutional failure is the most significant underlying answer to the question of 'why things are so... so shit'.

For some writers on the British constitution, belief in its glories trumps a reasoned view of how things work in reality. I admire greatly the work of constitutional scholars such as Anthony King, Peter Hennessy and Vernon Bogdanor, the constitutional lawyer Sam Fowles, and others quoted in these pages. But many constitutional commentaries revolve around a kind of sonorous vacuity; the bold enunciation of vague principles more appropriate for a religion than a users' guide to a modern, secular twenty-first-century state. In a world of believers, Ascherson is boldly asserting that there is no God. This chapter therefore begins with the constitutional implications of Brexit, not as an attempt to refight the referendum but as a means of understanding why the mechanism through which that referendum took place was always destined to cause the biggest constitutional mess any of us can remember. The make-it-up-as-we-go-along-and-pretend-it's-a-tradition constitutional charade proves that the United Kingdom needs a functioning, intelligible, relevant instruction manual for governing a complex, wealthy modern European democracy. If we cannot achieve that, then neither can we maintain balanced and respected institutions in our public life. Whatever the British constitution has done for the people of this country in the past, it is not an impossible dream to hope that Britain in the twenty-first century may one day become more democratic in the way we choose our elected politicians than Belarus. Brexit was even worse for traditional British democracy.

Make It Up, Call It a Plan

Leaving the European Union was never a salient issue in any British General Election until the Brexit vote. For years around election time pollsters asked voters what was on their minds. Few ever mentioned Europe. There was no popular demand to have a vote and no groundswell of opinion demanding that Britain should separate itself from the European Union. That changed in 2016. Just such a possibility suddenly found its way on to a ballot paper, without even the most ardent Brexit supporters agreeing among themselves what it meant. For Neal Ascherson (and for me) asking people to vote on leaving the European Union without defining the proposed terms of leaving, or at least offering a second referendum on those terms once they had been negotiated, proved to be a complacent error of judgement. That belief was true even for some of those in favour of Brexit, including Paul Goodman of Conservative Home: 'Voting to leave the EU was buying a pig in a poke,' Goodman admitted when celebrating the third anniversary of the Brexit deal. 'People couldn't give their verdict on a deal because none had been negotiated. This turned out to have baleful consequences. David Cameron's government willed the end of a referendum without preparing the means for leaving. This was irresponsible.'[2]

Irresponsible, yes. But not 'unconstitutional' because that term – as Anthony King and others argue – has almost no meaning in the United Kingdom beyond the idea that you don't like something and find it – as Goodman did in this case – wrongheaded or stupid. Only after the Brexit vote – not before – was the most important question asked, 'What does it mean?' David Cameron quit as prime minister rather than answer that question. We can avoid refighting the details of Brexit, but in terms of the existence or otherwise of the British constitution it's important to understand why there was no requirement for a prime minister to spell out in detail the implications of what people might be voting for in one of the biggest political decisions of our lifetimes. There's no requirement because a prime minister can do more or less what he or she wishes within the law, however 'irresponsible' it may seem, and laws about the powers of governments can be changed by the governments themselves. There are no significant constitutional rules limiting the freedom of a prime minister to ask voters to decide a vague question, claim it is 'advisory', quit the stage after losing, and then for everyone to be told they need to accept that what was once 'advisory' is now compulsory. Brexit became 'binding', a democratic mandate so strict that anyone who disputes it in detail was denounced as an enemy of democracy, thwarting the supposed 'will of the people'. That's how having a 'flexible' constitution works, although a synonym for flexible means that things can be bent. Rather than find himself stuck in tortuous negotiations with the European Union and the unbearable fractiousness of his own divided party, David Cameron told his Number 10 staff, with all the wisdom of a ten-year-old ordered to tidy his brother's bedroom: 'Why should I do all the hard sh*t for someone else, just to hand it over to them on a plate?'

Then the real rows began. Dominic Grieve, the Conservative former Attorney General, was absolutely clear: 'It is the case that all referendums are advisory – that's absolutely, abundantly clear.'[3]

Another Conservative former cabinet member, John Redwood, spoke for the ardent Brexiters. He was equally clear: 'This was not an advisory referendum.'[4]

The dispute went to the courts. Judges of the High Court sided with Grieve, affirming that in our representative democracy 'a referendum on any topic can only be advisory for the lawmakers in Parliament.' The House of Commons original briefing paper on the bill authorising the referendum also clearly demonstrated that Redwood was completely wrong. Redwood is a Fellow of All Souls who stood unsuccessfully twice for the leadership of the Conservative Party yet he appears to have been unable to comprehend the wording of the government briefing paper on the referendum bill which clearly states that it 'does not contain any requirement for the UK government to implement the results of the referendum'.[5]

Reflecting on this period the constitutional scholar Sir Anthony Seldon told me his misgivings about the entire process:

> Both sides [Leave and Remain] were putting out information that clearly was not properly fact-checked. The referendum was a dreadfully composed test on the most important issue in post-war British history. The risk when you hold a referendum is that it's so close. Talking to people today [2022] they still don't know what they were voting for and what the implications were. We will look back at the Brexit vote as a massive moment in British history, far more significant than the transition of the monarch. It was, by any measure, a dreadful contest that took place.

Seldon then insisted that treating the advisory vote as if it were mandatory 'ushered in the biggest domestic upheaval that this country has seen at the same time as the territorial integrity of the United Kingdom is at threat with Northern Ireland possibly uniting (with the Irish Republic) and Scotland breaking away'.[6]

Seldon's comments were uncannily prefigured two generations earlier by Margaret Thatcher. Four years before she became prime minister, and faced with the prospect of Harold Wilson's referendum on the UK remaining in the European Economic Community, in 1975 Thatcher made a carefully argued intervention in the House of Commons on the impact that a referendum would have on the British constitution:

> To use the referendum device at all is to ask the question: to what category of measure should referenda apply?... The implications for parliamentary sovereignty are profound... If the government cannot agree, gone is the discipline of resignation, gone is the principle of accountability to parliament. The new doctrine is to pass the buck to the people.[7]

Mrs Thatcher was channelling several centuries of British parliamentary tradition here, including that of Edmund Burke, about the sovereignty of parliament in a representative democracy. Put simply, we vote for MPs. MPs decide things. If we as voters don't like what they decide we get rid of them at the next election – but between elections MPs do not keep asking us for our opinions on specific issues through referendums. At this point you may conclude that in 2016 the British constitution was finally exposed for what it has been for years – flexible only in the ways in which a prime minister can manipulate it, and otherwise deliberately incomprehensible to the citizens of our democracy. It's instructive to see how very different the rules were on the other side of the Brexit argument. By that I do not mean those campaigning to remain in the EU. I mean the constitution of the European Union itself.

The European Union Constitution

First of all, the EU has a written constitution. That constitution is very clear about the mechanism for any nation choosing to leave. It says: 'The Constitution is divided into four parts, explaining respectively the constitutional architecture of the European Union, the Union's Charter of Fundamental Rights, the policies and operation of the Union and, general and final provisions. Part I is the core constitutional part.'

The EU constitution explains, very simply, how it came into being, with British experts playing a part in drafting this complex constitutional document:

> The Treaty establishing a Constitution for Europe was adopted by the 25 European Union Heads of State and Government in Brussels on 17 and 18 June 2004. Referendums are to be held in at least twelve of the 25 Member States. The European Constitution, if ratified by the Member States, will replace the current EU treaties with a single, new text. The main objectives of the Constitution are... to simplify the overlapping series of Treaties and Protocols providing the current legal constitution for Europe; to enhance and streamline decision-making in the Union; and to enable citizens to feel more part of the European Union. Critics of the Constitution point out that, compared to many existing national constitutions (e.g. the 4,600 word US Constitution), the European Constitution is very long, at around 265 pages and over 60,000 words in its English text. Nevertheless it remains considerably shorter and less complex than the existing set of treaties that it consolidates.

When the document explains that it was to be ratified by the citizens of many member states it means that those citizens, if they had any doubts about what the constitution really meant could (not very joyously, one assumes) read all 60,000 words and make up their own minds Yea or Nay. For all its flaws the union of democracies known as the EU wanted its own guide to how it should work. The historian of Britishness, Linda Colley, noted that around the world major countries having a written constitution is one of the signs of actually being a democracy: 'With only one major exception no polity has achieved what passes for full democracy without generating some kind of written constitution. That exception is of course the United Kingdom.' Colley then goes on to say: 'The flattering notion that the British were masters of good government helps to account for an apparent paradox. Although Britain has no written constitution, British lawyers, civil servants and diplomats have been conspicuously active in writing constitutions for other countries.'[8]

British constitutional experts did help write constitutions for other countries all around the world, from post-war Germany to numerous former British colonies and others. Yet those same experts were never called upon to provide such a good service for our own country. That's because we always considered ourselves better than the rest, even though the 'flattering notion that the British were masters of good government' has not worn well in the twenty-first century. No other country anywhere in the world looks at the British system of governance and says, 'That's what we want.' If imitation is the sincerest form of flattery, we are not flattered by anyone's desire to copy our 'exceptional' constitutional arrangements.

In terms of a constitution, then, the contrast between the 60,000 words which brought about major changes in two dozen European Union countries and the sixteen words of the Brexit referendum that brought about profound change in the United Kingdom could not be more obvious. Here's what the British voted on in 2016. Everything beyond this short sentence is merely opinion and argument:

'Should the United Kingdom remain a member of the European Union or leave the European Union?'

Nowhere in those sixteen words was there any guidance on how rapidly Brexit should begin, how long it would take nor in outline what it would look like. There was not even any guidance on the necessity or otherwise of implementing the result. But then, following the kind of constitutional mess Margaret Thatcher had predicted back in 1975, the British political class panicked. The government decided that what was sold as 'advisory' was now politically impossible to ignore. It became 'binding' even though whatever 'it' was could not be agreed. Listening to politicians talk, it reminded me of the notorious words of a candidate in a California Senate race decades ago. 'The people have spoken,' Dick Tuck said after losing in 1962. 'The bastards.'

Mrs Thatcher's wisdom was ignored, but she was proved correct. The principle of accountability to parliament had been abandoned. It is not fanciful to assume that 17 million Leave voters had almost as many as 17 million versions of what those sixteen words might mean for them and their families. What happened next was that both the Conservative and Labour parties deferred to the 'will of the people' by making up, in their own best interests, various versions of what 'the people' really meant. And this, once more, was just how the British system 'works'. An advisory vote on an unclear premise became a political and moral imperative. We were climbing Kilimanjaro, except that some were still yearning for Everest and Cameron's successor as prime minister, Theresa May, was taking a short walk alone in the Hindu Kush. Sir Anthony Seldon, who had the inside track on what was going on in government at the time, told me that Mrs May was in tears at the Brexit result and said to her joint chief of staff Nick Timothy that, 'The ones who voted for Brexit will be the ones who suffer the most.' In a meeting with the European Movement in Canterbury in March 2023 the former Attorney General Dominic Grieve said that prophecy turned out to be true. Academic research came to a similar conclusion. Older, poorer and less well-educated voters often chose to vote Leave:

Research published to date has concentrated on the high probability of voting 'Leave' among households living on less than £20,000 a year. The demographic that voted for Brexit was skewed towards older people rather than younger and poorer rather than richer... support for Leave was 30 percentage points higher among those with GCSE qualifications or below than it was for people with a degree.[9]

In terms of the British constitution (or lack thereof) it would be useful to understand why the two leading political parties in the United Kingdom did not mention before we voted that they would be bound to implement the result of a referendum that was clearly described in government publications as advisory. The answer, as it often is with British political disasters – appeasement of Hitler in the

1930s, Suez in 1956 – is profound arrogance and complacency plus a bit of political cowardice. Neither Labour nor the Conservatives thought that Brexit would actually happen. Even ardent Brexit campaigners thought a Yes vote unlikely. When it did happen no one dared to stand up to what appeared to be the 'will of the people', however fuzzily expressed and however flawed the basic premise. The constitutional scholar Peter Hennessy makes this ludicrous situation seem like a tradition. Unfortunately, it is:

> I have long suspected that one of the cardinal rules of the British way of government is that panic must always be portrayed as poise and desperate improvisation as the pragmatic product of centuries of wisdom and experience. 'Muddling through' is a polite expression of such realities.[10]

It's the Constitution, Stupid. Or Is It the Stupid Constitution?

When Theresa May eventually did come up with a response to 'What does Brexit mean?' many in parliament, including those in her own party, did not like her answer. We could leave the EU 'without a deal' one UKIP stalwart told me in a TV interview, like 'leaving your locker keys at the bar and walking out of the golf club'. It was an image repeated time after time, and very revealing of how ineptly any of this had been thought through. Walking out of the golf club in a huff was for some Option One, also called a 'No Deal' or a 'Hard Brexit'. Options Two, Three, Four, Five all the way up to Option Infinity were defined as less drastic. You could tell that 'panic must always be portrayed as poise' by the camouflage of repetitive constitutional tautologies, always a sign that no one really knew what they were talking about. The slogan 'Leave means Leave' gave way to 'Brexit means Brexit'. Whatever that meant, Theresa May insisted, 'We're going to make a success of it.' 'It' remained ineffable, undefined, the Holy Grail. Mrs May was rebuked by the European Commission President Jean-Claude Juncker for her simplistic rhetoric. Leaving a trading relationship with 450 million other people was not at all, Juncker said, like 'leaving a golf club'. Juncker was correct.

May's successor, Boris Johnson had a marginally better slogan, 'Get Brexit Done' but it is a slogan not a policy. Yet again Brexit remained just too good for coherent explanation. Successive British political leaders were falling not only into the trap Margaret Thatcher had pointed out but into the even worse hole in basic common sense spotted by that other Conservative prime minister Harold Macmillan: 'It would help us to get a little way on the road if we had a clearer idea of where we wanted to go.' Perhaps more alarming for the government was the analysis of the veteran British diplomat Sir Ivan Rogers. He tried to explode the pretence that Brexit was an event. It could never be such a thing. It was always going to be a process, and therefore the referendum risked becoming a 'neverendum', constantly being refought and relitigated. Sir Ivan was proved to be correct. But this was a period when heretics, especially well-meaning well-informed government advisers, were being burned at the stake.[11]

And that brings us back to Neal Ascherson's argument about our non-existent constitution. It is difficult to imagine any other profession – business? medicine? education? – in which a decision of the magnitude of Brexit would be taken based on 'rules' that were simply made up on the fly and then changed. In constitutional terms all the United Kingdom has is the political equivalent of situational ethics, the idea that the morality of right or wrong does not exist. There are no absolutes and what is right depends on the situation you face. But with Brexit we were not even told in advance anything of what that situation might look like. Two doctors who happened to be MPs, the Conservative Sarah Wollaston and the Labour MP Paul Williams, seized on this point. They likened the British constitutional process over Brexit to a surgeon performing an operation on a patient without telling them what it involved: 'To proceed without informed consent would not only be grossly unethical, it would also place the blame for the unintended consequences squarely at the feet of all those politicians who allowed it to happen.'[12]

Ordinary voters with scientific and medical backgrounds made the same point, exposing constitutional failure and double dealing. If we agreed to the principle of amputation of our European limb, no one mentioned that it would go from being advisory to compulsory, nor how painful it might be. Constitutional vagueness was our only anaesthetic.

> If a surgeon performed an operation on a patient without fully informed consent, knowingly used inaccurate data about the likely outcome, and then had no idea how to proceed after the initial incision, they would be struck off the medical register and not allowed to practise further. Isn't it time politicians too were held properly accountable for their individual actions?[13]

The flaw in this argument from the emeritus professor of medicine at Sheffield University Tony Weetman is of course that surgeons are regulated not merely by the Hippocratic Oath to do no harm but also by a General Medical Council rule book or code of conduct which if breached may cost them their career. British politicians do not work under circumstances of such rigour and constitutional clarity. Devoid of any discussion about constitutional principles, beyond the making-it-up-as-we-go-along Westminster traditions, British voters in good faith, thought they had voted For or Against a simple referendum proposition. The result was a tedious, embarrassing and at times infuriating mess of political, economic and constitutional wrangles. Of course plenty of other countries have constitutional wrangles too – the United States most obviously. But in the United Kingdom we were having a constitutional wrangle involving a constitution that – we can surely agree – if it exists at all, certainly does not exist in the manner in which the EU's own constitution of 60,000 words does, or the 4,500 words of the US constitution, or the General Medical Council's rules for surgeons. Margaret Thatcher's critique kept coming back to haunt us. Parliament, we were told, was 'sovereign'. But what did that mean any more? Parliament had conceded its decision-making power to 'the people' without the people agreeing precisely what that meant. And 'the people' in Scotland and Northern Ireland were a very different lot of people who definitely wished to remain in the EU. No thought in any of this was given to the disunity of the United Kingdom or indeed to much else either.

Then came the worst heresy of all. Some of us refused to accept this nonsense. I have never been a member of a political party but I joined with the Conservative MP Sarah Wollaston, and others formerly aligned with the Conservative and Labour parties plus those (like me) of no party affiliation to be part of the short-lived Change UK campaign. We had only one demand – a second referendum to ratify or reject the terms of any Brexit deal, once we knew what those terms were. No more buying a pig in a poke. But we failed. The prospect that Brexit could be overturned by another 'People's Vote' was too scary for those most in favour of leaving the European Union. The result was a series of political machinations brought to an end in December 2019 when Boris Johnson won his 'stonking' parliamentary majority in a General Election, with slightly less than 44 per cent of the vote. That returns us to the key point. What does the British constitution say about any of this? – assuming that Ascherson is wrong, and that a constitution, a series of documents and principles able to be understood by mere mortals, actually does exist.

A Constitutional Reformation?

The good news is that the British constitution does indeed exist. Sort of. The bad news is that reading through what some constitutional scholars say about it encourages empathy for illiterate peasants in Germany trying to make sense of the Reformation. Some English constitutional writing really is like being instructed by a priesthood of Illuminati. A learned and very direct response to Neal Ascherson appeared in *London Review of Books*. It came from a distinguished legal scholar, Sir Stephen Sedley, a former judge of the Court of Appeal of England and Wales and visiting professor at the University of Oxford. He offered this – dare I say, traditional – rebuke to Ascherson's assertion that under the British constitution no one knows who is in charge.

Sir Stephen wrote:

It is the Crown that is in charge, functioning through three separate but interlocking institutions: parliament, the courts and the executive. This paradigm long antedates the Tudors. It is depicted around 1300 in an illuminated manuscript showing Justinian on his imperial throne handing his legal code with his right hand to a kneeling lawyer and the sword of secular authority with his left hand to a kneeling knight.[14]

So, there we have it. Ascherson's government by metaphor has turned into a distinguished legal scholar's government by paradigm. You may judge for yourselves how helpful in our current predicament a pre-Tudor paradigm with roots in the years 'around 1300' may be. In the early fourteenth century, obviously, the United Kingdom did not exist. The Scots, Welsh and Irish were resistant to the charms represented by England. Most common English folk spoke early Middle English with a vocabulary based on Anglo-Saxon and Norse in the north of England. Anglo-Norman French was spoken among the ruling classes. But it is notable that if the Justinian in question is (as I assume) Justinian I 'the Great', the Byzantine Emperor from 527 to 565, then he is best known for his ambition of 'renovatio imperii' – the restoration or renewal of the Empire. Here was another leader who weaponised nostalgia, wanting to 'take back control' and 'Make Byzantium (or Rome) Great Again'. This may appeal to some constitutional scholars but, I would respectfully suggest, is of limited utility in deciding what to do about governments that have become 'lawless' in the twenty-first century. And – at the risk of disappearing down that recurring rabbit hole – what, if anything, does Sedley's return to the trope 'the Crown is in charge' mean in a constitutional monarchy in the twenty-first century? Few would doubt that Sir Stephen, a distinguished jurist, is correct in his description of the British constitution as being rooted in pre-Tudor English laws and customs, but in what sense is any of this generally 'understood' or even relevant to our current predicament? In what real sense is King Charles III, emblematic of the institution of 'the Crown', in charge of anything when, as we saw, he cannot even decide to go to a climate conference without approval? And if by the Crown we mean – and we do seem in reality to mean – mostly the executive, the government, then this circular constitutional argument – as usual – disappears up its own fundament.

The differences between Ascherson (the British constitution is unintelligible nonsense, deliberately obscure to stop people asking questions) and Sedley (the constitution is glorious and connects us to medieval England and with a Byzantine emperor) are nothing new. Nor is the sense that the 'Crown in charge' or the 'royal prerogative' are convenient phrases to paper over the cracks in a system where, as Ascherson argues, no one knows who is really in charge.

What is new is the mess we now find ourselves in and Ascherson's sense of lawlessness in government. But even that was predictable. It was predicted, at least in principle if not in detail, by the left-wing Labour MP Tony Benn three decades ago. In a series of BBC Radio programmes in the 1990s the constitutional historian Peter Hennessy – he of the Good Chap theory – interviewed leading thinkers of the day. With Benn he expanded on the dangers to democracy inherent within the British constitution, and the ideas floated by the Conservative peer Lord Hailsham. Benn and Hennessy reflected that phrases including the 'Crown in charge' and the 'royal prerogative' were vacuous terms rolled out to excuse anything the prime minister demanded. It is (of course) a tradition.

Benn said:

Every prime minister has grossly abused the powers of the Crown. [Clement] Attlee invited the Americans here, built the [nuclear] bomb without telling parliament. This isn't unique to the present era. It goes right back within my lifetime and probably even further... Power corrupts the Commons, You may come in with strong ideas. Within a week or two you realise that if you're going to get on you've got to please your leader... we do have a craven House of Commons... because the patronage of the Crown has spread like a virus into the party system.

The words 'royal prerogative' and 'patronage of the Crown', are used, in Benn's view, to dress up secrecy, allow executive power without obvious restraint and avoid accountability. Secrecy meant that MPs cannot know what they do not know. In that case they cannot do anything about it. And often they really do not know, as Benn noted:

You can't question what you don't know, and the Prerogative is the power that surrounds everything with barbed wire and klieg lights and mines the area. So the Commons, even if it wanted to question, could not know what it wanted to question because of the Prerogative... And if parliament isn't allowed to know what the Crown is doing through its ministers, the public doesn't know. And if the public doesn't know, they can't reflect their view in elections.[15]

Margaret Thatcher – hardly a political soulmate of Tony Benn – appeared to go some way towards agreement with him in her critique of plebiscitary democracy and the weakening of parliamentary sovereignty. There are two basic principles at stake – information and power. An uninformed democracy – either through MPs being kept away from secret information or citizens voting for something completely undefined like leaving the European Union – cannot be democratic. Turkeys probably would choose not to vote for playing the role they traditionally play at Christmas if they were properly informed; but if they are fed and watered sufficiently, they may not notice until it is too late. And then the squawking begins. Parliament cannot be 'sovereign' if it is fed nonsense and kept ignorant. Members of Parliament, especially those who are uninformed, are subject to the whims of a prime minister while forced to conform to those whims in the name of party loyalty. And this is just how the system works, apparently. But – again that nagging question – works for whom?

'Nobody Knows Who Is Ultimately in Charge'

Sir Stephen Sedley's other major point is worth thinking through. It is the traditional idea that somehow 'the Crown' is 'in charge' through 'three separate but interlocking institutions': parliament, the courts and the executive. British constitutional experts love their trinities. But admiration for those 'three separate but interlocking institutions' leads to one obvious question. What does any of this actually mean? Why are we in thrall to the idea that being governed by geometric metaphors – something which is 'not literally applicable' – is better than a system of governance with at least a basic rule book? Can we at least agree that the idea that 'the Crown' is 'in charge', sanctified by traditions dating back to a fourteenth-century illustration of a sixth-century Byzantine emperor, is of limited practical value in a twenty-first-century United Kingdom that only flickered into existence as 'Great Britain' in the seventeenth century and may be flickering out of existence before too long?

Can we also agree that we have a constitutional system few citizens understand – and few among us even try to do so? St Anselm was correct that faith may precede understanding, but once faith is lost – and faith in the British system of governance has certainly been lost – then without understandable rules and fundamental constitutional principles, faith in our democracy is unlikely to return. Voters may increasingly begin to suspect along with Ascherson that in reality we do not have a constitution at all. We have instead a con trick. It is based on admiration for a set of rules declared 'constitutional' or 'traditional' when they work to the advantage of those in power, and called 'flexible' when those in power need to change or remove them. This happens under the magic wand known as 'the Crown', the 'royal prerogative', or some other unquestioned phrase that signifies untrammelled executive privilege. Thatcher, Hailsham, Benn, Ascherson and others of widely different political views, see clearly the dangers in all this. In the wrong hands what passes for the British constitution is an instrument for potentially unlimited abuse. And we have already seen plenty of evidence of 'wrong hands' on the levers of power. That is where Britain now finds itself, although at this point we also need to understand why having a written constitution is no guarantee of good governance. There is no point in pretending there are easy answers.

The Rule Book for a State and the Good Chap Theory

University College London's Constitution Unit offers a simple definition: 'A constitution is the rule book for a state. It sets out the fundamental principles by which the state is governed.' In Britain rules are written down as Acts of Parliament or laws, but there is no one single document, no Basic Law as in Germany, no rule book. Any new British parliament can therefore rewrite the rules or laws created by its predecessors, without the fuss of constitutional change observed in other nations, including the United States where constitutional reform is complex and highly unusual. The US constitution has been amended twenty-seven times in 250 years, but the first ten amendments were added to it in the eighteenth century. They constitute the 'Bill of Rights' including the right to bear arms and the right not to incriminate oneself (by 'taking the Fifth Amendment'). The most recent amendment was in 1992 and it is relatively trivial, about the pay of members of Congress. Common to all democracies are constitutional 'conventions', precedents, traditions and norms of generally accepted behaviour. One convention in the UK is that a government minister caught out deliberately lying to parliament should resign. Such conventions are sometimes treated as if they were rules, but here again they may be changed, amended, adapted or ignored.

Peter Hennessy's Good Chap theory historically did often seem to hold true. The Foreign Secretary Lord (Peter) Carrington and two other Foreign Office ministers, Humphrey Atkins and Richard Luce, resigned in 1982 for failing to anticipate the Argentinian invasion of the Falkland Islands. It wasn't their fault, but a Good Chap does the right thing. But what happens when Good Chaps are in short supply and replaced by Not-So-Good-Men-And-Women who break conventions and ignore traditional norms of behaviour? The damage can be severe. Not having a 'written' or codified constitution comes with special problems when people in positions of power misbehave, as the veteran British Conservative politician and former government minister Kenneth Clarke observed in his own inimitable fashion. He referred once more to Lord Hailsham and the idea of Britain as an 'elective dictatorship' and nodded towards Peter Hennessy's Good Chap theory. Lord Clarke argued:

> We have relied for too long on a Victorian ideal of what we used to call 'decent chaps' doing the right thing to keep our constitutional principles intact. We have got to the point where we need a serious written constitution. We need to restore the strengths of the Commons and the Lords by putting their powers into statutory reforms. We are at the absurd point where it is up to the government whether extremely contentious pieces of legislation get to be debated at all... We are now getting dangerously close to the 'elected dictatorship' that Lord Hailsham, the former Lord Chancellor, warned us about half a century ago. He quite rightly identified it as the underlying risk of a totally unwritten constitution.[16]

But written constitutions have their problems too, of course. A codified, easily accessible written constitution is no guarantee that Ken Clarke's 'decent chaps' will observe conventions of good behaviour. They may turn out to be rather nasty chaps after all.

And bad people in power behave... badly. Constitutions, written or otherwise, may not be able to stop them. Two very different written constitutional settlements, that of the United States and Putin's Russia, point to the difficulties.

Why 'Norms of Behaviour' Matter

In Washington DC tourists can visit the Rotunda for the Charters of Freedom in the National Archives Museum where the original Declaration of Independence, the Constitution of the United States and the Bill of Rights are displayed. You can Google these documents and read them at home. They are truly inspiring. But nowhere does the United States constitution specify that a losing politician in a presidential election should concede gracefully or indeed concede at all, and yet that has always been a hugely important convention in sanctifying the American election process. In 2000, after a hotly disputed count in Florida, a state with a large number of Electoral College votes, vice president Al Gore eventually conceded defeat to George W. Bush. It was a very bitter pill for Gore. Winning Florida would have handed him the presidency and changed American history. He was, in the end, a Good Chap, and in an important moment for American democracy Bush entered the White House with – eventually – Gore's blessing. The unwritten norms of good behaviour were preserved. But in the November 2020 presidential election Donald Trump notoriously refused to concede to Joe Biden. He insisted that the election had been 'stolen' by Biden and the Democrats. By January 2021 mayhem ensued. Trump inspired the 'Stop the Steal' invasion of the US Capitol by a MAGA mob.

Having a written constitution did not stop Trump or the mob. But it did in the end make both accountable. Some MAGA protesters were jailed. Numerous investigations into Trump's activities, including his tax affairs, continue at the time of writing. US law will take its course, and the constitutional principle that no one is above the law appears to be intact. But having a written constitution did not prevent the collapse of democracy in Weimar Germany in the 1930s, or the imposition of authoritarian rule in 1990s Peru, or Hugo Chavez in Venezuela, military dictatorships in Chile or Argentina, or increasing authoritarianism in Brazil, India, Poland, Hungary and Turkey. Most strikingly Vladimir Putin's Russia has an excellent constitution. Article 29 of the post-Soviet Russian constitution is admirably clear: 'Everyone shall be guaranteed the freedom of ideas and speech... The freedom of mass communication shall be guaranteed. Censorship shall be banned.' Article 31 reads: 'Citizens of the Russian Federation shall have the right to assemble peacefully, without weapons, hold rallies, meetings and demonstrations, marches and pickets.'

Putting all this to the test, on 27 July, 2019, a seventeen-year-old woman, Olga Misik, attended one of the peaceful Moscow rallies 'For Fair Elections'. When we interviewed Olga for *The Big Steal* podcast series that I presented on Putin's crimes, Olga told us that she was so inspired by her country's written constitution that she decided to read sections aloud in public at the rally. She reminded Russian people of their rights in front of a large group of Putin's police in full riot gear. It did not go well. Olga's constitutional right to 'assemble peacefully' – or even to mention those constitutional rights – was cut short. The riot police carried her off. She was sentenced to a long period of house arrest.

What these accounts show is that no system is perfect or free from abuse. Whatever is written down in a constitution, or whatever in Britain may be understood as a convention, may or may not be regarded as worth the paper it is written on (or not written on) depending upon the behaviour of those in power. The ultimate question for a democracy is whether a rule breaker can be held to account through robust checks and balances in the system. In Britain in 2020 we had a much more genteel version of rule-bending or breaking, but rather than holding the person doing the bending or breaking the rules to account, the first casualties were not the rule breakers. They were the Good Chaps – the Ethics Advisers and outspoken civil servants. This is what Neal Ascherson meant by insisting that constitutional change is necessary in the UK 'because our governments are growing lawless'. He is right.

Boris Johnson's first Ethics Adviser Sir Alex Allan quit in November 2020. He did so because the 'convention' that a minister should resign if found in breach of the Ministerial Code was not observed, and that convention was not enforced by Boris Johnson. As prime minister, Johnson was the only person who could in practice enforce the code. He broke with convention by choosing not to do so.

Home Secretary Priti Patel had been accused of bullying her civil servants. Sir Alex Allan reported to Boris Johnson that bullying was indeed the case and the Ministerial Code had therefore been breached.

Ms Patel, a powerful senior government minister (as Home Secretary she was in charge of 'law and order') felt no obligation to resign. Her boss the prime minister shielded her from blame and refused to fire her. And so it transpired that it was the Ethics Adviser himself – a Good Chap – who felt compelled to quit when his advice about bad conduct was not taken seriously. In the Johnson administration the fox was now in charge of the chicken coop. The pattern was repeated two years later. You could almost say it became a tradition.

In 2022 Sir Alex's successor Lord Geidt quit after Prime Minister Johnson was yet again unwilling to observe some previously accepted norms of behaviour. That was particularly egregious because Johnson himself was one of those who misbehaved. The British system allows a prime minister latitude to be judge and jury of his own conduct. The story is depressingly familiar to most of us. In January 2022 Mr Johnson was accused of rule breaking at least eighteen times in connection with 'bring your own booze' parties in Downing Street during the coronavirus lockdown when the laws his own government had implemented were broken. Fined with a fixed penalty notice as a result of a police investigation into the Number 10 lockdown parties, Boris Johnson became the first prime minister in

British history proved to have broken the law while in office. He did not resign. He initiated an inquiry under a senior civil servant called Sue Gray. Mr Johnson was however Sue Gray's boss. That meant Gray was to report to Johnson on her investigation into conduct by people in Downing Street – including Johnson. I met Ms Gray on one informal occasion and all I can say is that she is someone who inspires trust. We can be sure she behaved impeccably. But being tasked with an inquiry by your boss into conduct including that of your boss for the ultimate judgement of your boss is once more the way the British system works. Or doesn't work. I was told by colleagues of Lord Geidt that he too behaved impeccably and stayed in post as Ethics Adviser only because he genuinely hoped to improve standards of behaviour within the Johnson administration. In the end he was another loyal public servant forced to admit failure. In his resignation letter Geidt's formal language barely masks his real anger. It's worth quoting at length:

> Despite being repeatedly questioned in the House of Commons about your obligations under the Ministerial Code [after paying a Fixed Penalty Notice], your responses again made no reference to it. I reported to the Select Committee yesterday that I was satisfied that you had responded to my Annual Report to explain your position. I am disappointed, however, that the account you gave was not fuller, as noted above. Moreover, I regret the reference to 'miscommunication' between our offices, with the implication that I was somehow responsible for you not being fully aware of my concerns. These inconsistencies and deficiencies notwithstanding, I believed that it was possible to continue credibly as Independent Adviser, albeit by a very small margin. This week, however, I was tasked to offer a view about the Government's intention to consider measures which risk a deliberate and purposeful breach of the Ministerial Code. This request has placed me in an impossible and odious position. My informal response on Monday was that you and any other Minister should justify openly your

position vis-a-vis the Code in such circumstances. However, the idea that a Prime Minister might to any degree be in the business of deliberately breaching his own Code is an affront. A deliberate breach, or even an intention to do so, would be to suspend the provisions of the Code to suit a political end. This would make a mockery not only of respect for the Code but licence the suspension of its provisions in governing the conduct of Her Majesty's Ministers. I can have no part in this. Because of my obligation as a witness in Parliament, this is the first opportunity I have had to act on the Government's intentions. I therefore resign from this appointment with immediate effect.[17]

One sign of the way things were shifting from the death of the Good Chap theory came when Johnson was followed into Downing Street in 2022 by a new prime minister, Liz Truss. She broke with convention in a different way – or perhaps she merely followed the Johnson invented 'tradition' of not caring what the previously observed conventions were. Truss decided not to have an Ethics Adviser at all. The answer to ethical problems in government was, therefore, to make sure that no ethical advice would be forthcoming. No Good Chaps and apparently No Problem. Simple.

The Good Chap theory is now dead. It cannot be resurrected by any trinity of interlocking institutions in whatever the British constitution is supposed to be. We need to replace the belief in good people (of whom there are plenty by the way) with something more substantial, belief in a written code of good practice, a rule book, or as the UCL Constitution Unit would call it... a constitution. One modern constitutional expert who wrote with great clarity and whom I've been quoting with considerable enthusiasm here, Anthony King, understood the weakness of the British system back in 2009. Put simply, if the person at the top of the constitutional tree – the prime minister – doesn't obey the generally accepted norms of good behaviour, the whole system is in trouble. And in particular 'in any governing body the powers of the whole body always tended to gravitate to the person in the chair'.[18] If the 'person in the chair', in this case Boris Johnson, loses a series of Ethics Advisers because he does not take their advice seriously, then the options for limiting the prime minister's abuse of power shrink considerably. In Johnson's case you could argue that the system did finally work, although it took the resignations of dozens of government ministers and the collapse of support for Johnson within his own MPs, to force him out. But Ascherson's scepticism is still important. What if Conservative MPs decided it was in their own best interests not to get rid of someone like Johnson but to tough it out and stick with 'the person in the chair', the most powerful of them all, the person to whom they might owe their future career prospects? What would the constitutional remedy be if a devious prime minister surrounded himself with equally devious MPs and they all stuck together? What would prevent this? Our constitutional metaphor?

There are many implications of this hypothetical situation. Conventions may or may not be observed. They are like traditions in that they can be invented or disinvented, made up to suit those in power, ignored or changed when 'the person in the chair' finds those conventions irksome or inconvenient. Vernon Bogdanor suggests that given such confusion about which conventions should be observed: 'This is the point at which you have to ask whether the conventions of the constitution might not be simply the conventions of the two-party system.'[19] Since Boris Johnson proved himself judge and jury in these investigations one might reconfigure Bogdanor's comment ultimately as 'the conventions of the constitution are the conventions acceptable to the leader of the party in government'. That is as close to Lord Hailsham's elective dictatorship or Ascherson's 'lawlessness' as any British person should wish to go.

Another constitutional historian, Anthony Seldon, reflecting on the events of the 2020s, told me that Johnson's approach was always to say that, 'If it's a law I can't change it, if it's a convention I can.'[20] It took me a while to realise that, rather typically for Boris

Johnson, neither part of that sentence is actually true. Johnson most definitely could and did change laws. He changed the Fixed Term Parliaments Act (2011) by getting rid of it, to his advantage. And he did not actually 'change' conventions. He broke them, including the convention that ministers who broke the Ministerial Code should resign and the convention that the advice of an Ethics Adviser should be given very serious consideration by the prime minister rather than summarily dismissed.

The point here is not that the United Kingdom is on its way to dictatorship. Nor is it that Boris Johnson breaking the norms of behaviour we had come to expect meant that he was to become a petty dictator. But in all democracies, especially in one with an uncodified constitution, conventions of behaviour are extremely important. They can easily be broken. Laws are obviously also important. Even if they are not broken, they can be changed by a prime minister with a big majority. An exceptionally flexible constitution is exceptionally open to abuse.

Our concern about the misbehaviour of a here-today-gone-tomorrow capricious politician like Johnson is real – but limited. Our real concern is how the broken British system of governance may provide a politician like Johnson with the tools for unchecked abuse. If Boris Johnson can chip away at conventions and norms of behaviour for years with relative impunity, worse may follow. Someone more ideologically driven, more attentive to detail and more ruthless in pursuit of his or her political goals can adopt Johnson's methods and push them much further. We need to start by recognising the problem is not the behaviour of a few politicians, but the generally incomprehensible nature of our national operating manual, our constitution, that allows such politicians to rise to the top and to be rewarded rather than punished. This leads to Neal Ascherson's provocative insistence that since we do not have an intelligible operating manual, we don't have, in practical terms, a constitution at all. It's not necessary to go quite that far to understand that what we do have is an enormous constitutional problem. Britain really could be much better than this.

'Nobody Knows Anything'

Anthony King argues that to describe the British constitution as non-existent or unwritten 'is simply bizarre. Britain's constitutional legislation runs to hundreds of pages. What Britain's constitution is, is uncodified, not both written down and formally gathered together all in one place.' But then King follows up with a most important caveat. So much of what we take for granted is astonishingly vague:

> That said, much of Britain's constitution is indeed unwritten. The role of the prime minister is not provided for by statute, the cabinet is not mentioned anywhere in statute law, and a Civil Service Act regulating the relations between civil servants and their political masters has yet to be passed... no single statute defines the role of local government in Britain's constitutional structure.[21]

King then nods significantly in Ascherson's direction by saying that the UK constitution cannot be 'amended' because there is nothing solid to amend. It's like trying to grasp your shadow. It does exist but you'd be hard put to grab hold of it. The British constitution can however be 'changed' because precedents, norms and traditions are easy to change – as Boris Johnson proved. All that is necessary is for a prime minister to do something different with the backing of a majority in a partisan House of Commons (and to repeat, a majority in the House of Commons is not the same as a majority of the British people). If that prime minister repeats his actions several times without penalty then these actions may become a 'new norm' or a tradition. But – and this is where we come full circle – if the role of the prime minister 'is not provided for by statute' then, while a prime minister cannot misbehave in any way they choose, if they do act in a wild fashion it may not be easy or even possible to stop them.

King notes that the British constitution:

Can be changed either as a result of changes in politicians' common understandings (often called 'conventions') or as a result of changes in ordinary statute law... the result is that the British constitution is in many ways remarkably easy to change, and sometimes politicians and others do not even notice that constitutional change is taking place. That also means that the word 'unconstitutional' has no precise meaning in the UK, because it would probably amount to no more than a vague term of abuse. [22]

Ascherson's blast of the trumpet about the hollow nature of the UK's constitution still has some force. If calling something 'unconstitutional' in Britain is vague, that is because the constitution is far from precise. We are indeed grasping at shadows. If the constitution can be changed as a result of changing 'conventions' and these conventions are merely 'politicians' common understandings' then changing politicians logically means changing their and our 'understandings' of what is permissible. Or misunderstandings. The notion that we truly do have constitutional rules moves closer to Ascherson's view that this is largely a 'myth'.

Boris Johnson had a different 'common understanding' of what was permissible in British public life from the 'common understanding' of any prime minister who preceded him in living memory. Ascherson insists that 'nobody knows who is ultimately in charge', although the whims of a capricious prime minister certainly play a large part. Perhaps the final word should go to the American screenwriter William Goldman. He famously said of Hollywood, in *Adventures in the Screen Trade* (1983): 'Nobody knows anything... Not one person... knows for a certainty what's going to work. Every time out it's a guess and, if you're lucky, an educated one.'

With the British constitution, everyone may have a view but in the end no one really knows anything. And that is just not good enough, especially at a time when 'governments are growing lawless'.

Why This Matters

Boris Johnson's rise was completely in accord with the Hansard survey showing British voters were ready for a leader 'willing to break the rules' to get things done. Cometh the Hour, Cometh the Man. Those voters got what they wished for. Beyond threats to renege on the Northern Ireland Protocol and break the law 'in a specific and limited way' there was an attempt to avoid international conventions of behaviour on refugee law concerning the proposed deportation of migrants to Rwanda. During the coronavirus pandemic the High Court found evidence of illegal contracts being awarded for PPE via a so-called 'VIP lane' for companies which were close to people in the government. Mrs Justice O'Farrell said the Good Law Project and EveryDoctor, two pro bono organisations that challenged the lawfulness of the way billions of pounds worth of contracts were awarded, had established that this was 'in breach of the obligation of equal treatment' and it was 'unlawful to confer preferential treatment in this way' and that 'there is evidence that opportunities were treated as high priority even where there were no objectively justifiable grounds for expediting the offer'.[23] Other matters, including those relating to political donations and friends of government ministers continue to be the subject of investigations. Daisy Cooper, the Liberal Democrat health spokesperson, summarised the High Court ruling bluntly: 'Not only did the Conservatives give their mates privileged access to lucrative covid contracts, they did it unlawfully.'

Anthony Seldon, who has written biographical sketches of every British prime minister since Sir Robert Walpole in 1735 was very blunt in conversation with me: 'Boris Johnson did more than any other prime minister to damage the integrity of democratic life,' he said. Part of Seldon's concern was directly related to the abuses involved in Brexit leading to constant clashes between government ministers and top civil servants. He told me he was alarmed by 'the attack on the civil service that Brexit has unleashed' with key personnel side-lined, ignored or encouraged to resign when they warned government ministers of the significantly negative consequences of their actions: 'We've seen a Permanent Secretary [the highly regarded Sir Tom Scholar] fired from the Treasury – and the civil service under attack as never before since the Northcote–Trevelyan reforms in the nineteenth century.' Seldon saw this as a deliberate attempt to undermine impartiality of advice and therefore 'a significant moment, as is the blithe disregard of the constitution by the out-going prime minister [Boris Johnson]'. The British 'convention' since the Northcote–Trevelyan reforms had been for experienced civil servants to give accurate and impartial advice. That no longer works, Seldon told me, 'if it's the head of government and cabinet ministers, who themselves are undermining the impartiality and attacking the objectivity of civil servants'.

Other constitutional scholars agreed with Seldon's characterisation of the dangers. Jill Rutter, Senior Research Fellow at UK in a Changing Europe, said that the sacking of the top civil servant at the Treasury, Sir Tom Scholar by Johnson's successor Liz Truss

> looks like an attack on the impartiality of the civil service, applying a new ideological compatibility test to appointments... They have lost an official with an unrivalled track record of managing the economic fallout of crises – in the middle of a major economic crisis. Externally, they are risking their credibility with markets, at a time when the pound is feeble, already spooked by their attacks on independent institutions such as the OBR and the Bank of England. And they have made life much tougher for any potential successor [to Scholar] who risks being seen as a yes-person. All in all it adds up to a difficult start at His Majesty's Treasury and an immediate challenge to the constitutional norms around the civil service from the new government.[24]

When it comes to 'constitutional norms of good behaviour' we all know that respecting such norms and encouraging good behaviour within the British system is clearly no longer normal.

See You in Court

The barrister Sam Fowles KC has been actively involved in some of the most tricky constitutional legal battles of the past decade. He does not subscribe to the provocative Ascherson argument that the UK 'has no constitution', although he does believe that 'our constitution is becoming ever more unbalanced and lawyers like me are increasingly unable to put things right'.[25] Fowles sees in his various court cases:

> A 'slow burn' crisis whereby the norms and institutions that underpin our democratic constitution are undermined by a lengthy war of attrition... Since 2010, those in power have increasingly chipped away at the ideas and institutions that safeguard our interests. Some of these attacks like the prorogation of parliament, are high profile, capturing the imagination of the nation. Others are far more subtle. They are suffered originally by only a few individuals. Taken together however they start to feel like an avalanche.

The Johnson government, Fowles argues, is not uniquely anti-democratic:

> [It is] merely symptomatic of a much deeper malaise. Our democratic crisis has been building for a long time... We are reaching a tipping point: the democratic essentials have been cut back so far that we must ask how long Britain will remain a genuinely democratic state.[26]

To take the most notable of these examples, the unlawful prorogation of parliament by the Johnson government in 2019 – a case in which Fowles was personally involved – was hugely controversial from the start not merely for what Johnson tried to do but for what it meant for democracy. The Johnson government found itself in difficulty over 'getting Brexit done'. They decided the best course of action was to close – 'prorogue' – parliament to cut down scrutiny and discussion. Proroguing parliament had a long history in times of trouble. Lord North had advised King George III to prorogue parliament in 1774 after the passing of the Quebec Act – and that led to the American War of Independence. In 1831 George IV prorogued parliament over the First Reform Bill at a time of great political ferment across the country. When Queen Elizabeth II did as Boris Johnson wished and prorogued parliament in 2019 the political and constitutional crisis was not quite up to that of the American revolution but the First Minister of Scotland Nicola Sturgeon did accuse Johnson, in language familiar in the time of Colonial America, of being a prime minister acting like a 'tinpot dictator'. The Commons Speaker suggested that prorogation was potentially unconstitutional because it 'represents not just in the minds of many colleagues, but to huge numbers of people outside, an act of executive fiat'. The First Minister of Wales Mark Drakeford said the prime minister had 'closed the doors' on democracy, while Donald Trump congratulated Mr Johnson. There were differences between England – where lower courts did not rule on the matter – and Scotland where an appeal went to the Outer House of the Court of Session, Scotland's highest court. In a unanimous opinion, Lord Carloway was very clear. The prime minister of the United Kingdom had lied when he claimed that closing down parliament for a few weeks had nothing to do with his desperation to push ahead with Brexit without parliamentary scrutiny: 'The circumstances demonstrate that the true reason for the prorogation is to reduce the time for Parliamentary scrutiny of Brexit at a time when such scrutiny would appear to be a matter of considerable importance given the matters at stake.'[27]

This, from a very senior judge, really was quite extraordinary. He asserted implicitly that Boris Johnson lied by not giving the 'true reason' for his actions. Not only that, logically he must have lied to the Queen. This was followed by a significant Supreme Court judgement in London delivered by the Supreme Court President, Lady (Brenda) Hale. She emphasised that the court was not there to judge whether leaving the European Union or the terms of departure were correct. That was a matter for the government and parliament. The Supreme Court was however to decide, 'Whether the advice given by the prime minister to Her Majesty the Queen on 27 or 28 August 2019 that parliament should be prorogued... was lawful.'[28]

The Supreme Court found that prorogation was not lawful. The judgement appeared to confirm the Scottish judgement that Boris Johnson, the prime minister, and head of the British government had indeed lied to our head of state. Mr Johnson denied it. Well, he would, wouldn't he? Others, including the legal expert David Allen Green were clear that the Queen had been deliberately misled. It was the most strategically important of strategic lies: 'In effect, the court held that Boris Johnson lied to the Queen.'[29]

More traditional constitutional scholars including Sir Stephen Sedley may argue that this shows how well the British system is working through its 'interlocking institutions'. The court verdict won through. Others – including judges I have talked with privately – suggest that various institutions including the courts, may work well despite flaws in the system rather than because of it. I happen to believe that British judges, male and female, really do tend to be Good Chaps or whatever the gender-neutral approximation might be. But after these verdicts the government and its allies were bent on revenge. The former Conservative leader Lord (Michael) Howard publicly called for reform of the judiciary. He claimed that courts sometimes 'distort' law to 'reach the result they want to achieve'. Lady Hale had said that prorogation, in effect decided by the prime minister, was not part of the proceedings in parliament. Lord Howard took a very different view. 'Prorogation was clearly, of any ordinary view of the language, a proceeding in parliament', Lord Howard said, adding that 'I think that judges have increasingly substituted their own view of what is right for the view of parliament and of ministers. The excellent Policy Exchange paper to which I have written the foreword makes some sensible suggestions for redressing the balance.'[30]

Policy Exchange is not quite what the neutral sounding name suggests. It's a right-wing think tank, one of many in Britain that seek to influence government policies and which are often funded opaquely. In November 2022, the funding transparency website 'Who Funds You?' gave Policy Exchange an E grade, the lowest transparency rating (ratings go from A – open – to E, not transparent at all). Policy Exchange runs something called the Judicial Power Project (JPP) which argues that British judges nowadays over-reach themselves and that a more 'traditional' view of executive power within the constitution should be restored. The paper to which Lord Howard refers is called 'Protecting the Constitution'. It calls, as the title suggests, for the constitution (that is, mainly the power of the government) to be 'protected' from judges by limiting judicial power. You may at this point conclude that the constitution – messy though it may be – requires to be protected from politicians instead, and that a constitution is supposed to protect us all as citizens from the abuses of governments who think anything they do is by definition 'constitutional'. Lady Hale felt moved to respond. In an unusual interview with the BBC *Today* programme she said of the judiciary:

> We have an independent, merit-based appointments system which most of us are extremely comfortable with. We don't want to be politicised, we don't decide political questions, we decide legal questions. In any event, parliament always has the last word. We are not politically motivated. I do not know the political opinions of my colleagues and they do not know mine, and long may it remain so.[31]

The constitutional lawyer Sam Fowles agreed with Lady Hale: 'The Supreme Court had struck down an attack on the Constitution. In the aftermath the government and its allies launched an attack on the constitution's most important moral value: truth.'[32]

Fowles traces the significance of truth in English law back to the Dooms (legal customs) of Athelstan (AD 924–39) in which anyone who lies shall 'ever after never be oath-worthy'. But Fowles saw something very troubling:

> Much relies on ministers understanding their error and 'doing the right thing.' In court we exposed the prime minister. We revealed how he tried to dispose of the elected parliament when it got in the way of his plans and then lied to the country about it... Yet public pressure for Johnson to resign was minimal. Listening to the prevailing winds of public discourse in October 2019 was to believe that the real threat to our constitution did not come from the executive, which had tried to govern without parliament, but rather from those who restored the representatives of the people to their rightful place. This is just one example of a public discourse that is no longer fit for purpose.[33]

Some eighteen months after the embarrassment of losing the prorogation case the Johnson government attempted to curb the powers of the court that had kept them in check by limiting judicial review of government actions. The Lord Chancellor Robert Buckland claimed that a review of the process independently by Lord Faulks had found 'a growing tendency for the courts in judicial review cases to edge away from a strictly supervisory jurisdiction becoming more willing to review the merits of the decisions themselves'. This was – to put it kindly – misleading. The Faulks review found the opposite, namely that we could 'be confident that the courts will respect institutional boundaries... politicians should in turn afford the judiciary the respect which it is undoubtedly due when it exercises these powers'. Buckland's comments to make the case for curbing judicial power do exactly the opposite. They show why honest and rigorous judges are needed to prevent politicians doing as they please and claiming that something is 'constitutional' merely because they did it.

The government, as Sam Fowles noted, 'altered the historical record to justify an attack on those it sees as its political opponents'.[34] This is very dangerous territory indeed.

As for the JPP, Fowles is scathing:

This purports to be a serious study of the constitution run by Policy Exchange. In practice it appears more intent on pushing an authoritarian narrative on the basis of misrepresentation... The JPP's work would unlikely survive the scrutiny of the court room or lecture theatre, but it is not intended for either. Its intended audience is politicians and through them the media and the public.

Fowles's assessment is echoed by others including Thomas Poole, Professor at Law at the LSE and editor of the *Modern Law Review*:

The [JPP's] targets seemingly include any institutional check on executive power. Authoritarian rather than conservative in disposition, for all the constitutional posturing the object of the power so directed is to make it easier to realise a purified version of an imagined past.[35]

Ah yes, the weaponised nostalgia again. The JPP view that British courts and judges are overstepping their powers is of course popular on the right of British politics, at least as long as the Conservative Party is in power. It may be less popular if we have a Labour government, especially is it is determinedly of the Left. As Anthony Seldon told me:

Democracy is under threat. Look at the eclipse of democracies and the quality of democratic life globally. What's happened in the United States is deeply worrying – to have a president (Trump) who doesn't accept the legality and the authenticity of the electoral process. That undermines a system where he is also the head of state. And it does show the fragility of democracy as we experienced in the 1930s. So could there be a similar march towards strong men – they are men, not women – who will 'solve the problems'? We've seen a lot of that in the last decade, and many moments of real concern in this country. Boris Johnson did more than any other prime minister to damage the integrity of democratic life.[36]

When we discussed Johnson's constructive dismissal of his two Ethics Advisors, Seldon became uncharacteristically cross at how Johnson's short-lived successor decided to push this contempt for any kind of oversight on ethical questions even further: 'And now Liz Truss apparently not wanting to appoint an Ethics Adviser!' he exclaimed. 'Who can champion the civil service if it's not the head of government – if it's the head of government and cabinet ministers, who themselves are undermining the impartiality and attacking the objectivity of civil servants?!'

Seldon asks a good question. Britain needs to find some good answers.

10

Hidden Persuaders: Media, PR and You

Nayirah's testimony was the most moving I have ever encountered. She was a Kuwaiti teenager who witnessed atrocities by Saddam Hussein's troops immediately following the invasion of Kuwait by Iraqi soldiers on 2 August 1990. The United States had made a catastrophic diplomatic error earlier that year, a blunder that led Saddam Hussein to assume he had a green light from Washington to invade his oil-rich neighbour. The US Ambassador to Iraq, April Glaspie, told Saddam Hussein that Washington had no strong views about inter-Arab disputes. Saddam interpreted this to mean the US would not be concerned if he invaded Kuwait, a state with which he had a long-running argument dating back decades. Kuwait was carved out after the First World War by the British and French from what Iraqis thought of as 'Greater Iraq'. At the time of the invasion, I was a member of the White House press corps travelling with US president George H. W. Bush as he met with Britain's prime minister Margaret Thatcher in the Rocky Mountain resort of Aspen, Colorado. Thatcher counselled Bush to take a strong line. She is said to have instructed him, 'This is no time to go wobbly, George.' Thatcher believed that the world had to be able to trust the sanctity of international borders and that they should not be redrawn by force. She told Bush that if Saddam Hussein was left unchecked, it would set a precedent that could lead to international chaos and possibly a Third World War. Bush agreed. The Iraqis were given an ultimatum to get out of Kuwait. When Saddam refused, the American-led military attack was to begin in January 1991, preceded by months of careful diplomacy and a lot of scare stories about Iraq's army being one of the largest in the world, a million strong, and full of combat veterans of the war with Iran. President Bush assembled an impressive coalition of allies, including Arab and Muslim states, but he faced one big obstacle – US domestic politics. The United States had been reluctant to become embroiled in foreign entanglements after the lies and failure of Vietnam. Bush had to convince the American people to trust his judgement. That's where Nayirah came in. Her performance at a hearing on Capitol Hill on 10 October 1990 helped turn the tide of US public opinion. She appeared before the

Congressional Human Rights Caucus chaired by Congressmen Tom Lantos and John Porter. It was a dramatic moment. Nayirah gave only her first name for fear of reprisals against her family who were still living in occupied Kuwait.

'I volunteered at the al-Adan hospital,' in Kuwait City, she told the caucus and the world, speaking in English, her voice trembling with emotion. 'While I was there, I saw the Iraqi soldiers come into the hospital with guns, and go into the room where... babies were in incubators. They took the babies out of the incubators and left the babies on the cold floor to die.'

The caucus room was silent except for Nayirah's sobbing. I immediately offered a report for BBC Television News and it ran on all available bulletins, at length. Similar reports ran on news stations across America and the world. Nayirah said this atrocity had happened to 'hundreds' of babies, a statement backed up by Amnesty International. Amnesty produced a report in December 1990 stating that 'over 300 premature babies were reported to have died after Iraqi soldiers removed them from incubators which were then looted'.

But there was a problem. In a relatively small society like Kuwait, the idea of having 300 premature babies in incubators should have set off alarm bells. Of course I did not realise it at the time, but Nayirah was a liar. My report and that of every other journalist who covered the story turned out to be what we now would call 'Fake News'. We were trusted and believed, in large part, because it was an accurate report of a televised Congressional inquiry into a horrendous act of aggression. In my case the broadcast I made was on the world's most trusted news source, BBC News, and the eyewitness was a fifteen-year-old girl. That veneer of credibility was the point of the fakery. I am recounting this embarrassing (for me) story as a reminder that Fake News and deliberate lying for political ends are not new. They did not begin with social media and they are always difficult to spot. Deconstructing this one cleverly conceived lie shows how we can reinvigorate British democracy through coming to terms with media literacy. That involves being able to spot fakery and expose those who would deliberately mislead us. It's a hard lesson, especially for journalists who do not want to appear gullible. We all need to be more media literate because otherwise the liars and truth twisters will always win.

Media literacy (sometimes called Media and Information Literacy or MIL) is the ability to analyse stories presented in the mass media or on social media and to determine their accuracy and credibility. Academic definitions vary, but they include skills of 'analysis, evaluation, grouping, induction, deduction, synthesis, and abstracting'.[1] In plain English, media literacy is the ability to evaluate what you see, read and hear, decoding the messages and the intent of the authors, and understanding how the authors may be biased or misled (as I was), and therefore either knowingly or unwittingly inaccurate and complicit. I'm quoting the Nayirah incident to demonstrate that even as a born sceptic, I fell for it, as did all my journalistic colleagues in Washington at the time. The BBC broadcast my report in good faith to tens of millions of people and three decades later I am appalled and aggrieved at the deception. Nevertheless it contains valuable lessons. A quick glance at Britain's daily newspapers or listening to commentaries on our TV and radio talk shows suggests that we urgently need to improve the quality of information, journalism and the media as well as leadership in British public life. That means as both transmitters and consumers of information we need to improve our ability to spot phoneys and liars. In the case of Nayirah, it wasn't easy.

In 1992, months after the invasion of Kuwait, after the music and memories of the victory parades had faded and American troops returned to their bases, journalists belatedly discovered the full name of Nayirah. She was Nayirah al-Sabah. The last name was the give-away. The al-Sabahs are the Kuwaiti royal family. Nayirah had not been a volunteer nurse in Kuwait at the time of the invasion. She had not witnessed babies being mistreated in any hospital. Her father was Saud Nasir al-Sabah, then Kuwait's Ambassador to the United

States. The Kuwaiti government-in-exile, through an organisation called 'Citizens for a Free Kuwait', paid the world's largest public relations firm, Hill+Knowlton, to help them overcome the 'Vietnam Factor' and persuade the American public of the case for war. Nayirah was one of the key weapons of persuasion. Citizens for a Free Kuwait was an 'Astroturf' organisation. Astroturf is phoney grass and Astroturf organisations appear to be grassroots organisations that give the impression they represent a popular movement. In reality they are created to advance a public relations aim. 'Free Kuwait' tee-shirts, posters and bumper stickers appeared all over Washington, on college campuses and elsewhere. At a moment of political crisis there is nothing wrong with people coming together to create an organisation to further a political cause by swaying public opinion in a democracy. It happens all the time, long before the invention of Astroturf in the 1960s. The British government engaged in these dark arts during the Second World War when Winston Churchill needed to persuade the United States to aid the fight against Hitler. This involved secret coordination between British intelligence, MI6 and the newly created Ministry of Information (or, perhaps we should say, Ministry for British Propaganda). The British government lied to the American public, and did so convincingly. Here's one very dramatic example:

> In June of 1941, Americans read about an extraordinary British mission into Nazi Occupied France. Newspapers, including the *Baltimore Sun* and *New York Post,* detailed how the British parachuted into an airfield with tommy guns and hand grenades, overpowered the guards and destroyed about 30 planes. All of the team members made it back to Britain alive via torpedo boats, along with 40 German prisoners in tow. It was an incredible story. It was also completely made-up.[2]

In the 'completely made up' case of Nayirah in 1990, journalists and human rights organisations like Amnesty swallowed the lie. We unknowingly gave the atrocity story the accelerant of credibility by reporting accurately the supposed 'facts' as Nayirah outlined them, perhaps because we all wanted to believe in the (otherwise well-documented) cruelty of Saddam Hussein's regime. Reinforcing the opinions already held by the general public is a longstanding and generally successful public relations technique. It was later revealed that up to US$12 million was paid by the Kuwaitis to the PR wizards at Hill+Knowlton. The company's Vice President Lauri Fitz-Pegado had coached Nayirah's testimony. From the point of view of the Bush administration wanting to influence public opinion and Congress, or for the Kuwaiti royal family-in-exile wanting their country back, it was cheap at the price.

When the truth emerged long after the war we found out that only a handful of incubators had been in the al-Adan hospital and that they were not looted in the way Nayirah described. Amnesty International and Middle East Watch concluded that her story was untrue, but by then it had served its purpose. The war was won. Saddam Hussein was guilty of many dreadful crimes, but not the specific atrocities that Nayirah had so eloquently described. 'Saddam Hussein – Baby Killer' was a reprise of effective British propaganda from the First World War when German troops were said to have bayoneted babies in Belgium. In 1991, just as in 1914, there was no easy way of verifying what Nayirah had to say, or of debunking her lies.

The point of rehearsing this story in the 2020s is not moral censure. It is to see how lies work in the hands of skilled public relations specialists. In each case the motive is the same. A convincing lie well told can change as well as reinforce public opinion and make it easier to justify difficult political decisions. Technologically of course there is a huge difference between 1914, 1990 and today. In the 2020s social media makes it much easier for falsehoods to spread and allows more sophisticated deepfake lies to be created which are tailored to individuals as well as mass groups of the general public. Yet social media can act as a disinfectant too. Had Google, Facebook and Twitter been available in 1990, we might have uncovered the Nayirah fakery almost immediately. Surely a school friend would have recognised her and outed her on Facebook as a member of the Kuwaiti royal family? Would a whistle-blower have offered a revelatory tweet? Would someone in Kuwait have mentioned that yes, the Iraqis committed atrocities but the incubator story was a lie? Probably.

The Iraq War lasted five weeks and ended in February 1991 but the truth took months to emerge. The PR wizards got their money. The Kuwaitis got their country back. The Bush administration got their victory and Members of Congress returned business as usual. No one was sanctioned, disciplined, arrested or publicly humiliated for colluding to help a teenager promote a war through stage-managed lies at the heart of American democracy. But in terms of media literacy and our loss of trust in media organisations, the key point is to remember how this lie was planted. A fifteen-year-old girl was taken to Capitol Hill to address the Human Rights Caucus. This was not a Pentagon briefing from authority figures with an obvious pro-war bias. There were no generals in uniform, no leaks from the CIA, and no off-the-record chat at the White House – all of which are treated by journalists with degrees of scepticism. PR professionals like Hill+Knowlton knew that a public hearing on Capitol Hill gives credibility. So does the use of someone who is still technically a child. The label 'Congressional Human Rights Caucus' helped enormously. In his study of information censorship and propaganda in the Gulf War, John MacArthur points out that 'lying under oath in front of a Congressional Committee is a crime. Lying from under the cover of anonymity to a caucus is merely public relations.'[3] To the untutored viewer – and almost everyone is untutored when it comes to the differences between a formal Capitol Hill committee and an informal Congressional caucus – all this looked at the time like an official part of the US government. We were duped by professionals.

The reason the story has resonance for our current predicament in Britain is because it illuminates most clearly how lies work, as well as when they may be forgiven or forgotten. Ask yourself if you remember the former British prime minister Tony Blair allegedly lying about the reasons for going to war against Iraq in 2003, which also involved exaggerations of Saddam Hussein's very real perfidy. Many Labour supporters still believe that the 2003 Iraq War was a blight on Blair's otherwise often admirable career. But does anyone remember Nayirah's lies? Most readers will never have heard of her. She is largely forgotten. That's because repelling the Iraq invasion was widely seen as a just cause and it certainly was a successful war. The US and its allies defeated what was described as the fourth or fifth largest army in the world in a hundred hours with minimal British, US or other allied casualties. The lies of 1990 are forgotten because the first Iraq War was a success on the ground and also on the war's 'second front', in the battlefield of public opinion. The same is true of the lies about Germans bayoneting Belgian babies in 1914 or the non-existent commando raid in 1941. The Blair allegations from 2003 stick in popular memory because the second Iraq War was a failure in both theatres of conflict. It led to the disastrous and bloody occupation of Iraq, it uncovered none of the weapons of mass destruction that were trumpeted as the reason for invading the country, it fuelled the rise of so-called Islamic State group (Da'ish) and the region today remains violent, divided and unstable. The reason the lie on the Brexit bus is remembered is precisely the same. Brexit lies are referenced repeatedly not because Brexit is a success, but because it is a profound failure. If Brexit had succeeded in making Britain better, the falsehoods on the way to victory would have become a footnote in history. One further note – Boris Johnson and Dominic Cummings were never as credible as Nayirah.

Hannah Arendt, as ever, is a trusted guide here. In a 1971 essay, 'Lying in Politics' Arendt wrote:

> Truthfulness has never been counted among the political virtues, and lies have always been regarded as justifiable tools in political dealings... Lies are often much more plausible, more appealing to reason, than reality, since the liar has the great advantage of knowing beforehand what the audience

wishes or expects to hear. He has prepared his story for public consumption with a careful eye to making it credible, whereas reality has the disconcerting habit of confronting us with the unexpected, for which we were not prepared. Under normal circumstances the liar is defeated by reality, for which there is no substitute; no matter how large the tissue of falsehood that an experienced liar has to offer, it will never be large enough, even if he enlists the help of computers, to cover the immensity of factuality.[4]

How prescient of Arendt to write more than fifty years ago of 'the help of computers' in manufacturing falsehoods. But the lesson is clear. In our suspicious century, media literacy means paying attention to lies and liars, especially when they are telling us what we want to hear: that the Iraq regime is cruel, or that it has access to weapons of mass destruction, or that membership of the European Union is a profligate waste of our money. It seems almost ludicrous and yet necessary to say this, but for Britain truly to be better than it is now, we need to stand up for the principles of truth and honesty in public life. It has not been going well. To understand what has gone wrong over the past twenty years, we therefore have to confront our own complicity in tolerating lies, deceit and incompetence. Change needs to begin not only with altering the actions of leaders and institutions but also with changing ourselves too. We need to become more critical and more sceptical of our sources of information, especially when they may be telling us what we want to hear.

In the United States, Fox 'News' viewers wanted to believe that Donald Trump won the 2020 US presidential election and that the violent Capitol Hill riot of 6 January 2021 was merely a peaceful protest. Fox News obliged by feeding viewers a diet of misinformation that backed up that lie. Britain is not yet in such a critical condition. But we have taken a few steps down this very dangerous road. And viewers, listeners and readers are becoming increasingly suspicious, that malevolent forces are capable of persuading us that what is false is actually true and that which is true might actually be false.

News You Can Use

Trust in mainstream British media organisations in the 2020s has fallen to the lowest levels since surveys began. A similar decline is not found in many other democracies, especially Nordic countries, where citizens remain much more stolidly trusting of their media and information sources. Scandinavia's populations are not more gullible than ours. In fact, Nordic news consumers are far more sceptical because they are also much more media literate. They are more likely to search out trusted sources and discount less reliable media outlets. British people can do this too, but research by the Reuters Institute for the Study of Journalism (RISJ) suggests that we have a long way to go to stop ourselves being fooled. The British increasingly often choose what might be described as the ostrich strategy called 'news avoidance'.

In 2022 Reuters surveyed 93,000 people in forty-six different countries with a focus on three democracies where trust in news sources was particularly problematic. Those three are the UK, US, and Brazil. The findings were alarming for Britain in three ways. Reuters found a significant decline in trust in British news media, a fall in the consumption of news and a rise in news avoidance, which they define as a decline in interest in reliable information. This comes in what might be considered interesting times full of highly significant news stories affecting all of us – a major turning point for our country, after Brexit, a succession of prime ministers, the war in Ukraine, a cost of living crisis, industrial unrest and serious economic dislocation. Even so, an increasing number of British people choose not to be informed (or fear they may be misinformed) and so turn off mainstream media altogether. You can understand why. If you do not trust what you read and hear in newspapers, on TV or on the radio, and the content is often depressing, then what's the point? News researchers talk of 'headline stress disorder', 'doomscrolling', and 'doomsurfing'. For some people, learning about bad news leads to increased social media activity to find even worse news. The RISJ findings confirmed that Nordic countries do much better than Britain in finding trustworthy sources of information. Britain is in the second division. After Brexit, our loss of faith in mainstream publications and broadcasts accelerated:

> Trust in the (UK) news is down by 16 percentage points since the Brexit referendum in 2016 amid increasingly polarised debates about politics and culture. The BBC has come under criticism from both left and right over perceived bias in its news coverage, with our data showing over a quarter (26%) have little trust in the news brand compared with 11% in 2018.[5]

Jair Bolsonaro's populist government in Brazil also witnessed an enormous decline in trust while post-Trump America, misinformed by Fox News, ideologically driven media, and a host of conspiracy theorists like QAnon, was bottom of the trust league.

But there was some good news:

> Finland remains the country with the highest levels of overall trust (69%), while news trust in the USA has fallen by a further three percentage points and remains the lowest (26%) in our survey... the proportion of news consumers who say they avoid news, often or sometimes, has increased sharply across countries. This type of selective avoidance has doubled in both Brazil (54%) and the UK (46%) over the last five years, with many respondents saying news has a negative effect on their mood.

The most trusted British news brands remain public service broadcasters. Both BBC and ITV news programmes were trusted by 55 per cent of viewers and listeners, yet for the BBC that was a huge drop from 75 per cent trust in 2018. Loss of trust is significant for the BBC since it relies on a universal tax, the Licence Fee. Having almost half the people who pay your salary unsure whether they trust you is an existential crisis for the world's greatest news organisation and those who work there.

In terms of Britain's least trusted news organisations there were no surprises:

> *The Sun* was the UK's least trusted news brand out of 15 major UK titles included in the survey, with 67% of people saying they didn't trust its news output versus 12% who did. The Rupert Murdoch-owned tabloid was joined by the *Daily Mail* (on 51% and 23% respectively) and the *Daily Mirror* (on 49% and 22% respectively) at the bottom of the trust ratings.[6]

It's a curious phenomenon that the three least trusted daily newspapers in the UK are the three most popular papers in the UK. What that says about *Sun, Mirror* and *Mail* readers and their view of the world is a matter for conjecture. But computer programmers have a useful phrase about what happens when a system is fed bad information. You cannot expect good results: 'Garbage In – Garbage Out'. If news consumers rely on sources that have proved themselves to be demonstrably untrustworthy then that is a problem for democracy. And if large numbers of voters also begin to doubt whether the news they read, watch or listen to can be trusted, then the idea of an informed democracy is also at risk. And perhaps to no one's surprise, the manufacture of lies can be good for some business plans.

Following Fox News' coverage of Capitol Hill riots on 6 January 2021, it was revealed in 2023 that some of the network's own 'journalists' were prepared to act as propagandists for Donald Trump while on air, despite what they actually believed and knew of the facts. When their private messages were made public as a result of a court case it was evidence that despite their public protestations some of them actively despised Trump and that they did not believe the nonsensical conspiracy theories they were promoting. Tucker Carlson, one of Fox's star anchors, sent a text message to another employee two days before Trump supporters stormed the US Capitol in January 2020. It read: 'We are very very close to being able to ignore Trump most nights. I truly can't wait. I hate him passionately... I can't handle much more of this.' Carlson described Trump as 'a demonic force, a destroyer... What he's good at is destroying things. He's the undisputed world champion of that. He could easily destroy us if we play it wrong.' Fox News averages around 2 million viewers in prime time. If a popular broadcaster with millions of viewers shamelessly repeats conspiracy theories that the broadcasters themselves do not believe, then it is hardly surprising that American democracy is extremely troubled.

British democracy is in trouble too. The only issue is the depth of the damage and how it can be repaired. What is clear is that media literacy is an acquired skill, much less in evidence in the US and UK than in Nordic countries. Finland does it better, and with good reason.

Finland and Media Literacy

Finland was invaded by half a million Russian troops in 1939. Nowadays it has a 1,340-kilometre-long border with one of the world's most difficult neighbours, the Russia of Vladimir Putin. Fake News from and about Russia is therefore an extremely sensitive subject for the Finns, the Baltic states and Scandinavian countries. As a result, they have all invested in education and media literacy. Finland also significantly outperforms the UK in measures of wellbeing, happiness, early-years childcare and in OECD 'Pisa' tests, in which fifteen-year-olds are tested on reading, mathematics and science. In 2023, for the sixth year in a row, Finland was the world's happiest country according to the World Happiness Report. The UK came nineteenth.[7] Media literacy is usually defined as the ability to critically engage with media in all aspects of life. Media literacy skills include differentiating facts from opinion and analysis, verifying sources, and understanding how the media works. According to the chief communications officer for the Finnish prime minister's office, 'The first line of defence [against Fake News] is the kindergarten teacher.'[8]

Media and Information Literacy means exploring critically both the role of media and communications, and the strategies of those who influence what we think we know of our world: leaders, politicians, journalists, businesses trying to sell us products and services, and public relations professionals. Finland is ranked first out of forty-one countries in Europe for this form of literacy, followed by Denmark, Estonia, Sweden and Ireland. The United Kingdom is at number eleven, in the second tier.[9] Meanwhile the Edelman Trust Barometer (2022) noted that loss of trust in the British media was not an accident. It was self-inflicted by the British media and government themselves as part of a worldwide pattern: 'We find a world ensnared in a vicious cycle of distrust, fuelled by a growing lack of faith in media and government. Through disinformation and division, these two institutions are feeding the cycle and exploiting it for commercial and political gain.'[10]

Finland is the world leading exception, actively inspiring critical scrutiny of information through education. In Finnish schools teachers show students TikTok videos and YouTube clips. They read newspaper articles together and discuss basic questions. What's the purpose of the article? Is it to inform, persuade or sell you something? How, when and why do you think it was written? What are the author's claims? Why should we believe them? How can we check if they are true? As we noted in our approach to the British constitution, media literacy is a form of literary criticism. In Finland the focus is less on the medium of communication than on providing a coherent critique of the content. It doesn't much matter if the information is on social media or in the 'dead trees' media of traditional print newspapers and magazines, upstart new TV stations or 'legacy' broadcasting organisations like the BBC, or even niche blogposts, tweets and podcasts. What matters is enabling children from an early age to deconstruct what they are being told by unpicking the communications strategies of those who have grabbed their attention. The result is that Finnish citizens take seriously all the key values of a successful democracy and are a happier, healthier and better-educated country too, while an uninformed or misinformed democracy risks becoming barely a democracy at all.

Ignorance is not bliss. It's ignorance. The United Kingdom, where almost half (46 per cent) the population selectively avoids news stories, clearly has a measurable problem with both messages and messengers. But blaming the mainstream media, news media or social media for failures of truth verification is only part of the problem. The overarching issue is the willingness of some of those in leadership positions to lie and the assistance provided to their disinformation by supporters and at times by accomplices in newspapers and other media, those who are prepared to transmit or report lies without verification, criticism or active scepticism. As consumers, readers, viewers and listeners at the end of the information food chain, perhaps we all need to recite Bill Clinton's favourite adage once more, 'Fool me once, shame on you. Fool me twice, shame on me.' Shame on all of us for tolerating being repeatedly fooled.

In that context, the way Nayirah's lie was choreographed reminds us that we are often in the hands of very clever communicators. The American writer Vance Packard called them 'hidden persuaders', the title of his 1957 book on public relations. As with Hill+Knowlton and Nayirah, persuasion often works best when the persuaders remain in the shadows.

But methods of persuasion go much further. What follows are two apparently benign examples from two prominent professional communicators. They help explain how different types of 'persuasion' work for those in positions of power. Just as with school lessons in Finland, once we begin to understand how and why hidden persuaders use these simple techniques, we can liberate ourselves from some of the tedium of trying to decrypt what we are being told.

The Professionals

Britain's former prime minister Tony Blair was a master of public relations. He understood that politics is theatre and, along with George Burns, intuited that 'authenticity' is so important that you may need to fake it. In his later years Blair was open about the absurdity of all this, but he also understood the need for soundbites and pictures to fit into the tight structure of television news. Some in New Labour called it a focus on 'messaging' as well as 'messages'. Knowing how to use the media to communicate with ordinary people is one reason Tony Blair won three general elections in a row. After his great success in the Northern Ireland peace deal, the Good Friday Agreement, Blair was ready to supervise the signing in April 1998 at Stormont Castle. He turned to the waiting cameras and told the world:

'A day like today is not a day for soundbites, really. But I feel the hand of history upon our shoulders. I really do.'

Blair crafted the perfect soundbite for the television age, on a day that he claimed was not for soundbites. A little of the facade of postmodern politics cracked. Blair knew it. His staff knew it and everyone tried not to laugh. It was such an obvious contradiction that as Blair recounted in his autobiography *A Journey*, 'In the corner of my eye, I could see Jonathan [Powell, his chief of staff] and Alastair [Campbell, his head of communications] cracking up.' But Blair also understood, in that other public relations phrase, the need to be 'relatable'. The prime minister of the United Kingdom needed to appear both a figure of authority and also – however unlikely this might be – a 'normal bloke'. When he left office Blair lifted the lid on the techniques he used to make this appearance of normality seem authentic. You could call it an honest deception:

With an election in the offing, it had been decided that I should do a regional tour to 'reconnect with the people'. There is always something a trifle dubious about the 'connecting with the people' business. In modern politics you have to pretend to be living the life the ordinary person leads, when of course you can't, and don't, do the shopping in the supermarket, fill up the car, go down the pub for a few beers, the quiz night and a bit of banter. But everyone nowadays has to go through the elaborate pretence that the prime minister could and should do all that, otherwise he or she is 'out of touch', the worst criticism that can ever be made. I can't tell you how many cafes, fish and chip shops and shopping malls I would go into... all in the interests of showing that I was a 'regular bloke'. One of the main reasons it's total rubbish is that prior to going in, the place is staked out by armed detectives, the shopkeeper is quizzed for security and politics, there are around twenty cameramen and film crews...

It's 'total rubbish' but it works. Blair then recounted another piece of staged authenticity at a time when unpleasant rows with his Chancellor Gordon Brown threatened to upset his re-election bid in 2005. Labour's public relations team wanted pictures of the two top members of the government being matey and 'authentically' united. They were instructed to do something photogenic and – the important word here – 'normal'.

'Go and buy ice cream from that van there, one for you, one for Gordon, to show togetherness and being normal,' Blair was instructed by an aide, Kate Garvey, who pointed him in the direction of a vehicle with Mr Whippy painted garishly on its side.

'No,' Blair protested. 'It's absurd... we're two guys in suits, one is the prime minister, the other is the Chancellor of the Exchequer. What's normal about it?'

'Just do it,' Kate Garvey said menacingly.

Blair did as instructed. He is scathing about the 'elaborate pretence', but understood it was necessary and (for him at least) useful. Kate Garvey did a good job. Blair's advisers also insisted that he should learn a price list of daily essentials for 'normal' people who might go to the supermarket:

I would have to go through a list of the price of everyday things like a pint of milk, a pound of butter, a shoulder of lamb. Bread used to produce lengthy debates about which type of loaf, white or brown, nothing too wholemeal, nothing too unhealthy, all of it done in the belief that if I knew such a fact, it would mean I might be going down to the shop near Downing Street (not that there was one) and collecting the groceries, which of course I wasn't. But people have great faith in the power of such trips to 'connect' with the public, and who's to say they're wrong.

Blair then accurately summed up twenty-first-century leadership, and its phoniness in a concluding wry phrase: 'It's about temperament, character and attitude. It's also about being authentic.'[11]

Authenticity is so important that Tony Blair clearly agreed not only with George Burns about faking it but also with Coleridge that 'human interest and a semblance of truth' made the fantastical seem real. If you push these leadership lessons just a little further, you end up with the language of division. The best guide here is one of the shrewdest communicators on Washington's Capitol Hill, Newt Gingrich.

The Third Wave

Newt Gingrich was the formidable Speaker of the United States House of Representatives from 1995 to 1999. Gingrich, whom I met on a number of occasions when I worked in Washington, was always charming, good company and provocative. He had a vast intellectual hinterland and he liked good-natured argument. He was a friend and admirer of Heidi and Alvin Toffler, the futurologists who wrote *Future Shock* (1970) and *The Third Wave* (1980). When Alvin Toffler died in 2016, Gingrich wrote an affectionate obituary, noting that the central thesis of *The Third Wave* had changed politics forever:

Its argument was that the first wave in human history was the shift from hunter-gathering to agriculture; the second wave was from agriculture to industry; and the third wave – which we were beginning to live through – was from industry to information... While I was in Congress, I brought the Tofflers into the Conservative Opportunity Society activist meetings I held among House Republicans, and the couple spent entire days brainstorming with us about how the world was changing, what it meant and how government should change.[12]

The Tofflers' ideas about the information revolution inspired Gingrich to think about how politicians could structure communications with voters in this new world. It worked. In 1994 Gingrich led his Republican party to an astonishing landslide in the mid-term Congressional elections. His conservative revolution was so successful that by 1996 President Bill Clinton had to admit in his State of the Union address that 'the era of big government is over'. Gingrich circulated a private document to Republican candidates entitled 'Language, a Key Mechanism for Control'. The word 'control' is a clue to what Gingrich was trying to achieve, and gestures to a language and vocabulary that is also at the empty heart of much of British politics. Gingrich recognised that if you can 'control' the vocabulary used in the media about you, your ideas, ideology and party, in a democracy you will win. This is the ultimate in techniques of 'messaging' being the key, whatever the content or wisdom of the message, or policy.

Gingrich's insight was based on the work of one of the United States's most highly respected political and public relations consultants, Frank Luntz, an Oxford University contemporary of Boris Johnson. An hour spent with Frank Luntz is never wasted. I attended focus groups organised by Luntz in which he tested language and tried to find words that resonate with voters to enable his clients to change public opinion and sell their ideas or products by changing the vocabulary that they use. Luntz suggested that Republicans opposed to an estate tax should call it instead a 'death tax'. ('High tax Democrats even want to tax the dead.') They were told to speak of 'climate change' rather than 'global warming'. ('Change can be good, right?') Inspired by Luntz, Gingrich offered a vocabulary of 'control' to less experienced candidates in his own party. There were two lists. The first list was called 'Optimistic Governing Words'. Gingrich said these 'can give extra power to your message'. The optimistic words Republicans were to use about themselves and their own party included: 'candid, care, challenge, change, children, courage, debate, dream, environment, family, hard work, legacy, liberty, opportunity, peace, proud, reform, share, tough, we/us/our.' Then Gingrich offered a selection of 'contrasting' words to define opponents, with a reminder of what the point of all this is supposed to be: 'Remember that creating a difference helps you... Apply these to the opponent, their record, proposals, and their party: bureaucracy, cheat, collapse, corrupt, crisis, cynicism, decay, destroy, destructive, failure, hypocrisy, incompetent, selfish, sick, steal, traitors, urgent, waste...'[13]

These words are value-loaded and deliberately divisive but, crucially, policy free. None of the Gingrich vocabulary tells voters anything about their lives, about governing or explaining policy. Instead, the vocabulary is entirely concerned with affirming that one team (Republicans) is composed of the Good Guys who share your values – family, hard work, and so on. The other team (Democrats) are the Bad People – they are associated with decay, they are destructive, selfish and sick. You may recoil at such cynicism, but rarely has it failed to be effective. The question is whether you or I will be impressed or fooled by it. The answer is – probably – yes. If you think about the speeches of politicians that you know, or see photos of them buying ice creams or drinking a pint of beer, visiting a local supermarket, or Boris Johnson driving a tractor through phoney bricks to 'Get Brexit Done', and then consider the way such stories are written for the evening news or on newspaper front pages, you will hear the words of Gingrich and see the 'authenticity' of the type Tony Blair mentions. Listen to Prime Minister's Questions, read opinion columns, especially in tabloid newspapers, and the echoes of the

Gingrich/Luntz vocabulary are everywhere, right down to the gutter media campaign calling judges 'Enemies of the People'. Donald Trump used the dim bulb version of the Gingrich vocabulary. He would make America 'great' again, and 'build' a wall while opposed by 'Crooked' Hillary who would 'destroy' American 'values'. Trump would often repeat the same 'positive affirming word' three times in three consecutive sentences: 'I'm the most successful person ever to run for the presidency, by far. Nobody's ever been more successful than me. I'm the most successful person ever to run.'[14] Trump's oratorical style is a constant reminder of the old Bette Midler joke about narcissism in the movie *Beaches*, 'But enough (of us talking) about me. Let's talk about you. What do you think of me?'

This vocabulary of love and hate inevitably bleeds into newspaper headlines. If you removed the words bureaucracy, cheat, collapse, corrupt, crisis, cynicism, decay, destroy, destructive, failure, hypocrisy, incompetent and many others in a similar vein from the news pages and opinion columns of the *Daily Mail* or *The Sun*, the tabloids would be even thinner than they are at present. For a flavour of the 'optimistic governing words' applied to those overtly or covertly endorsed by British newspapers, consider the headlines when the prime minister announced his 'Stop the Boats' anti-migrant policy in March 2023. Rishi Sunak, we learned, was prepared to 'battle' judges over whether it was legal (*Times*). 'Rishi Lays Down Law' because 'We Decide' (*Express*) while critics make 'jibes' (*Telegraph*) and 'face rebuke' (*Mail*). And so on. And on. Our decisive action man Rishi – 'Dishy Rishi' – in Number Ten is 'battling' the 'carping' critics, and the value-loaded words are given prominence long before the inconvenient facts make an appearance, if they feature at all. These facts include: people-smuggling in the Channel became a significant problem only after 2018 because Brexit ruined relationships with our European friends and neighbours, which meant we could no longer easily send migrants back to France; the UK takes far fewer refugees than similar European countries; the UK suffers from acute labour shortages and could actually use economic migrants – and so on. Such facts, if they are mentioned at all, can be presented in the

Gingrich 'contrasting' negative words – the idea that the 'carping critics' dislike 'being tough' on 'illegal migrants' in ways that merely seems 'virtue signalling' among the 'wokerati' who will 'open the floodgates' to 'millions' of 'illegal' migrants. Such words have a limited degree of rational meaning beyond the idea that the person calling you 'woke' and describing the migrants as 'illegal' doesn't like you, or them. One way, then, in which media literacy can work is to consider, rather like the oppositional Gingrich vocabulary, what the opposite of these words might mean. If you are not 'woke' are you 'asleep' to what is going on around you? If you are not 'virtue signalling' perhaps you are signalling that you prefer vice?

The benefit of media and information literacy is to signal to voters and citizens that such confidence tricks infect our news sources and reduce political debate to a series of unhelpful code words. This is especially true on wedge issues such as immigration, gender politics and re-evaluations of Empire. But once the first lessons in media and information literacy begin, then perhaps some British newspaper sales and TV audience figures will suffer, or – we can hope – perhaps editors and journalists may be encouraged to improve the quality of the information they provide, or face extinction. Either way, our responsibility as citizens is to become our own editors. It is in our own best interests to deconstruct the misleading messages that bombard us, and sometimes this is easy. For example there is the 'most successful' Donald Trump who told the American people in 2020 that he was a greater president for African-Americans than Abraham Lincoln, the president who actually freed the slaves: 'I think I've done more for the Black community than any other president', Trump said, 'and let's take a pass on Abraham Lincoln, cause he did good, although it's always questionable'. Or, slightly more subtly, there is Boris Johnson playing at being the scruffy but witty Latin-literate Old Etonian (with a degree in Classics, but he never mentions it) on *Have I Got News For You*; or there's the hapless wannabe Liz Truss in a battle tank pretending to be Mrs Thatcher during the Cold War. Artificial Intelligence, deepfakes and all the other products of modern technology are the most novel part of this mix of deceit from the hidden persuaders. But if we cannot see through shallow fakes, the stunts, photo opps and vacuous vocabulary of division, then we stand no chance with the deepfakes of the future. That means we also need to understand a profession intimately connected to politics yet often hidden in the shadows. It has a long and problematic history. It also has many names. One of those names is 'propaganda'.

Propaganda, Public Relations and Trust

If he were alive today the father of modern public relations, Edward Bernays, would understand the value of social media in spreading the word. But what most interested Bernays was the word itself. He called his profession 'propaganda' and was the author of a book with that name. Pope Gregory XV established the Congregatio de Propaganda Fide in 1622 – the congregation for the propagation of the faith. It was designed as a counter-blow in the information wars of the seventeenth century, between the Vatican and those considered by the pope to be spreading the theological fake news of the day. The Protestant Reformation was sweeping across northern Europe. Its most potent weapon was its own media and information literacy – the words of the Bible itself, with translations available in German, French, Dutch, English and other languages ordinary people could understand. By the twentieth century the word 'propaganda' fell into disrepute. The profession of spreading news and information for political or business purposes was renamed Public Relations. Nowadays PR companies are so aware that their profession is, like propaganda, not always trusted that they continually rebrand themselves. They have a variety of impressive titles including strategic communications, consulting, image management, marketing, corporate advertising, information consultancy, promotions, life coaching and other benign sounding synonyms. Rebranding, finding new words for tarnished products, is the key skill of public relations. In the 1990s Tony Blair spoke of 'New' Labour and Bill Clinton of the 'New' Democrats, while in 2000 George W. Bush rebranded himself as a 'Compassionate Conservative'. Bush said, 'It is compassionate to actively help our citizens in need. It is conservative to insist on accountability and results.' For a translation into plain English, at George Bush's Philadelphia Convention I asked a prominent Bush supporter what being a Compassionate Conservative, a New Democrat or New Labour really meant. He laughed and said: 'It means that whatever we were in the past that you don't like, we're not that any more. But whatever it was in the past that you do like, well, we're still that.'

The propagation of information is only good or bad depending on the content and the intentions, good or otherwise, of those communicating it. Trust in the British media enjoyed an uptick, for example, during the coronavirus pandemic. That's because we heard not only from politicians trying to sell us something 'authentic' using the Gingrich vocabulary and the Blair techniques. Instead we heard first hand from real experts, doctors, virologists and other scientists, who gave us fact-based and expertly presented information that might save our lives. They also gave us something politicians rarely do. Doubt. Real experts admit when they do not know the answer to a question. They explain why there is often no certainty in science. Politicians rarely publicly talk of their doubts. In years of interviewing frontline politicians, presidents and prime ministers from Brazil, Israel and Pakistan to Downing Street, the White House, the Élysée Palace and the German Chancellery, the only leading politician I have ever interviewed who said 'I do not know the answer to that' was David Miliband, former British Foreign Secretary (2007–10). He bluntly accepted that he did not immediately know what to do about a sudden crisis involving Libya. His admission of doubt made me trust Miliband all the more. Even from leaders trying to be honest, the distinction between information designed genuinely to inform and that created to misinform is not always obvious.

As the world saw with Donald Trump, the use of the phrase 'Fake News' can be effective, even though it merely follows the Gingrich vocabulary of 'controlling words' to abuse enemies rather than establish the truth. Trump shamelessly described awkward facts about himself as Fake News to blur the difference between truth and falsehood. In Britain in March 2023, a preliminary report for an important parliamentary disciplinary committee, the Privileges Committee (where Conservative MPs were in the majority) said that the evidence 'strongly suggests' that the former prime minister Boris Johnson knew that parties he held in Downing Street breached coronavirus lockdown rules in ways that were 'obvious'. Johnson's first response through a spokesperson was that this meant the committee 'will vindicate Boris Johnson's position', because 'the evidence will show that Boris Johnson did not knowingly mislead parliament'.

For all of us as citizens, therefore, trying to decide who is telling the truth or where the facts lie can unfortunately seem like a full-time job especially since the volume of information has increased exponentially. Technological changes also mean that the sophisticated delivery of fakery into our homes, phones, and social media groups is able to reach almost anyone. Hidden persuaders may have good or evil motives. Our task as citizens is to figure out how to separate the good, the bad and the ugly. As a PR professional would say, that's a 'challenge', especially when the hidden persuaders know their trade so well.

Edward Bernays worked during the First World War for Woodrow Wilson's benign sounding Committee on Public Information. His job was to promote US participation in the war against Germany to an American public sceptical of foreign entanglements, especially on the battlefields of faraway Europe. Bernays, like many excellent communications specialists, was originally a journalist, and a good one. He believed in herd instinct, a concept elaborated in his most famous work, *Propaganda*, written in the 1920s:

The receptivity of the great masses is very limited, their intelligence is small, but their power of forgetting is enormous.

In consequence of these facts, all effective propaganda must be limited to a very few points and must harp on these in slogans until the last member of the public understands what you want him to understand by your slogan.[15]

In fact that quote is not from Bernays. It is from another public relations genius of the same era, an Austrian writing in a Bavarian jail cell, a German ex-soldier from the First World War: Adolf Hitler. It's from Chapter 6 of *Mein Kampf*, written a few years before Bernays wrote *Propaganda*. These two men – one working for democracy, the other working to destroy it – were, in their very different ways, shrewd analysts of the power of persuasion to build trust in ideas, policies and individuals. Here is the real Bernays although it could just as easily have been his Austro-German contemporary:

The conscious and intelligent manipulation of the organised habits and opinions of the masses is an important element in democratic society. Those who manipulate this unseen mechanism of society constitute an invisible government which is the true ruling power of our country. In almost every act of our daily lives whether in the sphere of politics or business, in our social conduct or our ethical thinking, we are dominated by the relatively small number of persons... who pull the wires which control the public mind.[16]

Bernays was the nephew of Sigmund Freud, the founder of psychoanalysis. His insight about 'an invisible government which is the true ruling power of our country' is chilling. Almost a century before the words 'social media' entered our daily vocabulary, Bernays understood the significance of the 'unseen mechanism of society' while working as a skilful manipulator of public opinion for a democratically elected US president. We fret about Chinese ownership of TikTok, Elon Musk taking over Twitter or companies like Cambridge Analytica targeting selected voters with specific Brexit messages during the 2016 referendum, but there is nothing new in fearing that 'an invisible government' is pulling the strings. Our task as citizens in a democracy is to try to make the invisible more visible and thus accountable. The information age gives skilful twenty-first century manipulators a vastly bigger platform, an enormous potential audience and unlimited opportunities to inform or misinform a far wider national and international public. It also makes it more difficult for the rest of us to verify what we are being told. But the vocabulary – Gingrich's affirming words for political allies and nasty negative terms for enemies – doesn't change much. The techniques of manipulation don't change much either. These extend from coaching fifteen-year-old Nayirah for her TV performance, to twenty-first-century politicians in staged photo opportunities, and to prime ministers rehearsing their witty 'ad libs' as responses in Prime Minister's Questions in parliament.

Bernays is instructive about the real issue being the skill of the hidden persuaders in selling a message. That skill is much more important than the platform on which the message is made public or even the truth about the product they are selling. They will make the case for or against Brexit, for or against a sugar tax, fossil fuels, eating cornflakes, the Labour Party, a presidential candidate, or a new brand of car, and will be paid well for doing so. Their task may even be to make the case for war. And nowadays their key skill is to surf the waves of discontent in our suspicious century to offer a clear image of something we can, apparently, know for a fact, understand, relate to and ultimately trust. For an unknown politician the prize is to turn into a relatable Tom Hanks or Sandra Bullock, someone *Reader's Digest* subscribers will trust; or it's to be a Boris Johnson coached by Lynton Crosby to make headlines, distract from scandals, and employ buffoonery and Old Etonian charm to make himself seem amusing and charismatic. It's pure gold, especially when the reach of deceit has grown exponentially in the twenty-first century. I'm based in England, but I read British, Scottish and Irish print newspapers and magazines, online news sources such as the *New York Times* and the *Atlantic*, social media platforms, and news from Germany, *Deutsche Welle*, and from the Gulf, a newspaper called *The National*. The century-old medium of broadcasting also has a worldwide audience that has rapidly expanded across borders. The US presidency and the British royal family have always been international box office, from *The Crown* and *West Wing* to glimpses into their 'real' lives. The growth of that audience is astonishing:

> Twenty million watched Queen Elizabeth II's coronation in 1953. 300 million watched her sister's wedding in 1960. One billion watched her daughter in law's wedding in 1981. Two billion watched her daughter in law's funeral in 1997. A reality TV presenter became US president in 2016.[17]

For all of us as citizens, therefore, the challenge of improving our media literacy is daunting but necessary. As our own editors we have many choices – including the choice to trust those who are demonstrably untrustworthy. But there is one further complication. In the twenty-first century information business in Britain and elsewhere there are now more public relations specialists than journalists. There are more poachers than gamekeepers, and the rewards of poaching tend to be much greater.

Churnalism

In his book *Flat Earth News*, *Guardian* journalist Nick Davies recounts that when he began his career as a reporter in the 1970s it was rare to come across public relations specialists. By 2009, he discovered, Britain 'has more PR people (47,800) than journalists (45,000)'.[18] Research by Aeron Davis of City University in London[19] concluded that in 1979 only 28 per cent of the top fifty companies in *The Times* 1,000 list used PR agencies. By 1984 that number had risen to 90 per cent. By the twenty-first century it was presumed to be 100 per cent. Even paramilitary or terrorist organisations recognise the need for good public relations. They have their own press 'handlers'. In the case of the Provisional IRA, those I met during the Troubles were skilful and well-read. Since the IRA ceasefire, some of them have become elected politicians. Traditional politicians also understand the importance of corporate messaging. When Margaret Thatcher became prime minister in 1979 she promised to cut UK government bureaucracy. But spending on one area – government PR – went up almost six-fold from £27 million a year (at the Central Office of Information) to £150 million. The Blair government continued the trend by hiring 310 press officers in Blair's first two years in office, increasing the number of press releases by 80 per cent to 20,000 a year. This trend became known as 'spinning' the news although there is nothing new about it.

In Athenian democracy Plato disapproved of what he saw as 'rhetoric'. In the Socratic dialogues, notably *Gorgias*, he was suspicious of the skilful use of language to persuade the ignorant masses. Plato compared it to a chef masking bad food with good culinary skills. By the time of *Gulliver's Travels* (1726) Jonathan Swift could write 'there was a society of men among us, bred up from their youth in the art of proving, by words multiplied for the purpose, that white is black, and black is white, according as they are paid. To this society all the rest of the people are slaves.'

Two millennia since Plato and three centuries after Jonathan Swift, the *Columbia Journalism Review* (*CJR*) fretted about 'journalism in crisis' and the idea that newspapers, radio and TV were increasingly unable to offer a reliable critique of those in power. It came as a result of layoffs, cutbacks and bankruptcies decimating once trusted sources of information in the United States (where the *CJR* is based), but also in the UK, Australia, Canada and across Europe at a time when Fake News – the real mendacious fakery, not the inconvenient facts that populists denounce as fake – was spreading exponentially. The *CJR* quoted European Journalism Observatory research that chronicled 'cutbacks across Germany, Italy, the UK, Poland, Portugal, Latvia, Georgia and Spain. In Italy, many newsstands declared bankruptcy, with 1,410 closing in the first half of 2020 alone (some of this would undoubtedly be covid related). In Poland, some regional newspaper publishers reported revenue loss up to 80 per cent; local independent publications reported similar losses in Ukraine.'[20] Countless journalists moved into other sectors of the communications business, or became public relations specialists. I have met many journalists who have gone into PR. I have never yet met any PR professionals who have jumped in the opposite direction. If some do exist I'd be interested in hearing their stories. In twenty-first-century Britain, there are more spinners than those spinned against. Exact numbers are difficult to authenticate because so few PR people identify as PR people, but Statista calculated that there were 'approximately 61,800 people employed or self-employed as public relations professionals in the United Kingdom in 2021, compared with 37,500 in 2010'. Working from a different data set, in January 2022 the PR specialists Wadds put the figure at 94,000 in the PR 'industry'.[21]

The Labour Force Survey noted how financially unrewarding factual journalism may be, and how unstable. By 2015 some 36 per cent of self-employed journalists were claiming UK state benefits or tax credits because their pay was so low, even though journalist qualifications are often high. Roughly 80 per cent of journalists are graduates – but the average journalist's salary in the UK in 2022 was put at less than £28,000 (higher in London; lower elsewhere).[22] According to British government figures 'average weekly earnings were estimated at £621 for total pay and £578 for regular pay in September 2022', which is lower than the average wage.[23]

Both the numbers and salaries of journalists are eclipsed by (self-identified) PR specialists. According to a gushing report in the industry journal *PR Week*:

The PR sector has not just survived recession and its unconfident, penny-pinching aftermath, it has positively thrived. Turnover has increased by a staggering 28 per cent since the last PRWeek/ PRCA Census published in 2011, up from £7.5bn to £9.62bn. Headcount is up from 61,600 to 62,000, which in context means that productivity per head has rocketed from £121,753, which was pretty impressive, to £155,162 per head. Meanwhile salaries have increased to an industry average of just under £54,000, up some £5,500 on two years ago.[24]

All this happened at a time when the capacity of British journalists to verify and scrutinise the claims made to them by the PR industry has been significantly diminished. Some do not even attempt to do so. One result is that pressure to fill space in newspapers and on news bulletins, often from work overload rather than malice, leads some journalists to recycle or churn out 'news' based on press releases, PR offerings and stories lifted from wire services, sometimes without having the time or the ability to check the veracity of the contents. This is known as 'Churnalism'. The magazine *Private Eye* satirises this tendency with humorous 'news' reports written by their hard-working journalist 'Phil Space'.

As one study puts it, by 2005,

average staffing levels of Fleet Street [newspaper] companies were slightly lower than they had been in 1985. But the amount of editorial space which those journalists were filling in their papers had trebled. To put it another way, during those 20 years the average time allowed for national newspaper journalists to find and check their stories had been cut to a third of its former level... That is a disaster. It shoves a blade right into the heart of the practice of journalism.[25]

The same is true in television. In the BBC or independent TV and radio thirty years ago, a reporter usually began a career specialising in either television or radio, but generally not both. Now that same reporter in the BBC will – depending on their precise role – typically work for a combination of TV, radio, online, twenty-four-hour domestic British news, plus news aimed at a world audience, and may also be expected to write for the BBC News website, a blog, a podcast, and may be required to tweet and to use Facebook if appropriate for their role. Similar changes in work patterns apply to private sector broadcasters. Phil Space has a TV colleague called Phil Time. There are some advantages to all this. Personally, I benefited enormously from being able to work for a range of platforms, as do all journalists and editors who want to maximise the outreach and impact of their stories. But a Reuters Institute for the Study of Journalism report noted the potential downside: 'The increasing use of PR materials as an information or editorial subsidy may be one response to resource constraints in the newsroom.'[26]

What they mean by an 'information or editorial subsidy' is the idea that news organisations will print or broadcast PR material because it fills a space and costs them nothing, except perhaps their reputation. For a sense of how this may work, here's a one-size-fits-all PR template sent to a newspaper by mistake. The *Guardian* reproduced it in full to show how some PR companies make money by filling in blanks on behalf of clients, and sending the finished product to the mainstream media organisations that may publish the PR puff as if it were news:

> I am writing to you from (name of company) (URL of company) to let you know about (our product, new launch, event, award etc). It is (launching, starting, appearing, on sale etc.) from (insert date) and is available from (insert brief description). Don't hesitate to get in touch if you want more information. On (x date), (company name) (company URL) is (details of news – e.g. launching a new product, holding an event, won an award, new person starting a job. Insert line indicating why it is 'news' and what makes it interesting e.g. first time product/event, new launch, celebrity involved, award received. Insert line on what sets you apart – any personal angle or interesting facts/statistics? Other key points – list (bullet points) and other areas of interest (maximum 5 points). Insert prices and availability. Include stockist details if appropriate or location and timing of event. Please let me know if you use this story.[27]

The *Guardian* printed this nonsense for comic effect. You may have read some kind of press release or putative 'news' report that follows this style, especially in hard-pressed local newspapers. Here are four examples of what may result, taken from supposed 'quality' newspapers, and you can imagine what standards may be like in less esteemed publications.

The first three examples are from Rupert Murdoch's *Times*, from just one edition, 1 November 2013. The final example is from the *Daily Telegraph*. All four claim to be based on 'research'. This is a classic PR technique. Research is a Gingrich-style approved positive word to appeal to hard-pressed journalists and editors and therefore to readers too. That's because research is the sort of thing scientists do. Most of us still trust scientists especially when dressed up with a stock photograph of a 'scientist' who may be an attractive actor in a white lab coat pretending to 'do science'. Even if you missed these stories at the time, check your newspaper today and you will find similar research-based 'science' that, after a moment's reflection, you may suspect is hollow or covert advertising trying to sell you something. (The following 'research' stories were still available on the newspaper websites when I last checked in February 2023.)

STORY ONE: 'Women have always had different friends for different moods, but new research says their female sidekicks can be divided into ten types. The obvious characters – the patient Agony Aunt, the Childhood Favourite, the Cry-Baby who only calls when she is down.' The list featured in *The Times* also included 'the Samantha, from *Sex in the City*; the Nigella, a domestic goddess plus Married With Kids and the All Seeing Eye...' This 'research' was conducted by an online promotions site called Promotional Codes. They seek to encourage women shoppers. No mention was made of the methodology used to obtain the information.[28]

STORY TWO: On the same page of *The Times* on the same day as Story One, this appeared: 'For years, men suffering from a cold have had to put up with cries of "man flu" from the fairer sex -- the allegation that they collapse into bed at the first hint of a sniffle. However a survey reveals that women struggle to deal with colds the most and complain about it more.' This 'survey' was revealed to be 'research' commissioned by Beechams. No mention was made of the fact that Beechams makes cold and flu 'remedies', although use of the phrase 'fairer sex' is a classic red-alert that this is PR-Journalese-Churnalism nonsense. No normal person speaks like that.[29]

STORY THREE: *The Times* also published 'news' that 'Italian scientists have found that when dogs are content they wag their tails more vigorously to the right, while an anxious dog's wag will veer to the left -- and other dogs will respond to this.' There was a helpful graphic attached to show the difference between Left and Right.[30]

STORY FOUR: This is from the *Daily Telegraph* of 1 October 2014, under the headline: 'Could previous lovers influence appearance of future children?' To help you increase your trust in the content, the story was written not by some anonymous eccentric howling on the internet but by a *Telegraph* 'Science Correspondent'. The story was illustrated with a picture of an attractive family, mum, dad and two kids and was based, inevitably, on 'scientific research'. But unfortunately – if you got as far as paragraph six – you would discover that the research into whether your previous lovers could influence the appearance of your future children was conducted on... fruit flies. Unless *Telegraph* journalists have fruit flies as lovers (and who am I to judge?) the journalistic leap from the much-researched drosophila melanogaster to the sex life of homo sapiens is considerably greater than the supporting scientific evidence.[31]

All four stories reveal something of the techniques that lead to nonsense being dressed up as credible research in the legacy media, including 'quality' British broadsheet newspapers. If those newspapers, with supposedly robust editorial systems, rely even in part on stories like these, then you can imagine that in the Wild West of social and niche media, crackpot theories about coronavirus, the war in Ukraine, or 5G transmitters damaging your health may gain considerable traction. A moment's thought and a little research can often rapidly debunk the nonsense.

For example, I was contacted a few years ago by someone alerting me to the terrible consequences of 'chemtrails'. That person was genuinely alarmed by vapour trails from aircraft and spoke in doom-laden language about the consequences for all humanity. 'Facts' tumbled seamlessly out about the threat from unseen, unknown yet devious conspirators. Two minutes online uncovered a Harvard University report about the 'chemtrails threat':

'Chemtrails' refers to the theory that governments or other parties are engaged in a secret program to add toxic chemicals to the atmosphere from aircraft in a way that forms visible plumes in the sky, somewhat similar to contrails. Various different motivations for this alleged spraying are speculated, including sterilization, reduction of life expectancy, mind control or weather control. We have not seen any credible evidence that chemtrails exist. If we did see any evidence that governments were endangering their own citizens in the manner alleged in the chemtrails conspiracy, we would be eager to expose and stop any such activities... If you believe in chemtrails, ask yourself how you can be so certain that there is indeed a grand conspiracy. Consider alternative, simple explanations. Remember that the Internet is filled with people who are completely sure about stuff that just isn't true. Remember that while governments can keep secrets that involve only a few people they do a very bad job of keeping large-scale programs secret.[32]

I passed on this information to the person who raised the subject with me. I have not heard from him since. Perhaps he was embarrassed. Or perhaps he decided that I had joined Harvard University as part of the vast 'chemtrails' conspiracy. There are still those who believe that in 2016 during the US presidential election, a Washington pizza parlour was the headquarters of a vast conspiracy directed by Hillary Clinton, which involved leading members of the Democratic party and child sex trafficking. In December 2016 a twenty-nine-year-old North Carolina man fired an assault rifle inside the pizza parlour to 'save' the non-existent children trapped from the non-existent sex-slave ring. He was sentenced to four years in prison. Perhaps he also believes that Donald Trump's 2020 election victory was 'stolen'. As the nineteenth-century American showman P. T. Barnum is supposed to have said, 'There's a sucker born every minute.' Or maybe Barnum didn't say it. How do we know for sure?

These examples show that even with shallow fakes and ludicrous stories it is not always possible to separate believers from their potentially dangerous yet demonstrably false beliefs. Yet improving media literacy does offer endless ways that we as citizens can debunk nonsense and expose those who would fool us or misinform us. The truth is out there. At your fingertips. As a suggestion try Googling 'The (New) *Daily Mail* Oncological Ontology Project' (https:// dailymailoncology-blog.tumblr.com/). It was inspired to 'track the *Daily Mail*'s classification of inanimate objects into two types: those that cause cancer, and those that cure it'. The site takes delight in *Daily Mail* headlines and stories such as 'mistletoe, a new branch of cancer treatment' or 'the vitamin jab that shrinks tumours in a day', 'men should wake up and drink the coffee' ('in the battle against prostate cancer'), plus there is (they claim) cancer-fighting potential in Brussels sprouts, kangaroo cream (what?), green tea, and so on. For a fuller list you can try 'The Daily Mail's List of Things that Give You Cancer: From A to Z'.[33] The list, with helpful links, includes air travel, artificial light, babies, oral sex, being a man, being a woman, being a black person, fatherhood, menstruation and – my favourite – dogs. (I have two terriers. I am surely at risk.)

We can ridicule this stuff as 'clickbait' but it all appeared in a popular and professionally produced newspaper or on its website. The website, when I last checked, claims more than 218 million unique visitors per month. As citizens of an advanced but flawed democracy, we therefore have a choice. We can complain about Fake News, but buy into it anyway. We can pursue the ostrich strategy of news avoidance, and hope that sticking our head in the sand means the lions won't eat us. Or we can decide that, just like the food we eat, the information needed to nourish us is our own responsibility. Garbage In really is Garbage Out. The hidden persuaders – politicians, journalists, conspiracy theorists, PR people – will always be there. And good luck to them. Some do a great job. But to make our lives and our country better, the challenge is not to allow the hidden persuaders routinely to persuade us. It is to be sceptical and critical and truly informed.

The former US House Speaker Newt Gingrich once acidly observed that though most people are not stupid, 'they are ignorant'. That meant they were willing to tolerate ignorant politicians making an ignorant speech to be covered by an ignorant reporter and then 'shown in a forty second clip on television to an ignorant audience'.[34] We need not be quite so negative and perhaps instead should turn for guidance to another American politician, Thomas Jefferson: 'Whenever the people are well informed, they can be trusted with their own government; that whenever things get so far wrong as to attract their notice, they may be relied on to set them to rights.'[35]

Gingrich had a point. Jefferson had a vision. I'm with Jefferson and I believe that in sifting through information Britain really is better than some of the nonsense that swells the media in the information age. But that leads to a final big question. In a democracy, informed as well as misinformed, do we get the leaders we deserve?

II

The Leaders We Deserve

'Politics is perhaps the only profession for which no preparation is thought necessary.'

Robert Louis Stevenson, *Familiar Studies of Men and Books* (1882)

A few years ago, a teenage relative was involved in a debating competition against boys from Eton. At the end of the competition I asked her what she thought about the Etonians. She considered the question for a moment: 'They work very hard to make you like them', and then she added, 'so they can f*ck you over.'

I had never heard her swear like that before. But this insight from a teenager may explain in part the link between Edward Bernays' ideas about persuasion, public relations and the recent conduct of some of our leaders in the United Kingdom. The prominence of just one school, Eton, and one university, Oxford, in our political life is truly remarkable. For centuries, they have been key parts of the assembly line for making British leaders, and at times leaders on the make. More than a third of all the United Kingdom's prime ministers, twenty out of fifty-seven, went to Eton. Two of them held office within the past decade, David Cameron and Boris Johnson. They were soon joined in Downing Street by another product of an all-male boarding school, Rishi Sunak (Winchester). All three went to Oxford, as did our other two prime ministers since 2016, Liz Truss and Theresa May. That is five Oxford scholars in a row. This has been a pattern throughout our modern history. More than half, thirty British prime ministers out of fifty-seven, went to Oxford, and fourteen went to Cambridge.

You don't have to be a sociologist to work out that the British political system recruits leaders from a narrow and privileged group. You may wonder whether this shows natural selection from among Britain's best and brightest, or whether it is simply draining one part of the shallow end of the British talent pool as a result of their inherited wealth, connections and privilege. Many years of dealing with this group of politicians and a quick glance at any photograph of members of Oxford's (all male) Bullingdon Club (past luminaries include David Cameron and Boris Johnson) inclines me to the latter view. Either way, what is obvious is that leaders from these institutions do not always immediately empathise with the problems and ambitions of their fellow Britons. In earlier chapters we have used the individual character traits of politicians as a way of examining the inconsistencies and at times stupidities of the British system of governance. This chapter is about the character of the leaders themselves, and how that character may be shaped through their unusual or outstanding educational experiences.

To begin with the obvious, Old Etonians or otherwise, they all do indeed try to make us like them, and some of them seem to bear out the ruder part of my relative's insight. One thing we can be certain about is that, statistically at least, our leaders tend not to be much like you and me. No matter how hard their PR people work, they are not 'normal'. But they do try.

Since the Brexit vote in 2016 I have spoken about Britain's problems at public events all over the UK, from Shetland and Belfast to Kent, London and the west of England as well as dozens of places in between. One laughter line always works. I ask audiences, regardless of their political views, how do you get to be Chris Grayling? Or Boris Johnson? Or Liz Truss? In Conservative voting areas the audiences often laugh the loudest at these questions. I feel their pain. I then ask if any audience member would be happy if – for example – Boris Johnson or Liz Truss or Jacob Rees-Mogg offered to babysit their children or take over their business for a month. Again the usual response is laughter, and that turns the conversation to the question of how it might be possible to get better people at the very top of our political system who do represent the real talents of almost 70 million of us. How do we get representatives – MPs – who are perhaps more representative of our country? Do we get the best people in British politics? And – if not – do we get the leaders that we deserve?

The eighteenth-century Savoyard philosopher, monarchist and counter-revolutionary, Joseph de Maistre suggested the latter. That observation was not meant as a compliment. De Maistre was writing during the bloodiest period of the French Revolution, the Terror, and he was no democrat. He felt that the chaos and violence of life in France was inspired – and deserved – by the French people themselves. They had destabilised the monarchy and the natural hierarchical order of society. That permitted leaders such as Robespierre, Danton and Marat to indulge their taste for despotic anarchy. The reign of the guillotine was a logical outcome of the spread of atheistic and democratic ideas during the Enlightenment, and the instincts of the masses needed to be kept in check by what de Maistre called the great pillars of the 'national mind'. He defined those great pillars as another unholy trinity – Church, Throne and the Hangman:

> All known nations have been happy and powerful to the degree that they have faithfully obeyed this national mind, which is nothing other than the destruction of individual dogmas and the absolute and general rule of national dogmas, that is to say, useful prejudices… Government is a true religion; it has its dogmas, its mysteries, its priests; to submit it to individual discussion is to destroy it; it has its life only through the national mind, that is to say political faith, which is a creed.

What is interesting about de Maistre, the ultra-conservative supporter of 'the absolute and general rule of national dogmas' is that he saw these 'useful prejudices' working most admirably in the English constitution. He spotted that the vague nature of the relationship between the English government, monarchy and parliament was not a separation of powers but rather a consolidation of them at the very top which he called sovereignty. As he put it:

> However sovereignty is defined and vested, it is always one, inviolable and absolute. Take for example the English government: the kind of political trinity which makes it up does not stop sovereignty being one… The powers balance each other, but, once they are in agreement, there is then only one will which cannot be thwarted by any other legal will, and Blackstone [William Blackstone the eighteenth-century

English jurist] was right to claim that the English king and parliament together can do anything.[1]

The idea that an English sovereign government 'can do anything' was obviously appealing to an ultra-conservative counter-Enlightenment French thinker. His, after all, was the land that gave Europe the 'Sun King' Louis XIV who said of the French state, *L'état c'est moi*' – 'I am the state'. The other key envious insight from de Maistre is that while the institutions of government in England supposedly 'balance' each other, once they are in agreement they 'cannot be thwarted'. Things have changed greatly since de Maistre's day. No one pretends that a British prime minister is inviolable and absolute, but the 'balance' within the British constitution has most certainly tipped away from the Crown and parliament towards the prime minister and the government. De Maistre's envy of England is a reminder that the vagueness of the (English) constitution remains an asset to those in power, who ultimately – and with some diminishingly important caveats – 'together can do anything'.

At this point you may begin to understand why Jacob Rees-Mogg and our modern counter-Enlightenment advocates for leaving the European Union are channelling de Maistre when they argue so vociferously that EU membership limited British 'sovereignty'. They appear to believe that sovereignty is like virginity. It's either intact or broken, the position of de Maistre and those in his era who believed in the benefits of absolute monarchy. In modern life we would call this dictatorship. Perhaps we may even recall another unholy trinity in which sovereignty was regarded as inviolable and absolute – Ein Reich, Ein Volk, Ein Führer. Put simply, sovereignty in the twenty-first century can never be completely intact. We live in, and benefit from, a world in which membership of NATO, the United Nations, various principles of international law, the European Court of Human Rights, climate change protocols and the COP process, nuclear test ban treaties, trade agreements and other matters clearly demonstrate that sovereignty is never 'intact'.

De Maistre's other observation, that people get the leaders they 'deserve' is also worth considering. In what sense did even those who voted for him truly 'deserve' Boris Johnson? Did Americans 'deserve' Donald Trump? Since a majority of British voters never directly vote for a prime minister – we vote for our local MP – and since no single party in living memory has secured a majority of the vote, perhaps we get the leaders we deserve only because we have not been sufficiently energised to change a system that so frequently delivers politicians from the public school/Oxford assembly line, those who are mostly not like 'us'.

The good news is that in the past two decades British politics has become much more diverse. There are more women, people of colour, and openly gay or lesbian people entering politics and sitting in the House of Commons than ever before. The fact that Humza Yousaf became First Minister of Scotland while Rishi Sunak was prime minister led to jokes that a man of Pakistani descent and one of Indian descent may be about to agree the Partition of the United Kingdom. Yet many talented people simply do not play a significant part in public life. Most British people would never think of joining a political party. Only a tiny minority of a minority would ever consider running for parliament or even local government. In Britain the phenomenon of news avoidance is coupled with the avoidance of politics, especially in the presence of strangers:

> A majority of Britons (57%) say they have, at least sometimes, found themselves stopping themselves from expressing their political or social views for fear of judgement or negative responses from others. Conservative voters are more likely to say so than Labour voters (68% vs 53%), although notably most people in both groups feel this way. Women are also more likely to have held their tongue than men (62% vs 52%).[2]

The World Values Survey reported in April 2023 that while British people remain firmly in favour of democracy we are overwhelmingly disenchanted with British democracy as it currently operates.

Our satisfaction levels with the British system of governance were comparable to those of citizens in Nigeria and Russia:

> Few people in the UK think politics is working for them, with the country ranking firmly among the bottom half of an international league table for satisfaction with the political system... The research, by the Policy Institute at King's College London, also finds support for the idea that experts, rather than government, should make political decisions is at a record high, and is greater than in any other western nation included in the study... 17% of people in the UK indicate they are highly satisfied with how the political system is functioning these days – among the lowest of 23 countries analysed and on a par with satisfaction in Russia (16%), Mexico (17%) and Nigeria (15%).[3]

Rather than accepting de Maistre's view – that we get the leaders we deserve – perhaps we should reverse his insight and suggest that a broken system often gets the kind of politicians who are attracted to its weaknesses and opportunities. My personal observation is that most British people are engaged in political issues but take the entirely rational view that energetic involvement in the British political system is a waste of their time. Why prop up that which is clearly dysfunctional? What sort of people would wish to do that? Here's a clue.

Only 7 per cent of British people attend fee-paying private or so-called 'independent' schools. Just 0.7 per cent of British people have been to a boarding school. In contrast, in the 2019 General Election almost half (44 per cent) of the elected Conservative MPs and 38 per cent of Liberal Democrat MPs were privately educated, along with 19 per cent of Labour MPs and 8 per cent of those from the SNP.[4]

Four out of five of the most recent British male prime ministers, 80 per cent of the total, went to all-boys boarding schools – Tony

Blair (Fettes), David Cameron and Boris Johnson (Eton) and Rishi Sunak (Winchester). The Private Education Policy Forum's analysis of Boris Johnson's Cabinet of thirty people in June 2019 found that 'eleven went to private boarding schools [that's 37 per cent of the Cabinet compared with 0.7 per cent of the UK]. Three of those went to Eton; thirteen went to private day schools [that's 43 per cent of the Cabinet compared with 6 per cent of the UK]; six went to state schools [that's 20 per cent of the Cabinet compared with 93 per cent of the UK].'

One former boarder, Simon Partridge, has memorably recounted how he personally was damaged by the all-boys boarding experience:

> There is growing evidence from psychotherapists and developmental psychologists that sending children to boarding school at an early age does serious psychological damage. This has come to be formulated as 'boarding school syndrome' by psychotherapy experts Joy Schaverien and Nick Duffell. It is a form of post-traumatic stress disorder due to sudden attachment rupture from the family, frequently followed by abuse and bullying at school. The delegation of supervision in boarding schools to older pupils appears to have enabled a *Lord of the Flies* type of environment… More recently I have identified a more extensive but subclinical condition affecting many in the British upper-class… jokingly referred to as the 'stiff upper lip', signifying this social group's incapacity in the realm of emotional empathy. This incapacity can lead to arrogance, entitlement, misogyny (Cameron's infamous 'Calm down, dear!') and racism (Johnson's casual references to 'watermelon smiles' and 'piccaninnies').[5]

The implications for our public life of having so many leaders from such a narrow background inevitably results in some peculiar leaders doing some very peculiar things. 'Boarding school syndrome' is defined as:

Children sent to boarding school at an early age suffer the sudden and irrevocable loss of their primary attachments and this constitutes a significant trauma... To adapt to the system, a defensive and protective encapsulation of the self may be acquired; the true identity of the person then remains hidden. This pattern may continue into adult life, distorting intimate relationships.[6]

A psychological assessment of British leaders to determine whether they may often be products of a fundamentally damaged elite is beyond the scope of this book. But it is reasonable to conclude that in Britain we do get the leaders we deserve, if only by default, because the rest of us don't try to change the system through which they rise. A second observation is connected to the idea that actors of one sort or another, people who give a convincing performance, are those who build trust even if they are not themselves trustworthy. Joy Schaverien's definition of Boarding School Syndrome includes the telling phrase 'the true identity of the person then remains hidden'. It is worth considering the consequences of having as leaders those who try desperately hard to 'make us like them', and who, we may discover, subsequently try to 'f*ck us over' by keeping their 'true identity' hidden. Their 'true identity' is worth examining in detail.

The Leaders We Have

The Sutton Trust works with a UK government agency known as the Social Mobility Commission to analyse elitism in Britain. In a recent report they found (unsurprisingly) that 'power rests with a narrow section of the population – the 7 per cent who attend private schools and 1 per cent who graduate from Oxford and Cambridge'. The report reveals a 'pipeline' from fee-paying schools through Oxbridge and into top jobs. Some '52 per cent of senior judges came through this pathway. An average of 17 per cent across all top jobs, including 39 per cent of cabinet ministers... were independently educated.'[7]

In 2022 the Sutton Trust celebrated its 25th year of conducting this kind of research with an in-depth study of children born in one year, 1970. By the time of the study this cohort were presumably at the peak of their careers. By the 2020s most Westminster MPs were in their fifties or thereabouts. The report came at the same time that the Johnson government was focusing on their much used (and much derided) social mobility slogan, 'Levelling Up'. The report found that nothing was being 'levelled up'. Britain was in a state of social stasis:

> There is particular immobility at the bottom and top of the income spectrum. Children born into the highest earning families are most likely themselves in later life to be among the highest earners, while children from the lowest earning families are likely to mirror their forebears as low earning adults... 41 per cent of children born into the richest top fifth of homes stayed among the richest homes as adults.

The report uses phrases such as 'opportunity hoarding' implying that those at the top pass on opportunities and wealth to their children in ways unavailable to the less fortunate. The result is that:

> Privately educated elites have been remarkably persistent, making up around 50 per cent of leading people [in the UK] for at least half a century... The Trust has also exposed unpaid and unadvertised internships. Working for free is only fine if you are rich enough to cover the costs. Internships (and exclusive postgraduate courses) have become the gateways to starting a professional career across a range of industries. A tipping point in the modern era is observed also by economists... For much of history, economic growth ensured that each subsequent generation did better than the last. But this is no longer true.[8]

In 2006, 64 per cent of thirty and forty year olds exceeded or equalled their fathers' earnings in real terms at the same ages. But by 2019, this fell dramatically to 44 per cent. For generations growing up in the early twenty-first century the dream of just doing better in life, let alone climbing the income ladder, is disappearing.[9]

For others the dream of doing better is like a family heirloom. Opportunity is not so much hoarded as passed on through the generations. It has even given rise to the term 'nepo babies', originally directed at the progeny of Hollywood stars but now used more generally about those for whom nepotism ensures success. The author Richard Beard is one of the tiny minority of British men who were sent to an all-boys boarding school (in his case, Radley) at an early age. Beard's book *Sad Little Men – How Public Schools Failed Britain* is an account of the childhood of an isolated, privileged and yet emotionally starved elite, many of whom have risen to the top in British politics and other institutions. You may hear echoes of the language Beard uses – the insulation from modernity – in ideas popular with recent British leaders:

Forty years later those school experiences and attitudes have a magnified effect on the country, and in England it isn't difficult to look back and see where the nation's leaders were formed [p. 13]... In 1975, for the boys in the private prep schools of the nation, World War II hadn't ended yet. The last two Japanese soldiers had surrendered from their Philippines jungle in 1974 but small boys in the uniform shorts in the converted country houses of England held out. In the House of Commons private schoolboys of my generation continue to fight World War II even today. Their background is absolutely to blame. [p. 27]... We merged with the past assiduously protected from modernity. Which, as a side effect, kept us insulated from modern Britain. Tom Brown's schooldays at 19th century Rugby were more relatable to us than Tucker's troubles at TV's *Grange Hill*. Our intimacy with history included a kind of ancestor worship. [p. 36]... We favoured Battles of Britain that saved Europe for freedom and democracy proving that because we were English we were special; we were exceptional. Whatever the national question British national identity was the answer. [p. 41]

Beard's book is a personal memoir, not a psychological or political treatise, but his characterisation of emotional starvation and casual cruelty as an essential ingredient in the struggle to 'get on' in Britain is stark and informative. A consideration of the most heated British political debates of the past decade, most notably around Brexit, often includes evocations of the 'Blitz spirit', of national suffering, of standing up to foreign domination rather than cooperating with neighbours, and the idea of English exceptionalism. Beard's notion of ancestor worship comes up repeatedly in the nostalgic pessimism that runs through modern British political discourse. Both Leave and Remain politicians in 2016 used references to the Second World War in their campaigns for and against leaving the European Union, although the lessons they drew were a study in stark contrasts. The UKIP leader Nigel Farage spoke in terms of Brexit as 'the Great Escape'. This was a reference to the celebrated 1963 film about a break-out from a Nazi wartime prison camp. The former Conservative MP and later Brexit Party member Ann Widdecombe claimed on BBC Radio 4 that a No-Deal Brexit would be 'nothing compared to the sacrifice' made in the Second World War 'to ensure Britain's freedom'. Some 880,000 British military personnel died in the Second World War, 6 per cent of the adult male population, one in eight of those in uniform. How lucky we are that Brexit isn't up to those levels of suffering. Meanwhile another Brexit masochist, Ant Middleton, the former special forces soldier and instructor on Channel 4's *SAS: Who Dares Wins* told British people that a No-Deal Brexit 'for our country would actually be a blessing in disguise. It would force us into hardship and suffering which would unite & bring us together, bringing back British values of loyalty and a sense of community! Extreme change is needed!' A researcher from the Department of

War Studies at King's College London discovered that Middleton's rhetoric resonated throughout British culture:

> Particularly on the political right, [British] citizens continue to draw on Britain's military mythology to explain who 'we' are as a people. People explained to me – erroneously – that Britain has never been invaded. They also explained that Britain's imperial wars began to defend new trade routes rather than to plunder existing ones. Some think Britain is the world's leading provider of peacekeepers (it is 36th as of May 2019); others that Britain usually fights alone since they rarely hear about Britain's allies in the media. The idea of Britain standing alone in the Second World War looms large – as one participant explained to me, in comparison, 'America turns up late to any war. Then they think they've won it.' Common stereotypes are that European countries are too cowardly, America is too gung-ho, and other countries are either too ruthless or incompetent. Brexit further reveals the importance of the idea of being at war to other aspects of national life... EU leaders have been bemused at right-wing British politicians suggesting that it is 1940 once more and the EU are the Nazis Britain should stand alone against rather than longstanding allies. This would not have been surprising for the interviewee who, sat in his living room in Birmingham, explained to me that he saw the EU as representing the final conquest of Europe Germany has always wanted.[10]

Other historians of the Second World War noted a similar series of delusional tropes, including one articulated by Peter Hargreaves. He is cofounder of one of the UK's biggest stockbroking companies, Hargreaves Lansdown, and one of Britain's richest men (twelfth richest by some estimates). He was also a major financial backer of the Brexit campaign. Hargreaves compared leaving the EU to the British evacuation from Dunkirk in late May 1940:

It would be the biggest stimulus to get our butts in gear that we have ever had. It will be like Dunkirk again. We will get out there and we will be become incredibly successful because we will be insecure again. And insecurity is fantastic.[11]

My father was a British Expeditionary Force veteran. He was rescued in 1940 from a small boat on which he and others paddled out from Calais as the Wehrmacht stormed the city, then eventually evacuated from Dunkirk by the Royal Navy. I cannot tell you how much William John Esler disapproved of the use of Dunkirk and the supposed Dunkirk spirit for political ends by people who were not in northern France in May 1940. He particularly despised – that is not too strong a word – those who do not seem to recall that the Dunkirk evacuation was the result of a colossal and humiliating defeat. It's rather like saying shooting yourself in the foot is character building because you were originally trying to put the bullet in your head.

The Ladybird View of British History

Richard Beard's memoir is insightful about more than his own life. It raises serious questions about the cultural experiences of those privileged boys who end up in parliament and leading our country. I can't be certain about all the books I read as a child, although Ladybird books, war comics, *The Beano* and *The Hotspur* competed with Just William, Billy Bunter, Jennings and Biggles in my preteen childhood imagination. There were certainly a lot of battles against 'the Hun' and Spitfires taking on Messerschmitts in endless dogfights over white cliffs. What we do know is that David Cameron (Old Etonian) was born in 1966; Nigel Farage, the most consequential politician who never made it to parliament in recent years, was born in 1964 (he attended Dulwich College, a school where he said he was 'terrified'). Boris Johnson (Eton) was also born in

1964; Michael Gove (Robert Gordon's, Aberdeen) on 26 August 1967; Theresa May was born in 1956 (she attended a girls' grammar school which later became a comprehensive) and Keir Starmer (grammar school) was born on 2 September 1962. I stumbled on a clue to the formative years of that generation of leaders in the late 1960s and 1970s when I came across a copy of Ladybird's *Flight Five: Africa*. That specific title may not have been on their reading lists (or mine – I certainly do not remember it). But the vocabulary, certainties and assumptions of life in that period as depicted by the Ladybird history of British colonialism are revealing.

First published in 1961, the book then cost two shillings and six pence (12.5 pence nowadays). *Flight Five: Africa* is a guide to some of the illusions and myths that children born in the 1960s imbibed with hot milky drinks at bedtime and are regurgitated by prominent people in public life even in the twenty-first century. It follows a group of wealthy white British children being shown what the book describes as 'the dark continent'. (Incidentally, I've been to north, south and east Africa and can report that it tends to be sunny and light rather than dark. That notion of the 'dark continent' has its own history of European assumptions about Africa as a zone of ignorance and savagery.)

The book begins with 'an Arab in the Sahara desert' seeing a modern British Comet airliner bearing the visiting children as they fly above him heading south. He looks up at the sky with wonderment. On arrival in East Africa 'Daddy' explains that 'the British came here to stop the slave trade'. There were many reasons why the British conquered Africa from the Cape to Cairo but stopping the slave trade was not the goal that immediately comes to mind for most twenty-first-century historians. No mention is made in the book of the British coming to Africa to profit from the slave trade. Royal approval for slave trading was granted to British merchants in 1663. The trade was theoretically abolished in 1807 across the British Empire but continued until the Slavery Abolition Act of 1833. It lasted even beyond that in areas run by the East India Company, where the practice continued until 1838.

More than 3 million African people were trafficked on British ships. At the time it was the greatest forced migration in history. When the trade ended, Britain compensated slave owners for loss of their 'property'. No slaves were ever compensated. In *Flight Five: Africa* British exceptionalism means 'we came here to stop the slave trade', while others – 'the Portuguese' and 'Arabs', we are told – continued to fight over its riches.

At Victoria Falls the children's conversation turns to Dr Livingstone. Daddy explains: 'He was a doctor, a missionary and a very brave explorer... he made very careful maps, healed the sick, made friends with the Africans, who were all savages then... a great and wonderful man.' The casual dismissal of African culture – 'all savages' – was typical of the time. So was the idea that Cecil Rhodes was a great and wonderful man. Rather than plundering the riches of Africa, we learn that Rhodes 'made peace with the African chiefs and used his fortunes and energy to develop the country. That is why it is called Rhodesia.'

It's a lovely story. It's also mostly nonsense. Cecil Rhodes had a leg-up even as a teenager. He began in the diamond trade as an eighteen-year-old in Kimberley. He founded De Beers in South Africa in 1888. By 1891 his company was mining 90 per cent of the world's diamonds. We may hazard a guess that whatever Rhodes put into Africa, he took considerably more out. The book ends with paternalistic pride: 'In all the countries which have been under British control they are being given their independence as soon as they are able to manage their own affairs.'

Flight Five: Africa, the Ladybird history of an entire continent aimed at British children in the 1960s, was published fourteen years after the partition of British India which – the best estimates suggest – led to around a million deaths and 15 million or more people forced to flee their homes. And yet the tone and the language resonates for some in the twenty-first century. Africa is even now sometimes discussed as if it were one country, one people with one culture. At the 2016 Conservative party conference the then British Foreign Secretary (the Foreign Secretary!) Boris Johnson instructed his party in language which could have come from the Ladybird version of world affairs: 'Life expectancy in Africa has risen astonishingly as that country has entered the global economic system.' There are currently fifty-four countries and 1.3 billion diverse people on the African continent. Britain's role in slavery is still mentioned much more often in relation to abolition rather than in the context of the slave trade's economic role in the growth of the Empire. And there's more.

Here is Boris Johnson writing in the *Spectator* in 2002, forty-one years after the Five flew to Africa. His article employs Ladybird history for the education of readers of one of the United Kingdom's supposedly sophisticated news magazines. The title of Johnson's column is 'Africa is a mess, but we can't blame colonialism'. He writes: 'It is just not convincing... to blame Africa's problems on the "lines on the map", the arbitrary boundary-making of the men in sola topis.' (A sola topi (sic) is a pith helmet of the sort worn in India more often spelled 'solar topee'.) Johnson continues:

> The continent may be a blot, but it is not a blot upon our conscience. The problem is not that we were once in charge, but that we are not in charge any more... Consider Uganda, pearl of Africa, as an example of the British record. Are we guilty of slavery? Pshaw. It was one of the first duties of Frederick Lugard, who colonised Buganda in the 1890s, to take on and defeat the Arab slavers.

Pshaw? For those who do not speak Etonese, 'pshaw' is an expression of contempt or disbelief. As for Frederick Lugard, he was a very able soldier and administrator. Here's a slightly different version of what he was up to in Uganda:

> Within eighteen months—not without a brief use of his one operative Maxim gun—Lugard imposed peace, carried out an immense march to the west, and won a treaty of allegiance from the kabaka (the king). Hearing that his company meant to abandon Uganda because of mounting expenses, he hurriedly

returned to England to fight a successful two-pronged campaign to defend, first, the retention of Uganda in addition to imperial annexation and, second, his own reputation against accusations of harshness and injustice... Though to modern critics of colonialism there may seem much to criticize in his ideas and actions, there can be no questioning the great range and effectiveness...'[12]

Two centuries of British slave trading before 1890 were not worth mentioning either by our future prime minister or his editors at the *Spectator* apparently all content to write off an entire continent as a 'blot'. Then Johnson really gets into his stride:

If left to their own devices, the natives would rely on nothing but the instant carbohydrate gratification of the plantain. As one British official said: 'I've been in Africa for ages and there's one thing I just don't get. Why are they so brutal to each other? We may treat them like children, but it's not because of us that they behave like the children in *Lord of the Flies*... The best fate for Africa would be if the old colonial powers, or their citizens, scrambled once again in her direction; on the understanding that this time they will not be asked to feel guilty.

One (anonymous) British official in the twenty-first century supposedly said this to Boris Johnson. Really? And he wasn't finished: 'The Queen has come to love the Commonwealth, partly because it supplies her with regular cheering crowds of flag-waving piccaninnies.'[13]

And this on Prime Minister Tony Blair's visit to the Congo in 2002: 'No doubt the AK47s will fall silent, and the pangas will stop their hacking of human flesh, and the tribal warriors will all break out in watermelon smiles to see the big white chief touch down in his big white British taxpayer-funded bird.'[14]

When challenged years later in the House of Commons, Prime Minister Johnson responded merely that he had been misunderstood:

'I have commented many times about the words that I've said in the past and I think the house understands how you can take things out of context.'[15]

Johnson never explained what 'context' would make any of these comments anything less than ill-informed and cartoonishly racist. What they reveal – even if Johnson himself never read *Flight Five: Africa* – is that a particular historical mindset imbibed from childhood still persists in British public life in the twenty-first century. Johnson has frequently written for the *Spectator* and the *Telegraph*, and perhaps we can infer that some of their readers find geriatric racist stereotypes in some way entertaining or incisive.

This mindset persists in the weaponised nostalgia over – for example – the statues of British heroes from the past who turn out to have made their money from the slave trade and other forms of colonial exploitation. Bristol's Edward Colston (1636–1721) is often described as a wealthy slave trader and philanthropist. This is an extraordinary conjunction of activities when you think about it. Colston's statue was defaced, toppled and thrown into Bristol harbour in 2020 during protests related to the Black Lives Matter movement. Similarly the campaign to remove, or oppose the removal of, the statue of Cecil Rhodes in Oxford University led to a long-running debate in Oriel College. The South African historian and Oxford professor William Beinart examined 'whether Rhodes contributed to racial segregation in the Cape Colony; and how to characterise the violence in the conquest of Zimbabwe in the 1890s'. His investigation concluded that: 'with respect to the Cape, the evidence shows that Rhodes made a number of important decisions, or supported developments, that intensified racial segregation in the late nineteenth century. He had some power to influence an alternative political direction in the Colony but advocated a racially restrictive franchise, punitive racially based Masters and Servants legislation, a labour (poll) tax for African people only, a segregated local government system and segregation in the South African cricket team. He was increasingly in favour of segregated urban "locations" and "rural districts".'

Beinart continues:

In respect of Zimbabwe, 1890–97, Rhodes and his Company were responsible for extreme violence against African people. Wars were fought in 1893 and 1896–7: unbridled use was made of the Maxim gun; cattle were looted by the Company and its agents on a large scale; in the 1896–7 war, grain stores and crops were appropriated or destroyed over a sustained period as a deliberate strategy; many Ndebele soldiers were shot in flight; supposed rebels were sentenced and hung or shot without due process of law. Over a period of nine months in 1896–7, African men (including armed men), women and children sheltering in caves were blown up with dynamite, when it was clear that many were being killed. Rhodes was well aware of these practices, at times participating or present while they were taking place, and involved in strategic discussions. Although these are difficult to quantify, it is likely that African deaths in the conquest of Zimbabwe in the 1890s were over 20,000 and perhaps closer to 25,000.[16]

The point here is not to refight so-called Culture Wars battles. It is to insist that a Ladybird version of British history persists in the minds of Boris Johnson and others of his era and background, including those who publish and uncritically enjoy his racist maundering. The idea that the people of 'Africa' are a homogeneous group who have somehow missed out on having British administrators make their lives better would be laughable if it were not so dim-witted and offensive. It is hardly surprising that when weaponised nostalgia meets historically accurate re-evaluations of Britain's imperial past, rhetorical gunfire continues. This historical re-evaluation has produced a rich literature. It includes Beinart's work, Sathnam Sanghera's *Empireland*, Caroline Elkins's research on imperial violence, Kavita Puri's *Partition Voices*, the excellent writings of Manchester University's David Olusoga and many others. These writers touch a raw nerve in British politics because history has become a convenient wedge issue in the UK just as it has in the United States, where the inane *Gone With the Wind* version of the supposed honour and civility of the Confederacy, built on slavery and brutality, is challenged by a host of scholars. Their work, however, has had little impact on politicians including Donald Trump and Ron DeSantis, those who for their own advantage remain prepared to weaponise nostalgia and sanitise the history of slavery as a sop to white, rural, southern voters. Writers who re-evaluate the British Empire by telling the stories of the colonised rather than the imperial colonisers are rarely challenged by coherent counterarguments. Instead they are attacked for being 'woke' or even in some peculiar way 'anti-British', the kind of words and abuse from the Gingrich playbook of division. Rewriting history is not a sin. It is literally the definition of being a historian. History is always changing, while heritage is more rigid. It's the accretion of statues, monuments, castles and ideas from the past, and undeniably, as the British Council has reported, it sells.

In that sense, *Flight Five: Africa* is itself an interesting historical document and an all-too-living part of our heritage. But for the purposes of a critical examination of British governance, the key point is to demonstrate that in twenty-first-century Britain we are still promoting to the highest positions of power (and in sections of the media) people for whom the Ladybird history fantasy even now appears to inform their world view, their judgements and vocabulary. Change, however, is ultimately unstoppable.

Is Britain Better Than This?

In trying to answer the question at the heart of this book – whether Britain truly is better than we appear to be now – I have maintained a veneer of optimism. Good cheer however is often difficult to sustain. Two letters, both to *The Times* newspaper, sum up the British dilemma about our traditions and also about the many good people who make up our country. The first letter is seventy or so years old, although it re-entered our political debate in the past few years. It encapsulates both the idea that good people try to solve problems even if they do so by making up their version of the British constitution. That remains part of the nonsensical, but often well-meaning, vacuity at the heart of the British system. The second letter also captures the basic decency of many of our fellow citizens including those who have served at the highest level as public servants and as Members of Parliament from different political parties.

The first letter was written in 1950 and returned to prominence in October 2019. That month then prime minister Boris Johnson had a very slender majority in the House of Commons. In the depths of despair among pro-Brexit MPs about their dream of Brexit ever being 'done', and following Johnson's failed attempt to suspend parliament through the prorogation measure overturned by the Supreme Court, the Johnson team tried all kinds of backstairs manoeuvrings. Some MPs suggested that a vote of no confidence in the government should be held with the aim of forcing an election. Then anonymous 'sources' in Downing Street suggested that if Johnson did lose a no confidence vote, he would neither step down as prime minister nor would he call a general election. *The Sun* translated this complex political principle into the suggestion that Boris Johnson would tell Queen Elizabeth that she 'can't sack him'. The royal prerogative didn't seem any kind of prerogative any more. Others suggested that this was not the case. And that's when constitutional scholars began quoting the 'Lascelles Principles'. They were named after Sir Alan Frederick 'Tommy' Lascelles GCB, GCVO, CMG, MC, undoubtedly one of British history's Good Chaps. He even featured as a character portrayed by the actor Pip Torrens in the TV series *The Crown*. With a long lineage in the aristocracy, Lascelles had been a boarder at the then all-boys Marlborough School. His education took him along the familiar route to Oxford University from where he became a trusted adviser for British monarchs from the 1920s until the 1950s. Upon retirement in 1953 Lascelles refused a peerage. He opted instead for a GCB (Knight Grand Cross of the Order of the Bath) because he rated this gong much more highly than being sent to the House of

Lords. Yet his place in British constitutional history, and the reason his 'principles' were quoted in 2019 and again when Johnson faced his final crisis as prime minister in 2022, was a letter he wrote under a pseudonym to *The Times* in 1950 when he was King George VI's private secretary. The constitutional dilemma then was also about the monarch calling an election.

The Labour government of Clement Attlee had been elected in the 1945 post-war landslide with a majority of 146. In the subsequent General Election on 23 February 1950, Labour was returned to power but with an overall majority reduced to just five. Amid fears of political instability, speculation grew at Westminster that King George VI would dissolve parliament to enable fresh elections. Could he? Should he? What were the constitutional rules? No ordinary person – and no newspaper political correspondent – had a clue. The Lascelles letter was published on 2 May 1950 to settle the matter, insofar as anything is ever settled in the British constitution. The pseudonym Lascelles chose was 'Senex' (Latin for Old Man). Here is how the supposedly relevant part of what passes for the British constitution was spelled out in the letters pages of *The Times*:

> Sir, It is surely indisputable (and common sense) that a Prime Minister may ask—not demand—that his Sovereign will grant him a dissolution of Parliament; and that the Sovereign, if he so chooses, may refuse to grant this request. The problem of such a choice is entirely personal to the Sovereign, though he is, of course, free to seek informal advice from anybody whom he thinks fit to consult. In so far as this matter can be publicly discussed, it can be properly assumed that no wise Sovereign— that is, one who has at heart the true interest of the country, the constitution, and the Monarchy—would deny a dissolution to his Prime Minister unless he were satisfied that: (1) the existing Parliament was still vital, viable, and capable of doing its job; (2) a General Election would be detrimental to the national economy; (3) he could rely on finding another Prime Minister who could carry on his Government, for a reasonable period,

with a working majority in the House of Commons. When Sir Patrick Duncan refused a dissolution to his prime minister in South Africa in 1939, all these conditions were satisfied: when Lord Byng did the same in Canada in 1926, they appeared to be, but in the event the third proved illusory.

I am, &c.,

SENEX. April 29

The wisdom of what then became known as the Lascelles Principles seems obvious. Lascelles was doing his best for his country, his monarch and for British democracy. But take a step back. The relevant part of the British constitution in a political discussion about Brexit in the twenty-first century was, we were told, based on a letter published anonymously seventy years earlier under a Latin pseudonym in a British daily newspaper. These constitutional principles were articulated by an unelected royal appointee, the private secretary to the king telling the British people under what circumstances they might get a chance to vote for or against a government in difficulty, based on precedents involving two (by then) foreign countries – Canada in 1926 and South Africa in 1939 – former parts of an empire which no longer existed. There was no General Election in 1950 but Clement Attlee did call one in October 1951 and lost, even though his Labour party not only won the popular vote, but also achieved the highest-ever total vote for any party in history, surpassed only by the Conservatives in 1992. Yet Labour in 1951 still lost power because, despite the enormous Labour vote, they won fewer seats. The Conservatives had a majority of seventeen.

There may be readers who believe that publishing in 1950 an anonymous letter from an unelected royal flunkey in a newspaper that was formerly read by the establishment and nowadays is owned by the family of an Australian-turned-American billionaire Rupert Murdoch is a satisfactory way to arrive at a constitutional decision in British democracy, and that all this somehow remains relevant in 2019 and 2022. Personally, I think we really have to consider how to do better than this.

And that's where the second letter comes in. It is another letter to the *Times* which appeared in 2023 from another fine British public servant, reminding us of some of the strengths of our very peculiar country. It was from Sir David Normington. From 2011–16 he was the Commissioner for Public Appointments, a person who, as the government describes it, 'regulates the processes by which ministers make appointments to the boards of national and regional public bodies. The commissioner aims to ensure that such appointments are made on merit after a fair, open and transparent process.'

Sir David chose to write about precisely the key constitutional area where Britain is most vulnerable to abuse, namely the way in which the executive, the government, the prime minister (and even a royal aide like 'Senex') can change the rules of our public life very easily because – stripped of constitutional mumbo jumbo – that which is 'constitutional' in Britain is in reality what the people in charge say it is. Sir David Normington's letter was restrained but clearly somewhat cross. His former job was to be a gamekeeper in a world of poachers. He was particularly exercised by the appointment of Richard Sharp as chairman of the BBC. Mr Sharp, as we saw, had been Rishi Sunak's boss at Goldman Sachs and contributed £400,000 to Conservative party funds. He was also the man who helped fix an introduction to secure a loan of £800,000 for Boris Johnson. Subsequently Mr Sharp was appointed to his top job at the BBC by Johnson himself. No one broke any law of course. Legally all this was just fine. But Sir David's letter suggests we really can do better.

Sir,

In 2016 the government changed the public appointments rules after an independent report by Gerry Grimstone who subsequently became a Conservative peer and government minister. Those changes gave the government the power to write its own appointments rules, appoint the advisory panels, intervene at every stage to get their candidates appointed, ignore the panels' advice and appoint their friends and cronies. The public appointments commissioner, a regulator with few powers, was reduced to a commentator whose advice is easily discounted. The resulting system depends largely on the self-restraint of ministers and the prime minister. Those who want to appoint political donors and allies can do so with impunity. This is how we ended up with a BBC chairman who, whatever his other merits, is a large scale donor to the Conservative party and we now learn a go-between in arranging a loan for Boris Johnson. Is it any wonder that the public have little confidence in either our politicians or those they appoint to lead our most important public bodies?[17]

The Normington and Lascelles letters, taken together, answer Elizabeth's question: 'Why are things so... so shit?' The rules in the Lascelles case were spelled out because Lascelles took the time to consider what they should be, sent his letter to *The Times* and our 'unwritten' constitution had another bit of wisdom added to the accretion of constitutional spaghetti. In the Grimstone case, the rules were changed to give the British government even more power to write its own rules, appoint its own cronies and donors to high office. The person who changed the rules was – on merit – rewarded with a lifetime position in the House of Lords. The result has been that a British government minister is given the power to 'intervene at every stage' in public appointments. The checks and balances of the British system were often in the past merely flimsy constitutional camouflage. Now they mean that the public appointments commissioner has so few powers that the job is not that of a regulator at all, but of a 'commentator'. Normington does not say it, but the spectre of the kind of abuse the Northcote–Trevelyan reforms ended in the nineteenth century has returned. Lascelles and Normington were Good Chaps. Others in our public life are not. Until we find a better way to broaden the talent pool in British public life, to reward those who behave ethically and weed out the others, then de Maistre is indeed correct. We do get the governments we deserve. But can we agree this is an idiotic way to run a country? We really are better than this. Aren't we?

About the Author

GAVIN ESLER is a journalist, television presenter and author. He was a main presenter of the BBC current affairs show *Newsnight* for 12 years until 2014. Since then, he has been a public speaker, political commentator and writer, and currently serves as the Chancellor of the University of Kent.

Acknowledgements

I'd like to thank all the constitutional experts, civil servants, politicians, lawyers, academics and – most of all – voters and citizens whose knowledge, opinions and experiences helped guide this work. I would particularly like to thank those quoted in the text, especially Anthony King who sadly passed away in 2017. Anthony's wit, wisdom and straightforward common sense are sorely missed. Any omissions or errors are mine. I am hugely indebted to two people who championed this book from the start, my agent Andrew Gordon at David Higham Associates and Neil Belton at Head of Zeus. Both helped me emerge from the thickets of research into what I hope is the sunlight of the extraordinary story of the idiosyncrasies of the British constitution, and why it matters. I am also grateful to conversations with countless Members of Parliament, members of the House of Lords, MSPs, and both the Mayor of Greater Manchester Andy Burnham and the Mayor of the West Midlands Andy Street for illuminating some of the areas where the United Kingdom can do better. We have no lack of talent, and no lack of ideas. We need to remember our past, not try to emulate it. Even for those who disagree with the more contentious points in the book, I hope I have at least managed to explain why the peculiarities of the British constitution matter in our daily lives. Finally, I'd like to thank 'Elizabeth', the woman at Dartington Hall who asked me in very blunt terms what had gone wrong in the country she loves. I hope that in searching for an answer I may be of some assistance to all those good people in British public life who prefer to solve problems rather than create them.

Notes

Part One: Inspirations and Irritations

Chapter 1: 'Why are things so... so shit?'

1   'UK immigration routes for Afghan nationals', House of Commons Library, 26 January 2023, https://commonslibrary.parliament.uk/research-briefings/cbp-9307
2   Tim Tonkin, 'NHS in midst of workforce shortfall', www.bma.org.uk/ news-and-opinion/nhs-in-midst-of-workforce-shortfall
3   Office for National Statistics, 'Trust in Government, UK: 2022', 13 July 2022, https://www.ons.gov.uk/peoplepopulationandcommunity/wellbeing/bulletins/trustingovernmentuk/2022#
4   Sam Fowles, *Overruled: Confronting Our Vanishing Democracy in 8 Cases* (Oneworld/London, 2022), p. 5.

Chapter 2: A State of Disunion

5   OECD, 'Paying the Price of War: OECD Economic Outlook, Interim Report September 2022', https://www.oecd.org/economic-outlook/september-2022/
6   The Health Foundation 2020, 'Health Equity in England – the Marmot Review 10 Years On', https://www.health.org.uk/publications/reports/the-marmot-review-10-years-on
7   'NHS vacancy rates point to deepening workforce crisis', *The Health Foundation* (1 Dec. 2022), https://www.health.org.uk/news-and-

comment/news/nhs-vacancy-rates-point-to-deepening-workforce-crisis

8   Hannah White, *Held in Contempt: What's Wrong with the House of Commons?* (MUP/Manchester, 2022), p. 9.

9   Mark Elliott, '"Law in Focus"' – Does the Northern Ireland Protocol Bill Breach International Law?', *Cambridge Faculty of Law* (17 Jun 2022).

10 Andrew Blick, 'What is the Union?', https://publications.parliament.uk/pa/ld201516/ldselect/ldconst/149/14905.htm

11 *Ibid.*

12 Nation Cymru, 'Support for Welsh independence nudges upwards in latest poll before Wrexham march', YouGov poll, https://nation.cymru/news/welsh-independence-poll/

13 Bloomberg TV, 23 September 2022.

14 Michael McDowell, *Irish Times* (5 Oct. 2022).

15 'Ireland GDP', *Trading Economics*, https://tradingeconomics.com/ireland/gdp

16 World Economics, 'Ireland's GDP PPP per Capita', https://www.worldeconomics.com/Wealth/Ireland.aspx

17 World Economics has reassessed Ireland's GDP by adjusting for any base year age and size of the informal economy to estimate GDP PPP at $629 billion – 12 per cent larger than official estimates. The population of Ireland is estimated to be 5 million which gives a GDP per capita PPP of $125,292. This places Ireland in 5th place in the World Economics Global Wealth rankings and 1st for Europe. https://www.worldeconomics.com/Wealth/Ireland

Chapter 3: Idiosyncrasies

1   Departmental Select Committee Factsheet, House of Commons Information Office, August 2010.

2   Electoral Reform Society, 'Analysis: Millions of votes go to waste as parties need "wildly" different number of votes per MP', https://www.electoral-reform.org.uk/latest-news-and-research/media-centre/press-releases/analysis-millions-of-votes-go-to-waste-as-parties-need-wildly-different-number-of-votes-per-mp/

3   Office for National Statistics, 'Electoral statistics, UK: 2019', https://www.ons.gov.uk/peoplepopulationandcommunity/elections/

electoralregistration/bulletins/electoralstatisticsforuk/2019

4 Scolari Federico, 'Why are there still hereditary peers in the House of Lords?', www.electoral-reform.org.uk/why-are-there-still-hereditary-peers-in-the-house-of-lords/

5 Matthew Smith, 'Public opinion of Boris Johnson's competence and trustworthiness reach new lows', https://yougov.co.uk/topics/politics/articles-reports/2022/02/22/public-opinion-boris-johnsons-competence-and-trust

6 UK Parliament 2022, 'Parliament and Crown', https://www.parliament.uk/about/how/role/relations-with-other-institutions/parliament-crown/

7 House of Commons Library, 'The Crown and the Constitution', https://commonslibrary.parliament.uk/research-briefings/cbp-8885/

8 Anthony King, *The British Constitution* (OUP/Oxford, 2007), p. 16 and p. 342.

9 E. M. Syddique, 'This Sceptred Isle', *Guardian*, Research and Information Department, Electoral Reform Society, https://www.theguardian.com/notesandqueries/query/0,5753,-2036,00.html

10 Peter Kellner, *Democracy: 1,000 Years in Pursuit of British Liberty* (Mainstream Publishing/Edinburgh, 2009), p. 223.

11 'Ministerial Code investigation', Gov.uk November 2020, https://www.gov.uk/government/news/ministerial-code-investigation

12 Charles Hynes, *The Daily Telegraph* (20 Oct. 2020)

13 Geidt resignation letter, 15 June 2022.

14 Hannah White, 'What Boris Johnson taught us about the UK constitution', *Prospect* (17 Aug. 2022).

15 King, *op. cit.*, p. 1.

16 Transparency International UK, 'Corruption and the UK', https://www.transparency.org.uk/corruption-and-uk see also https://www.transparency.org.uk/corruption-and-uk/Money%20and%20Politics and https://www.transparency.org.uk/corruption-and-uk/Dirty%20Money

17 Ashley Cowburn, 'Three quarters of public concerned about corruption in government, poll shows', *The Independent* (17 Nov. 2021).

18 *Observer* and *Led By Donkeys* (26 March 2023)

19 Kate Samuelson, 'A timeline of the Tory sleaze allegations', *The Week* (9 Nov. 2021); Halliday, Josh, 'Scandal after scandal: timeline of

Tory sleaze under Boris Johnson', *The Guardian* (1 July 2022); James, Liam and Middleton, Joe, 'Why did Boris Johnson resign as prime minister? Timeline of his biggest scandals as he plots comeback', *The Independent* (23 Oct. 2022).

20 UCL, 'What is the UK Constitution?', https://www.ucl.ac.uk/constitution-unit/explainers/what-uk-constitution

21 King, *op. cit.*, pp. 6–9.

Chapter 4: Innovations

1 Edmund Burke, 'Speech to The Electors of Bristol, November 1774' in Burke, E., *Works 1*, pp. 446–8.

2 Jonathan Jones, speech 6 November 2022, copy kindly passed to the author by Sir Jonathan.

3 Phil Hickley, 'Recreational Fishing in England and Wales', https://www.fao.org/3/W0318E/W0318E20.htm; 'Fascinating facts and figures about the National Trust', *National Trust*, https://www.nationaltrust.org.uk/who-we-are/about-us/fascinating-facts-and-figures

4 Peter Kellner, *Demcracy*, (Mainstrream Publishing, 2009, p. 27).

5 Anthony King, *The British Constitution*, (Oxford University Press, 2009, p. 2).

6 'Ian Paisley accuses Tories of "betrayal" for choosing "English nationalism" over unionism', *The Journal* (8 Feb. 2022).

7 Rob Merrick, 'Brexit: "I fear for my country" says Tory grandee as he brands Boris Johnson as "English nationalist"', *The Independent* (12 Dec. 2020).

8 George Osborne, 'Unleashing nationalism has made the future of the UK the central issue', *Evening Standard* (19 Jan. 2021).

9 Mark Drakeford quoted in report by Gary Flockhart, *The Scotsman* (4 March 2021)

10 Gordon Brown, *Daily Telegraph* (24 Jan. 2021).

11 Akash Paun, 'Brexit, Westminster and Scotland: when constitutional worlds collide', Institute for Government, 20 December 2016, https://www.instituteforgovernment.org.uk/article/comment/brexit-westminster-and-scotland-when-constitutional-worlds-collide

12 King, A., *op. cit.* p. 2.

13 Tom McTague and Robbie Lawrence, 'How Britain Falls Apart', *Atlantic* (5 Jan. 2022).

Part Two: Ideals – Truth, Trust, Tropes and Tradition

Chapter 5: Truth Decay: Strategic Lying, Dead Cats and Our Democratic Recession

1 Bastian Herre, Esteban Ortiz-Ospina and Max Roser, 'Democracy', *Our World in Data*, https://ourworldindata.org/democracy

2 Freedom House, 'Freedom in the World', https://freedomhouse.org/report/freedom-world

3 Sam Delaney, 'How Lynton Crosby and a Dead Cat Won the Election,' *The Guardian* (14 March 2017). Also quoted by Isabel Hardman, *The Spectator* (9 April 2015).

4 Kate Lyons, 'Mesmerising', *The Guardian* (26 June 2019).

5 Emer O'Toole, 'Boris Johnson says £350m Brexit bus figure was an "underestimation"', *The National* (7 July 2021); Nick Hardinges, 'PM claims £350m figure on side of Brexit bus was actually "a slight underestimate"', *Leading Britain's Conversation* (7 July 2021).

6 Edmund Burke, 'Letters on a Regicide Peace 1796', in Burke, E., *Select Works of Edmund Burke: Letters on a Regicide Peace* (Liberty Fund Inc., 1999).

7 Maya Yang, 'More than 40% in US do not believe Biden legitimately won election – poll', *Guardian* (5 Jan. 2022).

8 Joe Biden, 'Remarks by President Biden on the Continued Battle for the Soul of the Nation', https://www.whitehouse.gov/briefing-room/speeches-remarks/2022/09/01/remarks-by-president-bidenon-the-continued-battle-for-the-soul-of-the-nation/

9 Ivor Gaber and Caroline Fisher, '"Strategic Lying": The Case of Brexit and the 2019 U.K. Election', *The International Journal of Press/Politics*, https://journals.sagepub.com/doi/10.1177/1940161221994100

10 Hannah Arendt, 'Lying in Politics', *New York Review of Books* (Nov. 1971), https://www.nybooks.com/articles/1971/11/18/lying-in-politics-reflections-on-the-pentagon-pape/

11 Ivor Gaber, 'Strategic lying: the new game in town', https://www.electionanalysis.uk/uk-election-analysis-2019/section-1-truth-lies-and-civic-culture/strategic-lying-the-new-game-in-town/

12 Jennifer Kavanagh and Michael D. Rich, 'Truth Decay: An Initial Exploration of the Diminishing Role of Facts and Analysis in American Public Life', https://www.rand.org/pubs/research_reports/RR2314.html

13 Garry Kasparov, tweet 13 December 2016.

14 Kim Darroch, *Collateral Damage* (William Collins, 2021), pp. 5–6.

15 *Ibid.*, p. 261.

16 Isabelle Kirk, 'Eight in 10 Britons say Boris Johnson lied about lockdown parties', *YouGov* (21 Apr. 2022).

17 Jon Stone, 'Boris Johnson widely regarded as a 'liar' by voters, poll finds', *The Independent* (18 April 2022).

18 Wes Streeting Labour MP live blog, *Guardian* (29 March 2022).

19 YouGov, 'Boris Johnson trustworthiness', https://yougov.co.uk/topics/politics/trackers/is-boris-johnson-trustworthy

20 https://boris-johnson-lies.com

21 *The New European* (1 Sept. 2022).

22 Hannah White in conversation with author, October 2022.

23 'Strategic Lying' is a phrase which appears to derive from a paper written for the University of California (San Diego) in 2003. It was defined as 'lying for strategic advantage about planned actions, or intentions', which the author pointed out 'is a common feature of economic and political as well as military life. Such lying frequently takes the extreme form of active misrepresentation, as opposed to less than full, honest disclosure' (Crawford, Vincent P., *Lying for Strategic Advantage: Rational and Boundedly Rational Misrepresentation of Intentions* (University of California/San Diego, 2003)).

Chapter 6: Trust and the Suspicious Century

1 Finances Online, '53 Important Statistics About How Much Data Is Created Every Day', https://financesonline.com/how-much-data-is-created-every-day

2 Ryan Holiday, *Trust Me, I'm Lying: Confessions of a Media Manipulator Portfolio* (Profile Books/London, 2013).

3 Mike Brewer and Thomas Wernham, 'Income and wealth inequality explained in 5 charts', https://ifs.org.uk/articles/income-and-wealth-inequality-explained-5-charts

4 John Burn Murdoch, 'Britain and the US are poor societies with some very rich people', *Financial Times* (16 Sept. 2022).

5 Judith Thurman, 'Philip Roth E-mails on Trump', *The New Yorker* (30 Jan. 2017).

6 Aaron Young, 'The Des Moines Register', https://eu.desmoinesregister.com/story/news/politics/2018/01/11/donald-trump-speaks-fourth-

grade-level-factbase-analysis-herbert-hoover-iowa-united-states-
president/1024002001/

7   Sarah Repucci and Amy Slipowitz, 'The Global Expansion of
    Authoritarian Rule', https://freedomhouse.org/report/freedom-
    world/2022/global-expansion-authoritarian-rule

8   National Intelligence Council, 'Who We Are', https://www.dni.
    gov/index.php/who-we-are/organizations/mission-integration/nic/
    nic-who-we-are#:~:text=Since%20its%20establishment%20in%20
    1979,Intelligence%20Community%20collaboration%20and%20
    outreach

9   Global Trends 2040 – A More Contested World National Intelligence
    Council (NIC) (March 2021).

10 'Edelman Trust Barometer UK Findings 2021', Edelman (21 Feb.
    2021), https://www.edelman.co.uk/edelman-trust-barometer-2021-
    uk-findings

11 House of Commons Library: Research Briefing, 'Political
    Disengagement in the UK: Who Is Disengaged?' See also Trust,
    politics and institutions', *British Social Attitudes*, https://www.bsa.
    natcen.ac.uk/latest-report/british-social-attitudes-30/key-findings/
    trust-politics-and-institutions.aspx)

12 Peter Kellner, 'No of course Boris Johnson didn't get Brexit done',
    The New European (1 Sept. 2022), https://www.theneweuropean.
    co.uk/peter-kellner-polls-boris-johnson-did-not-get-brexit-done/

13 'Impact of Brexit on economy "worse than Covid"', BBC News (27
    Oct. 2021), https://www.bbc.co.uk/news/business-59070020

14 Jacob Rees-Mogg, 'I want Sun readers to write to me and tell me of
    ANY petty old EU regulation that should be abolished', *The Sun* (9
    February 2022).

15 James Gale, 'Which celebrities can we really trust? Top ten most
    trusted famous faces revealed', *The Daily Record*, https://www.
    dailyrecord.co.uk/news/uk-world-news/celebrities-can-really-trust-
    top-11801783 *The Independent* (5 January 2018).

16 Ruth Fox and Joel Blackwell, 'The public think politics is broken,
    and are willing to entertain radical solutions', *Hansard Society* (8
    April 2019).

17 *The Independent* (19 Apr. 2022).

18 NHS Digital, Health Survey for England, 'Adult Obesity in England',
    House of Commons Library (12 Jan. 2023).

19 Dominic Ponsford, 'Piers Morgan returns to News UK to join

TalkTV and Sun on three-year "£50m" deal', *Press Gazette* (30 Sept. 2022),

20 Lesley Stahl, *Reporting Live* (Simon & Schuster, 1999), quoted Gavin Esler, *Lessons from the Top* (Profile Books 2012), p. 45.

21 Megan Foley, 'Rethinking the Fragmentation of Speech from Fragments to Fetish', *Rhetoric and Public Affairs* (15:4), pp. 613–22).

22 Richard Nordquist, 'Sound Bites in Communication Glossary of Grammatical and Rhetorical Terms', https://www.thoughtco.com/sound-bite-communication-1691978 11.3.20

23 Michael Bywater, *The Chronicles of Bargepole* (Jonathan Cape, 1992)/ Richard Nordquist, 'Sound Bites in Communication', Thought & Co, https://www.thoughtco.com/sound-bite-communication-1691978

24 Jon Whiteaker, 'Opinion: The UK is better off for Boris Johnson's departure', https://www.internationalaccountingbulletin.com/comment/boris-johnson-departure-uk-brexit-better-off/

25 Edelman Trust Barometer UK, 'UK Nations Fracture as Government Trust Bubble Deflates 2021', https://www.edelman.co.uk/research/uk-nations-fracture-government-trust-bubble-deflates

Chapter 7: Tropes and How Others See Us

1   *The Art Newspaper* (2 Nov. 2021).

2   John Arbuthnot, *The History of John Bull*, 'Law is a Bottomless Pit (John Arbuthnot. Full Title: "Law is a bottomless-pit: Exemplified in the case of the Lord Strutt, John Bull, Nicholas Frog, and Lewis Baboon. Who spent all they had in a law-suit. Printed from a manuscript found in the cabinet of the famous Sir Humphry Polesworth.")' 1712.

3   Jacques-Bénigne Bossuet, 'Sermon pour la fête de la Circoncision de Notre-Seigneur', in *Oeuvres complètes*, Volume 5, Ed. Outhenin-Chalandre, 1840, p. 264.

4   *Talking Humanities*, 'Perfidious Albion: Britain's shameful role in blocking a non-racial franchise in the Union of South Africa', https://talkinghumanities.blogs.sas.ac.uk/2016/08/16/perfidious-albion-britains-shameful-role-in-blocking-a-non-racial-franchise-in-the-union-of-south-africa/#:~:text=Perfidious%20Albion%20is%20a%20phrase,her%20diplomacy%20and%20treaty%2Dmaking

5   Quoted in Keith Somerville, 'Perfidious Albion: Britain's shameful role in blocking a non-racial franchise in the Union of South Africa', *Talking Humanities* (16 Aug. 2016).

6   Matt Withers, 'Hardline Brexiteer tells EU it faces 'Perfidious Albion on speed,' *The New European* (9 April 2019).

7   Will Self, 'Mark Francois' Spartan Victory is illiteracy on parade', *The New European* (21 Jan. 2022).

8   Irving, W., *The Sketch-Book of Geoffrey Crayon, Gent* 1819 (OUP/ Oxford, 2009).

9   John Henley, '"Vain, fickle, hypocritical": how Europe sees Boris Johnson after partygate', *The Guardian* (13 Jan. 2022)

10 Amelia Hadfield and Nicholas Wright, 'Fog in Channel? The Impact of Brexit on EU and UK Foreign Affairs', *European Union Institute for Security Studies* (11 Jun. 2021).

11 See Josep Borrell tweet, 30 January 2021, and blog https://europa. eu/!hm84Yh

12 Peter Ricketts, *Hard Choices* (Atlantic Books/London, 2021), p. 12.

13 *Ibid.*, p. 119.

14 *Ibid.*, pp. 118–20.

15 Patrick Wintour, 'Former FCO head lambasts UK foreign policy under Boris Johnson', *Guardian* (7 Nov. 2017).

16 Boris Johnson's first speech as prime minister, 24 July 2019.

17 Ricketts, *op. cit.*, pp. 188–9.

18 David Axe, 'The Royal Navy Keeps Shrinking – Frigates To Drop By Three Over Five Years', www.forbes.com/sites/ davidaxe/2021/02/12/the-royal-navy-keeps-shrinking-frigates-to-drop-by-three/?sh=38711e166621

19 Laurence Dollimore, 'British Army is "only big enough to tootle around at home" so needs proper funding, says Defence Secretary Ben Wallace', *Mail Online* (28 Nov. 2022); George Grylls, 'UK has "deep vulnerabilities", admits defence secretary', *The Times* (25 Nov. 2022).

20 Ricketts, *op. cit.*, pp. 8–9.

21 George Kennan, 'The Sources of Soviet Conduct', *Foreign Affairs* (January 1947). (George Kennan 'American Diplomacy', *Foreign Affairs magazine*, July 1947, based on his 'Long Telegram' to the US State Department February 1946 and published as 'Mister X'.)

Chapter 8: Traditions: They're Not What They Used to Be

1 'Black Rod', *UK Parliament*, www.parliament.uk/about/mps-and-lords/principal/black-rod/
2 Rajeev Syal and Hélène Mulholland, 'Queen attends cabinet meeting in Downing Street', *The Guardian* (18 Dec. 2012).
3 Jonathan Rauch, *Demosclerosis: The Silent Killer of American Government* (Times Books/New York, 1995).
4 Ipsos Survey for The British Council, 'How The World Sees Britain', *IPSOS* (23 Nov. 1999).
5 British Council 'A "Special Relationship"?', *British Council*, www.britishcouncil.org/research-policy-insight/insight-articles/a-special-relationship
6 Gov.uk, 'Applying a crown symbol to pint glasses', www.gov.uk/guidance/applying-a-crown-symbol-to-pint-glasses
7 Joshua Askew, 'UK to revive imperial measurements to bring back 'British culture and heritage', says MP', *Euronews* (1 Jun. 2022).
8 Andrew Roberts, 'It's Time to Revive the Anglosphere', *Wall Street Journal* (8 Aug. 2020).
9 International Trade Committee Report, 'The International Trade Committee publishes its verdict on the UK's trade deal with Australia', *UK Parliament* (6 July 2022).
10 International Churchill Society, 'The Sinews of Peace ("Iron Curtain Speech")', winstonchurchill.org/resources/speeches/1946-1963-elder-statesman/the-sinews-of-peace/
11 Penny Wong speech, 'An enduring partnership in an era of change', *Australian Ministry of Foreign Affairs* (31 Jan. 2023)
12 'Some Facts on the Canadian Francophonie', Government of Canada, https://www.canada.ca/en/canadian-heritage/services/official-languages-bilingualism/publications/facts-canadian-francophonie.html
13 Jonathan Kirkup and Stephen Thornton, *The Deputy to the British Prime Minister: A Mystery of Role, Responsibility and Power* (Routledge/Oxfordshire, 2015).
14 Eric Hobsbawm and Terence Ranger (eds), *The Invention of Tradition* (Cambridge University Press/Cambridge, 1983), p. 101.
15 David Cannadine,'The British Monarchy 1820–1977', in Hobsbawm and Ranger (eds), *op. cit.*, p. 102.
16 Statista, 'Monthly reach of leading newspapers in the United

Kingdom from April 2019 to March 2020', www.statista.com/
statistics/246077/reach-of-selected-national-newspapers-in-the-uk/
17 Cannadine, *op. cit.*, p. 101ff.
18 UK Parliament, 'The architects: Charles Barry and Augustus
Pugin', www.parliament.uk/about/living-heritage/building/palace/
architecture/palacestructure/the-architects/
19 White, *op. cit.*, p. 145ff.
20 Hannah White, *Held in Contempt*, p146ff.
21 Rob Hakimian, 'Palace of Westminster restoration could take over
half a century and cost £22bn', *New Civil Engineer* (24 Feb. 2022).

Part Three: Institutions and Constitutions

Chapter 9: The British Constitution

1 Ascherson, Neal, 'Scribbles in a Storm', *London Review of Books*
43:7 (2021).
2 *The Independent* (17 Oct. 2016); see also The Constitution Society,
'Dominic Grieve – A Backbencher's View of Brexit', consoc.org.uk/
publications/dominic-grieve-backbenchers-view-brexit/
3 Robert Merrick, 'UK Government agreed referendum could not be
legally binding', *Indepenent* (17 Oct. 2022).
4 John Redwood MP, 'This was not an advisory referendum', 7
November 2016; see also https://fullfact.org/europe/was-eu-
referendum-advisory/ and John Redwood's own account /blog
https://johnredwoodsdiary.com/2019/04/07/what-the-government-
said-about-the-referendum/
5 Government briefing paper on the European Referendum Bill, June
2015.
6 Conversation with author, 19 September 2022.
7 Margaret Thatcher, 11 March 1975, House of Commons speech.
8 Linda Colley, *Acts of Disunion* (Profile Books/London, 2014), p. 143.
9 LSE Blogs, December 2016, blogs.lse.ac.uk/politicsandpolicy/brexit-
inequality-and-the-demographic-divide/
10 Peter Hennessy, *Muddling Through* (Weidenfeld & Nicolson/
London, 1996), p. 14.
11 Ivan Rogers, *9 Lessons in Brexit* (Short Books Ltd/London, 2019).
12 *British Medical Journal* 2018;363:k4816 15.11.18.
13 Tony Weetman (Emeritus professor of medicine at Sheffield

University), *The Times* Letters (29 Jun. 2016), referring to the Brexit campaign.

14 Stephen Sedley, 'Knife, Stone, Paper', *London Review of Books* 33:13 (2021), p. 17.

15 Hennessy, *op. cit.*, interview with Tony Benn, pp. 29–32.

16 *The New European* (18 Nov. 2021).

17 Seth Thévoz, '18 times Boris Johnson was accused of breaking rules – and got away with it', www.opendemocracy.net/en/opendemocracyuk/boris-johnson-broke-rules-no-punishment/

18 King, *op. cit.*, p. 24.

19 Hennessy, *op. cit.*, interview with Vernon Bogdanor, p. 39.

20 Interview with author, September 2022.

21 King, *op. cit.*, p. 6.

22 *Ibid.*, pp. 8–9.

23 Haroon Siddique, 'Use of 'VIP lane' to award Covid PPE contracts unlawful, high court rules', *Gaurdian* (12 Jan. 2022).

24 Jill Rutter, 'Sacking Tom Scholar – a move that undermines the Treasury, the civil service and the government', https://ukandeu.ac.uk/sacking-tom-scholar-a-move-that-undermines-the-treasury-the-civil-service-and-the-government/

25 Sam Fowles, *Overruled: Confronting Our Vanishing Democracy in 8 Cases* (OneWorld, 2022, p. 3).

26 *Ibid.*

27 Judgement of the UK Supreme Court, 24 September 2019, R (on the application of Miller) (Appellant) v The Prime Minister (Respondent) Cherry and others (Respondents) v Advocate General for Scotland (Appellant) (Scotland) 24.9.2019 UKSC-2019-0192-judgment

28 *Ibid.*

29 David Allen Green, 'The question of whether Boris Johnson lied to the queen', https://davidallengreen.com/2022/08/the-question-of-whether-boris-johnson-lie-to-the-queen

30 Michael Howard, quoted in Mattha Busby, 'Michael Howard claims judges "distorted" law in prorogation ruling', *Guardian* (28 Dec. 2019).

31 BBC *Today* programme (26 Dec. 2019); also see Adam Forrest, 'Lady Hale warns government against US-style 'politicisation' of court appointments', *Independent* (27 Dec. 2019).

32 Fowles, *op. cit.*, p. 31.

33 *Ibid.*, p. 33.

34 *Ibid.*, pp. 42–3.
35 *Ibid.*, p. 46.
36 Conversation with the author, 19 September 2022.

Chapter 10: Hidden Persuaders: Media, PR and You

1   James W. Potter *Theory of Media Literacy: A cognitive approach* (SAGE/California, 2004), p. 68.
2   Becky Little, 'The Secret British Campaign to Persuade the US to Enter WWII', www.history.com/news/wwii-us-entry-secret-british-campaign-mi6
3   John MacArthur, *Second Front: Censorship and Propaganda in the 1991 Gulf War* (University of California Press/California, 2004).
4   Maria Popova, 'Lying in Politics: Hannah Arendt on Deception, Self-Deception, and the Psychology of Defactualization', www.themarginalian.org/2016/06/15/lying-in-politics-hannah-arendt/
5   Nic Newman, 'United Kingdom', https://reutersinstitute.politics.ox.ac.uk/digital-news-report/2022/united-kingdom
6   Andrew Kersley, 'Trust and interest in news falls in UK with Sun, Mail and Mirror bottom of table', https://pressgazette.co.uk/news/trust-in-news-uk/
7   John Helliwell, Richard Layard, Jeffrey D. Sachs *et al.*, 'World Happiness Report 2023', https://worldhappiness.report/ed/2023/
8   The Australia Institute, Nordic Policy Centre, 'Media literacy education in Finland', www.nordicpolicycentre.org.au/media_literacy_education_in_finland
9   European Policies Initiative, MIL league table (2022), in 'Finland, Denmark and Estonia top the Media Literacy Index 2021', *Education Estonia* (15 March 2021).
10 Edelman, '2022 Edelman UK Trust Barometer: The Cycle of Distrust', https://www.edelman.co.uk/2022-edelman-uk-trust-barometer
11 All Blair quotes from Esler, G., *Lessons from the Top* (Profile Books/London, 2022), pp. 104–6.
12 Gingrich, Newt, 'Toffler obituary', *Politico* (31 Dec. 2016).
13 GOPAC Republican Party memo, 1990.
14 *Des Moines Register* (6 Feb. 2015).
15 Hitler, A., *Mein Kampf* (trans. Ralph Manheim), (Houghton Mifflin Company/Boston, 1943).
16 Edward Bernays, *Propaganda* (Ig Publishing/New York, 2004).

17 Tom Fletcher, *Ten Survival Skills in a World in Flux* (William Collins/Glasgow, 2022), p. 56.

18 Nick Davies, *Flat Earth News* (Vintage/New York, 2009), p. 85.

19 Nick Davies, *Flat Earth News* (Vintage, 2009, pp. 85–6).

20 *Columbia Journalism Review* (31 Mar. 2021).

21 Stephen Waddington, 'UK PR employment data shows industry in good health', https://wadds.co.uk/blog/2022/1/30/uk-employment-trends-for-public-relations-and-communications

22 Payscale, 'Average Journalist Salary in United Kingdom', www.payscale.com/research/UK/Job=Journalist/Salary

23 Office for National Statistics, 'Employment and labour market', www.ons.gov.uk/employmentandlabourmarket/

24 Ruth Wyatt, 'The PR Census 2013', www.prweek.com/article/1225129/pr-census-2013

25 Davies, *op. cit.*, p. 63.

26 See Neil Thurman, Alessio Cornia and Jessica Kunert, 'Journalists in the UK', Reuters Institute for the Study of Journalism; and Nic Newman with Richard Fletcher, Craig T. Robertson, Kirsten Eddy, and Rasmus Kleis Nielsen, 'Digital News Report 2022', Reuters Institute.

27 Media Monkey, '#PRfail: fill in (all) the template before sending out your press release', *The Guardian* (7 Jan. 2015).

28 Katie Gibbons, 'The ten friends who make a woman tick', *The Times* (1 Nov. 2013).

29 Tom Knowles, 'Facing up to the cold truth', *The Times* (1 Nov. 2013).

30 Hannah Devlin, 'Happy to see you? How wagging dog has sting in the tail', *The Times* (1 Nov. 2013).

31 Sarah Knapton, 'Could previous lovers influence appearance of future children?' *The Telegraph* (1 Oct. 2014).

32 Harvard University: David Keith's Research Group, 'Chemtrails Conspiracy Theory', https://keith.seas.harvard.edu/chemtrails-conspiracy-theory

33 Anorak, 'The Daily Mail's List of Things That Give You Cancer: From A To Z', www.anorak.co.uk/288298/tabloids/the-daily-mails-list-of-things-that-give-you-cancer-from-a-to-z.html

34 Newt Gingrich, *Window of Opportunity: A Blueprint for the Future* (New York, Tor Books, 1984).

35 Thomas Jefferson letter to Richard Price, 8 Jan. 1789, Library of Congress, *Thomas Jefferson Papers*.

Chapter 11: The Leaders We Deserve

1 de Maistre, Joseph, *The Generative Principle of Political Constitutions* (*1794*) (Routledge/Oxford, 1965).
2 Matthew Smith, 'Cancel culture: what views are Britons afraid to express?', https://yougov.co.uk/topics/politics/articles-reports/2021/12/22/cancel-culture-what-views-are-britons-afraid
3 UK in the World Values Survey, 'UK satisfaction with politics internationally low – but support for democracy has still risen', https://www.uk-values.org/news-comment/uk-satisfaction-with-politics-internationally-low-but-support-for-democracy-has-still-risen
4 Richard Cracknell, Richard Tunnicliffe, Cassie Barton *et al.*, 'Social background of Members of Parliament 1979-2019', Commons Library, https://commonslibrary.parliament.uk/research-briefings/cbp-7483/
5 Simon Partridge, 'The 0.7 per cent problem is much worse than the 7 per cent problem', www.pepf.co.uk/opinion/the-0-7-per-cent-problem-is-much-worse-than-the-7-per-cent-problem/
6 Schaverien, Joy, 'Boarding School Syndrome: The Psychological Trauma of the "Privileged" Child', https://www.britishpsychotherapyfoundation.org.uk/insights/blog/joy-schaverien
7 Andrew Eyles, Lee Elliot Major and Stephen Machin, 'Social Mobility: Past Present and Future', www.suttontrust.com/our-research/social-mobility-past-present-and-future/
8 *Ibid.*
9 *Ibid.*
10 Thomas Colley, 'War, Brexit and National Identity', https://blog.press.umich.edu/2019/07/war-brexit-and-british-national-identity/
11 Andrew MacAskill and Anjuli Davies, '"Insecurity is fantastic," says billionaire funder of Brexit campaign', www.reuters.com/article/uk-britain-eu-donations-hargreaves-idUKKCN0Y22ID
12 Margery Purham, 'Frederick Lugard', https://www.britannica.com/biography/Frederick-Lugard
13 Boris Johnson, 'If Blair's so good at running the Congo let him stay there', *Daily Telegraph* (10 Jan. 2022).
14 *Ibid.*
15 Peter Davidson, 'Boris Johnson says his 'racist content' about Africans was taken out of context', *Daily Record* (14 July 2021).

16 William Beinart, 'Cecil Rhodes: Racial Segregation in the Cape Colony and Violence in Zimbabwe', www.oriel.ox.ac.uk/cecil-rhodes-racial-segregation-in-the-cape-colony-and-violence-in-zimbabwe/

17 *The Times* Letters to the Editor, *The Times* (14 Feb. 2023).

Index